Bank mergers and acquisitions in the Asia-Pacific region

Corporate Finance and Governance

Edited by Dirk Schiereck

Volume 16

Zur Qualitätssicherung und Peer Review der vorliegenden Publikation

Die Qualität der in dieser Reihe erscheinenden Arbeiten wird vor der Publikation durch den Herausgeber der Reihe geprüft.

Notes on the quality assurance and peer review of this publication

Prior to publication, the quality of the work published in this series is reviewed by the editors of the series.

Sascha Kolaric

Bank mergers and acquisitions in the Asia-Pacific region

An investigation of the shareholder wealth effects of the financial sector consolidation and its impact on the acquirer's cost of debt

PL ACADEMIC RESEARCH

Bibliographic Information published by the Deutsche Nationalbibliothek
The Deutsche Nationalbibliothek lists this publication in the Deutsche Nationalbibliografie; detailed bibliographic data is available in the internet at http://dnb.d-nb.de.

Zugl.: Darmstadt, Techn. Univ., Diss., 2015

D 17
ISSN 1869-537X
ISBN 978-3-631-67054-5 (Print)
E-ISBN 978-3-653-06268-7 (E-Book)
DOI 10.3726/978-3-653-06268-7

PL Academic Research is an Imprint of Peter Lang GmbH.

Peter Lang – Frankfurt am Main · Bern · Bruxelles · New York · Oxford · Warszawa · Wien

This publication has been peer reviewed.

www.peterlang.com

Overview

Table of Contents

List of tables

List of figures

List of abbreviations

AAR	Average abnormal return
ACAR	Average cumulative abnormal return
AR	Abnormal return
ARCH	Autoregressive conditional heteroskedasticity
ASC	Adjusted/abnormal spread change
BHC	Bank holding company
bps	basis points
CAR	Cumulative abnormal return
CASC	Cumulative adjusted/abnormal spread change
CDS	Credit default swap
CEO	Chief executive officer
CMA	Credit Market Analysis
EGARCH	Exponential generalized autoregressive conditional heteroskedasticity
FDIC	Federal Deposit Insurance Company
Fitch	Fitch Ratings
GARCH	Generalized autoregressive conditional heteroskedasticity
GDP	Gross domestic product
M&A	Merger and acquisition
MCASC	Mean cumulative adjusted/abnormal spread change
Moody's	Moody's Investors Service
OLS	Ordinary least squares
ROE	Return on equity
S&P	Standard & Poor's
SCAR	Standardized cumulative abnormal return
SIC	Standard industry classification
TBTF	Too-Big-to-Fail
UK	United Kingdom
US	United States
US$	United States dollar

1. Introduction

1.1 The importance and relevance of bank mergers and acquisitions in the Asia-Pacific region

The economic growth and development of the Asia-Pacific region since the year 2000 has been remarkable. According to the World Bank, between 2000 and 2013 the average GDP growth of the East-Asia and Pacific region was 4.12%, compared to 1.40% for the European Union and 1.92% for the United States. In line with this development, per capita GDP of the region more than doubled. During the same time, foreign direct investment in the region almost quadrupled and stood at more than 632 billion US$ in 2013. The increasing number of customers and demand for banking services, coupled with the need to finance the continued economic growth of the Asia-Pacific region creates profit opportunities for banks and other financial institutions. Banks can realize these opportunities either through offering traditional banking services, such as lending or depository activities, or through brokerage or investment banking services.

Moreover, in the wake of the 1997–1998 Asian Financial Crisis, the stability and integration of Asian financial markets came into focus. Several major initiatives were launched to avoid future crises and further integrate markets.[1] Research now shows that the integration of Asian financial markets, especially equity markets, is well underway (Yu, Fung, & Tam, 2010). This, combined with increasing harmonization of international financial markets, for example through the Basel Accords, should allow international institutions to more easily gain access to these markets and engage in mergers.

The relative importance of the banking sector in the Asia-Pacific region in regard to merger and acquisition (M&A) activity increased over time as well. The US banking sector is largely consolidated and merger activity decreased remarkably, especially since the 2007 Financial Crisis. Similar patterns can be observed for European bank M&As (see Figure 1-1). At the same time, the total deal volume is down since the 2007 Financial Crisis, but the Asia-Pacific region plays a more prominent role than before. In 2013 the total deal volume was 24.95 billion

1 These initiatives include, among others, the Chiang Mai Initiative, launched in May 2000, the Asian Bond Fund Initiative, introduced in 2002, and the Asian Bond Market Initiative, launched in August 2003.

US$ in the Asia-Pacific region, compared to 22.58 billion US$ in Europe and 18.42 billion US$ for bank mergers in the United States (see Figure 1-1). This translates to a relative deal volume of 37.83% for mergers in the Asia-Pacific region, 34.24% for Europe and 27.93% for the United States. For 2014 the numbers are similar, albeit with overall slightly lower deal values than in 2013. These numbers underscore that mergers among financial institutions in the Asia-Pacific region have gained in importance and are likely to continue to do so in the future. This is probably due to there being further room for consolidation within the region, in particular compared to banking markets in Europe and the United States.

Figure 1-1: Bank M&A activity in Asia-Pacific, Europe, and the US 1995–2013

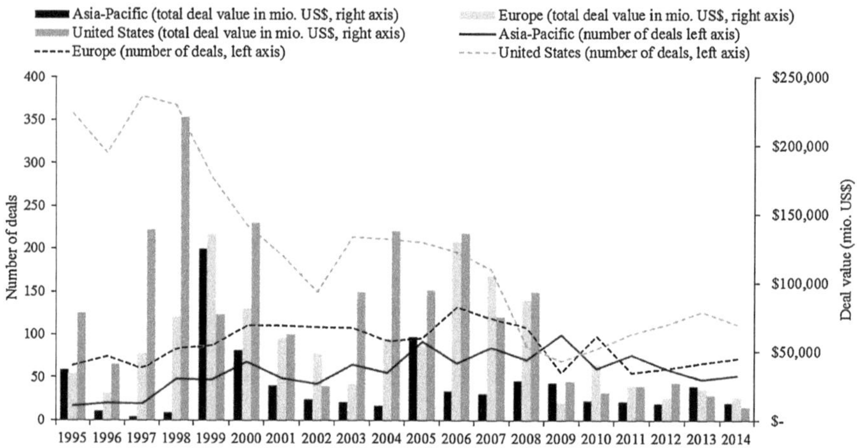

This graphic shows M&As between banks and financial institutions with Standard Industrial Classification codes between 6000 and 6282 and Standard Industrial Classification codes 6712 and 6733. Only majority acquisitions which are completed are considered and deals for which a deal value was recorded in the Thomson Reuters SDC Mergers and Acquisitions database.

Source: Thomson Reuters SDC Mergers and Acquisitions database

Bank mergers among US and European financial institutions have been examined for more than two decades now. Research on mergers and acquisitions in the Asia-Pacific region, however, is still scarce. Yet, the existing results indicate that there may be substantial differences to prior research for other regions, which centers on the largely consolidated and mature banking markets of the United States and Europe. For this reason, the present study applies event study methodology and analyzes the capital market reactions of the bidding and target banks to merger announcements in the Asia-Pacific region. In addition, in order to obtain a more complete picture of the impact of M&A announcements on the financial sector in the region, the capital market reaction of the acquiring as well as target bank rivals are also observed. Furthermore, multiple aspects that influence the returns of the bidding banks and their rivals are investigated in detail to better understand what the key factors of successful mergers are. Finally, the reaction of debtholders to M&As is also examined by observing CDS spread changes surrounding merger announcements. In this way this study provides an encompassing analysis of the effects of the financial sector consolidation in the Asia-Pacific region. In addition, in light of the rapid economic development and increasing international efforts to harmonize global financial markets, the question arises for investors and bank mangers, whether mergers and acquisitions in the region can create shareholder value. It is therefore relevant for the management to know which requirements the merging institutions should fulfill prior to the M&A transaction in order to make the takeover as successful as possible.

The first part of the present study, chapter 2, provides a comprehensive analysis of the literature on bank mergers and acquisitions with an emphasis on the last decade. More than 135 publications focusing on that subject are reviewed and grouped along their regional focus and the three main empirical methodologies used in the literature, which are event studies, dynamic efficiency studies, and performance studies. The results of prior event studies indicate that, as national banking sectors mature over time, it is becoming continually more challenging for banks to create shareholder value through takeovers. Banking markets in the emerging economies of Asia and Latin America, on the other hand, appear to still offer opportunities for shareholder value creation through mergers. The empirical findings of previous studies also suggest that performance differentials between acquirer and target, the financing method and higher levels of regulatory efficiency and quality are some of the main drivers of successful mergers. It remains unclear, whether geographic or product focus or diversification offers more benefits. In addition, there is some empirical evidence that banks benefit from mergers that allow them to become "Too-Big-to-Fail" and that they may engage in regulatory arbitrage.

The analysis of the shareholder wealth implications of the financial sector consolidation in the Asia-Pacific region in chapter 3 shows that Asian bidding banks stand to gain more from takeovers than their non-Asian peers. Moreover, the rivals of Asian bidders also profit from further consolidation, indicating that market power considerations play an important role when investors value bank mergers within the region. Non-Asian bidders, on the other hand, perform significantly worse than their Asian counterparts and earn negative returns, while their rivals' share price remains largely unaffected. In addition, significant gains to takeover targets and their rivals are documented, especially to those of non-Asian bidding banks. Asian acquiring banks are most successful when engaging in M&A transactions with private targets, while the opposite is true for non-Asian banks. Furthermore, larger transactions are associated with significant losses in shareholder wealth. Overall, the results suggest that the consolidation of the financial sector in the Asia-Pacific region was successful and that shareholders of Asian institutions were able to reap significant benefits from the process, whereas their non-Asian peers were not able to profit in the same fashion.

Chapter 4 is dedicated to the examination of bidding banks' CDS spreads surrounding merger announcements in the Asia-Pacific region. The results show that merger announcements are associated with significant widening of CDS spreads for the acquiring institution. Therefore, bank mergers appear to be perceived as overall risk increasing events by market participants. Moreover, non-Asian bidders experience larger increases in their CDS spread levels than their Asian peers. However, despite M&As being overall risk increasing corporate events, acquiring institutions, which are comparatively larger than their closest national rivals, are actually able to obtain highly significant reductions in their CDS spreads due to the takeover announcement. This finding can be interpreted as evidence of "Too-Big-to-Fail" considerations when market participants value these mergers, as the newly formed institution is more likely to receive a government bailout in case it falls into financial distress.

Overall, the results suggest that for equity markets the origin of the bidding banks is a decisive factor for successful mergers, while from the perspective of credit markets, relative size of the bidder compared to national competitors appears to be most relevant. Bidding bank shareholders, especially in Asian national transactions, appear to benefit from further consolidation in the financial sector. The same holds for the shareholders of the bidding banks' rivals. Investors appear to anticipate that the remaining banks will be able to either increase their efficiency or benefit from lower levels of competition, as fewer banks remain in the market. This points towards market power considerations playing a role when investors value bank mergers. In this case, regulators should carefully assess these developments, as possible collusion due to increased market power may lead to undesirable outcomes for consumers and the financial system. For debt markets, the origin of the bidding bank appears to be irrelevant. However, even though M&As appear to be overall risk increasing events, banks that have a comparatively large market capitalization in relation to their competitors are able to significantly decrease their borrowing costs. This points towards the existence of implicit "Too-Big-to-Fail" expectations by debtholders.

1.2 Thesis structure

This thesis is divided into three main parts. The first one (chapter 2) provides a comprehensive overview of the empirical research on bank mergers and acquisitions. The second part (chapter 3) offers an in-depth analysis of the shareholder wealth effects of the financial sector consolidation in the Asia-Pacific region. The third part (chapter 4), in turn, examines the impact of bank mergers in the region on the acquirer's cost of debt by investigating the CDS market reaction to M&A announcements.

The literature review given in chapter 2 introduces the three most frequently used research methodologies, the event study, the dynamic efficiency, and the performance study approach. The three research designs are briefly described and their advantages and disadvantages are highlighted. Section 2.2 provides a detailed overview on the empirical research carried out on bank mergers so far, separated into the findings of the three different methodologies. In addition, the results of the research on Asian bank mergers so far are examined, followed by an assessment of the empirical results achieved so far. Section 2.4 presents the main research results on the determinants of successful merger transactions, divided into characteristics related to the acquirer and target, those specific to a transaction and to the regulatory and economic environment. This section also includes the effects of a bank's management on merger performance and the effect of regulatory arbitrage considerations and "Too-Big-to-Fail" mergers. Section 2.5 looks at the wealth effects of mergers on rival firms within the same industry and briefly explains the three main hypotheses advanced by this strand of research. Prior empirical evidence on the rival effects of bank mergers is also presented in this context. Section 2.6 then offers an overall assessment of the research on bank mergers and acquisitions conducted so far.

Chapter 3 provides a comprehensive analysis of shareholder wealth effects of bank M&As in the Asia-Pacific region. The reaction of bidding and target banks and their closest rivals to the announcement of an M&A transaction is examined. Section 3.1 briefly outlines the most relevant results of the prior literature on bank mergers with a particular focus on the results from emerging markets. Section 3.2 describes the event study methodology in detail, including the relevant tests of statistical significance. Section 3.3 presents the results of the empirical investigation, divided into the results for bidding and target banks and their respective rivals. Section 3.4 assesses the overall observed return patterns, while section 3.5 examines the drivers of the observed returns for the sample of bidding banks and their rivals. This is followed by multiple robustness checks of the results in section 3.6. Section 3.7 briefly evaluates the main results of the empirical analyses.

Chapter 4 then turns from the equity analysis of bank M&As to the impact of mergers on the bidding bank's cost of debt using a CDS event study approach. Section 4.1 reviews the prior research using CDS event study approach and the research conducted so far on the effect of bank mergers in regard to the acquirer's cost of debt. Section 4.2 explains the CDS event study methodology and also includes an in-depth description of the CDS spread data and the M&A data set. The next section, Section 4.3 presents the results of the empirical investigation on the impact of M&A announcements on the bidder's CDS spreads. This includes an investigation of the drivers of the observed results as well as robustness checks. The final section of chapter 4 discusses and evaluates the main results.

Chapter 5 summarizes the results of the empirical investigations. The main conclusions of this study are discussed and the implications for financial markets and the banking sector in the Asia-Pacific region are described. In addition, the limitations of the empirical analyses are briefly discussed and avenues of future research outlined.

2. Literature review of the performance of bank mergers and acquisitions

Mergers and acquisitions among financial institutions are a worldwide phenomenon and the rapid pace in which the financial sector underwent consolidation has been compelling.[2] This consolidation process, especially in the United States and Europe during the late 1990s and early 2000s, has spurred a vast body of empirical research on bank mergers and acquisitions, their key success factors, and the implications of this consolidation process for the financial system in general. The 2007 Financial Crisis, however, dramatically slowed down the consolidation rate and called prior research findings into question. Mergers among banks between the years 2000 and 2014 were usually large and characterized by high transaction values. Mergers among US banks had a combined transaction value of more than 911 billion US$, those of intra-European transactions exceeded 650 billion US$, and mergers among Asian institutions exceeded 330 billion US$. As banking markets mature over time, it becomes increasingly difficult for the acquiring institution to outperform its rivals. In this case, the takeover market becomes more competitive and bidding banks may be forced to pay a comparatively high premium for a target. This in turn will lead to a more critical evaluation of the transaction by capital market participants and will likely lower the financial performance of the newly combined institution. Moreover, increasing regulation in light of the 2007 Financial Crisis and a more competitive market environment make it more important than ever for bank managers and shareholders to know how mergers and acquisitions affect their stock prices and which factors play a decisive role in making the transaction an overall success or failure for the involved financial institutions.

This chapter provides a comprehensive review of the empirical evidence on the success of bank mergers and acquisitions, giving a special focus to the research findings since the year 2000. During this time span the research offers a vast amount of new empirical evidence, which partly deviates significantly from older insights. The recent findings on M&A success and the most frequently observed success factors are documented, and the main methodologies that are employed to derive the empirical results are contrasted. Yet, the focus of empirical studies is overall still relatively narrow, as almost all methodologies mainly describe success

---

2 I am thankful to Prof. Dr. Dirk Schiereck for his helpful comments and insights. An abbreviated version of Section 2 is published in Kolaric and Schiereck (2014).

from the viewpoint of the owners of the acquiring and target institution. The consequences that bank M&As have on the financial system and its stability have just recently become a focus of empirical research. A prominent topic in this area is empirical investigation in regard to regulatory arbitrage due to "Too-Big-to-Fail" (TBTF) bank M&As.

2.1 Scope of empirical research methodologies

In order to measure the success of M&A transactions among banks, the three most frequently employed empirical methodologies are: (i) event studies, (ii) efficiency studies, and (iii) performance studies (Beitel & Schiereck, 2003; Kolaric & Schiereck, 2014). Besides these three main approaches, survey and case studies also exist, but they are rarely used and hence hardly merit a more detailed discussion in this context.

The event study approach directly measures the impact of M&A transactions on the stock price of the involved institutions and hence documents the shareholder wealth effects. Therefore, a successful merger or acquisition is a transaction in which shareholders obtain returns that are significantly higher than the expected return in a given event window. Efficiency studies, on the other hand, consider an M&A transaction to be successful if the post-merger efficiency of the combined institution moves closer to the efficient frontier, usually considered to be the most efficient institution in the sample. Finally, performance studies regard improvements in accounting ratios to be a sign of a successful M&A transaction. Over the last three decades all three approaches were continuously used and have been modified to incorporate the more recent advances in econometrics and statistics.

2.1.1 The event study methodology

Event studies have been used for more than four decades now. The first time this methodology was specifically employed in an empirical study was by Fama, Fisher, Jensen, and Roll (1969) and since then it has become one of the most prominent approaches for evaluating the success of mergers and acquisitions. An acquisition is identified to be successful if the transactions results in an increase in the share price for both target and acquiring firm. To this end the stock returns of the bidding and target institution during the days surrounding the official announcement day are examined. A larger than expected change in shareholder value, or abnormal return, is generated if investors receive a stock return in excess of the projected one.

Expected returns are usually calculated according to one of the three basic models: (i) the market and risk adjusted return model, or short just market model, (ii) the mean adjusted return model, and (iii) the market adjusted return model (Bühner, 1990). The market model, as initially proposed by Dodd and Warner (1983) and Brown and Warner (1985), is by far the most frequently used model in empirical research. The return during the event period is calculated by an ordinary least squares regression of the form:

$$R_{jt} = \hat{\alpha}_j + \hat{\beta}_j R_{mt} + \varepsilon_{jt} \tag{1-1}$$

where R_{jt} is the return of firm j on day t during the event period, $\hat{\alpha}_j$ and $\hat{\beta}_j$ are the model parameters obtained from a predefined estimation period (e.g. 252 trading days), usually prior to the event date, R_{mt} is the rate of return of an industry or country benchmark index, which serves as proxy for the market return, and ε_{jt} is the regression residual. The abnormal return AR_{jt} is then calculated as the difference between the actual return R_{jt} and the expected return:

$$AR_{jt} = R_{jt} - (\hat{\alpha}_j + \hat{\beta}_j R_{mt}) \tag{1-2}$$

The mean or market adjusted return models are nowadays used only by few empirical studies.[3] Cable and Holland (1999) compare the three approaches and find that the market model should be preferred in an event study analysis. Furthermore, measuring returns against an industry specific or a country index is of little significance to the overall result (Brown & Warner, 1980). A small number of studies (Houston et al., 2001; Houston & Ryngaert, 1994, 1997) use a "leakage" date, the date on which the information about the impending transaction approximately first reached capital markets, instead of the official announcement date. However, the majority of studies account for information leakage simply by increasing the event window for several additional days (e.g. Amihud, DeLong, & Saunders, 2002).

Along with these three classical methods for calculating the expected return, three additional approaches are recently gaining popularity for event studies in general: (i) the three-factor model of Fama and French (1993, 1996), (ii) a four-factor model developed by Carhart (1997), which adds an additional momentum

3 The mean adjusted return model is used by, among others, Sushka and Bendeck (1988), Zhang (1995), and Lorenz (2006). Dubofsky and Fraser (1989), Kane (2000), and Houston, James, and Ryngaert (2001), on the other hand, use the market adjusted return model.

factor to the three factor model of Fama and French (1993, 1996)[4], and (iii) a generalized autoregressive conditional heteroskedasticity (GARCH) model as proposed by Frame and Lastrapes (1998), and Brockett, Chen, and Garven (1999).[5]

The Fama and French (1993, 1996) three-factor model generally takes the following form to estimate the expected return:

$$R_{jt} = \hat{\alpha}_j + \hat{\beta}_{1j} R_{mt} + \hat{\beta}_{2j} SMB_t + \hat{\beta}_{3j} HML_t + \varepsilon_{jt} \tag{1-3}$$

and for the four-factor model, including the moment factor introduced by Carhart (1997), the model takes the following form:

$$R_{jt} = \hat{\alpha}_j + \hat{\beta}_{1j} R_{mt} + \hat{\beta}_{2j} SMB_t + \hat{\beta}_{3j} HML_t + \hat{\beta}_{4j} MOM_t + \varepsilon_{jt} \tag{1-4}$$

where R_{jt} is again the return of firm j on day t during the estimation period, MKT_t is the market or benchmark return on day t, SMB_t is the return difference between a portfolio of companies with a small and large market capitalization on day t, HML_t is the return difference between a portfolio of stocks with a high and low book-to-market value on day t, MOM_t is the return difference between a portfolio of past stock return winners and losers on day t, $\hat{\alpha}_j$ is constant and, $\hat{\beta}_{1j}$, $\hat{\beta}_{2j}$, $\hat{\beta}_{3j}$, $\hat{\beta}_{4j}$, are the coefficients for the respective factors of firm j, and ε_{jt} is the regression residual. The calculation of the abnormal return AR_{jt} follows equation:

$$AR_{jt} = R_{jt} - (\hat{\alpha}_j + \hat{\beta}_{1j} R_{mt} + \hat{\beta}_{2j} SMB_t + \hat{\beta}_{3j} HML_t) \tag{1-5}$$

for the Fama and French (1993, 1996) three-factor model and

$$AR_{jt} = R_{jt} - (\hat{\alpha}_j + \hat{\beta}_{1j} R_{mt} + \hat{\beta}_{2j} SMB_t + \hat{\beta}_{3j} HML_t + \hat{\beta}_{4j} MOM_t) \tag{1-6}$$

for the Carhart (1997) four-factor model.

However, for the calculation of the factors in these models financial firms are generally explicitly excluded (Fama & French, 1992, 1993, 1996) and therefore these models do not appear to be appropriate for the investigation of bank mergers and acquisitions. Among others, Kiymaz (2004) and Al-Sharkas and

---

4 In the most recent development in regard to multi-factor models, Novy-Marx (2013) adds a profitability factor to the Fama and French (1993, 1996) three-factor model in place of the momentum factor of Carhart (1997).

5 A multi factor model for bank M&As is used by Al-Sharkas and Hassan (2010), by Lensink and Maslennikova (2008) and by Choi, Francis, and Hasan (2010). The GARCH approach is utilized by Crouzille, Lepetit, and Bautista (2008) and Lepetit, Patry, and Rous (2004), while Al-Sharkas and Hassan (2010) use an Exponential GARCH (EGARCH) model. No bank M&A specific literature has employed the four-factor model yet.

Hassan (2010) employ multi-factor models with banking specific factors for US mergers. Specifically, Kiymaz (2004) uses the change in the 3-month US T-bill rate in addition to the market factor, while Al-Sharkas and Hassan (2010) use the return on the 1-year US T-bill index and the return on the US foreign exchange index in addition to the market factor. However, the data required for the calculation of these factors is often not available for countries other than the US. Therefore, for studies focusing on US bank mergers, these models may be appropriate, but not for international studies that include financial institutions from multiple nations.

Zollo and Leshchinkskii (2000) compare the market model as well as the Fama and French (1993) three-factor model, but are not able to find significant differences in the results. Cyree and DeGennaro (2002) develop a comprehensive model to estimate the expected return by relaxing some constraints of the classical models. Their approach allows for heteroskedastic variances, firm-specific event windows, multiple events, as well as short-term and permanent changes in systematic risk. The latter two occasions describe "risk-shifting events". Additionally, they employ a log-likelihood function for each company instead of a simple linear regression model. The resulting abnormal returns of acquiring institutions differ slightly in significance compared to the classic event study approach. Nonetheless, Cyree and DeGennaro (2002) concede that the classical event study methodology is still robust enough to obtain valid results.

Starting with Houston and Ryngaert (1994), research frequently combines the abnormal returns of the acquirer AR_{tA} and target AR_{tT}, based on their respective market capitalization MV_{tA} and MV_{tT}, to obtain the abnormal return of the transaction for the newly merged entity:

$$AR_{t,transaction} = \frac{AR_{tA} \times MV_{tA} + AR_{tT} \times MV_{tT}}{MV_{tA} + MV_{tT}} \tag{1-7}$$

This approach allows for the estimation of the absolute and relative total shareholder wealth creation due to an M&A transaction.[6]

6 Other studies, which employ this approach include, among others, Zhang (1995), Toyne and Tripp (1998), Becher (2000), Houston et al. (2001), Beitel (2002), Beitel, Schiereck, and Wahrenburg (2004), Becher and Campbell (2005), Lorenz (2006), Mußhoff (2007), Brewer and Jagtiani (2013), and Al-Sharkas and Hassan (2010).

2.1.2 Dynamic efficiency studies

The use of dynamic efficiency studies for the investigation of the effects of mergers and acquisitions in the banking industry has its origin in the beginning of the 1990s (e.g Rhoades, 1993; Shaffer, 1993). The empirical approach of efficiency studies, which are also described as sophisticated benchmark methods (Berger & Humphrey, 1997), differs markedly from the event study methodology. Based on accounting data, research using efficiency studies employ an econometrical technique known as the frontier methodology. The most common approach is to estimate either the cost or profit function of the most efficient company in the sample and to subsequently regard this function as the efficient frontier to which the remaining firms in the sample are compared to. The further away a company is from the efficient frontier, the less efficient it is considered. However, at the same time, the potential for efficiency improvements is considerably higher. The majority of static efficiency studies shows that mergers and acquisitions among financial firms should lead to large gains in the efficiency of the involved institutions.[7] Yet, the actually observed gains from M&A transactions are frequently significantly smaller than the potential suggests (Berger, 2000; Berger & Humphrey, 1994). The efficiency can be estimated by either parametric or nonparametric techniques. Berger and Mester (1997) point out that the parametric techniques should be chosen over the nonparametric ones, as their focus lies on economic optimization rather than technological optimization. Therefore, they better reflect the concepts of cost and profit efficiency.

The three most important and commonly employed economic efficiency concepts are (i) cost efficiency, (ii) standard profit efficiency, and (iii) alternative profit efficiency (Berger & Mester, 1997). Berger and Mester (1997) suggest that standard profit efficiency is a preferable starting point for the analysis of the success of M&A transactions, but they also test cost and alternative profit efficiency and various estimation techniques, as well as different functional forms. They show that it makes nearly no difference which of the techniques is used, as they all yield qualitatively similar results and can therefore be considered to be robust.[8] Therefore, significant distortions due to methodological difference appear to be unlikely. Furthermore,

---

7 For a comprehensive review of the literature using the static efficiency methodology see Berger and Humphrey (1994), Berger, Demsetzc, and Strahanc (1999), and Berger (2000).

8 The one notable exception to this general statement is the treatment of equity capital. If it is not properly accounted for a scale bias may arise, which makes large banks appear to be more profit efficient than small ones (Berger & Mester, 1997).

efficiency studies allow researchers to simulate hypothetical M&A transactions in the financial sector (Altunbaş, Molyneux, & Thornton, 1997; Hughes, Lang, Mester, & Moone, 1999; Lin & Huang, 2009; McIntosh, 2002; Shaffer, 1993). In this way, the theoretically possible efficiency gains can be observed and recommendations can be made as to which institutions stand to increase their efficiency the most and should therefore consider to carry out an M&A transaction.

2.1.3 Performance studies

Performance studies, similar to efficiency studies, primarily use accounting ratios to test whether there is a significant change in the financial performance of the merging banks following merger transactions. An M&A transaction is considered successful if the investigated accounting ratios exhibit significant improvements and if these improvements are attributable to the merger transaction itself, and not to other external or internal factors, such as the general economic climate. In order to avoid noise from not directly transaction-related sources, several studies use a paired analysis (e.g. Chamberlain, 1998; Hoshino & Turnbull, 2002; Rose, 1987), while other studies employ a control group to mitigate this issue (e.g. Auerbach, 2009; Knapp, Gart, & Becher, 2005; Kwan & Wilcox, 1999; Linder & Crane, 1993).

Due to the relative simplicity of this approach compared to event studies and efficiency studies, only few different techniques and methods can be observed. Studies by Elsas (2007), Kondova Georgiev and Burghof (2007), and Auerbach (2009) employ more specific estimation methods based on the larger panel data sets. In addition, as with efficiency studies, performance studies enable researchers to simulate hypothetical mergers to show which banks will gain the most by undertaking an M&A transaction. The studies by Boyd and Graham (1988) and Boyd, Graham, and Hewitt (1993) use this approach. Moreover, performance studies find frequent application in the context of case studies, either as the primary method of analysis, as in Drees, Keisers, and Schiereck (2006), or as supplementary analysis to provide more in-depth information (Mußhoff, Jahns, & Schiereck, 2007a, 2007b).

Kwan and Wilcox (1999) make several adjustments to their data in order to take into consideration for the different accounting methods that banks are able to use when adjusting their books to reflect an M&A transaction. They consequently obtain "cleaned" accounting data after reflecting all one-off expenses that occur as a result of the merger and which do not reflect the actual performance of the bank. Kwan and Wilcox (1999) specifically point out that the chosen accounting method does not only alter the cost performance of the acquiring bank in the merger year, but also in the years following the merger. Therefore, it is important to consider the chosen method in order to obtain the actual merger related performance changes. Yet, other studies simply omit the data of the merger year from their calculations (e.g. Cornett, McNutt, & Tehranian, 2006; Drees et al., 2006; Linder & Crane, 1993). Cornett et al. (2006) emphasize the fact that the choice of financing method by the acquirer (cash, debt, equity, or a mix of those) can have a fundamental effect on the post-merger performance of the acquiring and target institution. Therefore, prior to choosing the relevant performance ratio on which to base the empirical analysis, this choice ought to be carefully examined.

2.1.4 Evaluation of the different empirical methodologies

All of the described methodologies have their distinct advantages, but also exhibit some limitations. Among the most obvious differences among the three methodologies is their definition of merger success, which is also one of the main points of criticism. They generally center on the owner (e.g. shareholders) of the acquiring bank in order to judge the success of a merger transaction. However, it is by no means clear whether added shareholder value, increased efficiency, or improvements in various accounting rations are actually the appropriate measure to evaluate the success of a merger. In addition, there is little evidence in the empirical literature whether successful bank M&As actually benefit consumers, for example through lower lending costs, or lead to more stable financial markets. In addition, particularly performance studies need to be interpreted carefully, as they are based on accounting data, which is subject to different rules in different jurisdictions and over time. Another major issue in any empirical study that examines one specific event, such as an M&A transaction, are potentially confounding events, which makes it more difficult to estimate the true effect of the investigated event. The majority of empirical research, however, reviews newspaper articles and company statements during the days surrounding the event to control for this issue.

Event studies commonly use the market model in order to investigate the shareholder wealth effects of M&A announcements. A criticism of this single-factor model is its generally relatively weak explanatory power. Yet, research shows that the overall results of more sophisticated multi-factor models do not differ significantly from the ones obtained by using the single-factor model (Cyree & DeGennaro, 2002; Zollo & Leshchinkskii, 2000). Generally, only the height of the abnormal returns changes, but the significance of the results largely remains the same. Some studies use advanced GARCH (e.g. Frame & Lastrapes 1998) and EGARCH models (Al-Sharkas & Hassan, 2010), but still arrive at qualitatively similar results to those obtained by using the classic market model. Therefore, the results obtained by using a single-factor model should not be dismissed entirely. Pilloff and Santomero (1998) argue strongly in favor of using the event study methodology, as it uses stock market data, which is forward looking and hence provides a reasonable estimate of the expected future performance of the merging institutions.

Dynamic efficiency studies, on the other hand, do not consider a bank's market performance. Their estimations are entirely based on accounting data. Beitel (2002) even argues that dynamic efficiency studies are error prone, since they rank among the most complex methodologies, which need a large number of accounting variables to approximate the models. In addition, there still is an ongoing debate as to whether deposits should be considered as an input or an output of the production function of a bank (see also Berger and Humphrey (1997) for a more detailed discussion on this topic). Therefore, the conclusions drawn by these studies need to be examined carefully. Nonetheless, the overall results seem to only partially depend on the way in which deposits are treated (Berger & Humphrey, 1997). One of the key advantages of efficiency studies is their ability to more clearly examine the origins of efficiency changes (Berger et al., 1999) and to use simulation studies to predict the outcome of potential mergers. This allows researchers to compare the outcomes of simulated mergers with actual ones. Rhoades (1994) argues in favor of efficiency studies, as they can be used to assess M&A activity and the corresponding industry consolidation from the vantage point of public policy and long-term industry performance.

Finally, DeLong and DeYoung (2007) prefer using performance studies. They favor the use of accounting data as it captures the actual past performance of a company as opposed to the expected future performance, as done by stock market data. Therefore, accounting data can be used to support or refute the observed stock market reaction and to examine and compare the most important profit and cost metrics directly. Pilloff and Santomero (1998), however, argue that accounting data may be incorrect in many cases and therefore lead to misleading results, which do not properly reflect the actual impact of a merger. In addition, accounting rules in most jurisdictions offer multiple options in the way that costs associated with an M&A transactions are treated.[9] Therefore, managers have some

9 Kwan and Wilcox (1999), for example, point to the differences in bank holding companies employing either the purchase or the pooling accounting method. In the purchase method, the premium paid to the target is put on the balance sheet of the acquirer as goodwill, which can then be amortized, thus reducing profits and lowering the tax rate. The pooling method, on the other hand, simply combines the assets of both institutions and hence does not allow for subsequent tax savings.

leeway to influence them. Overall, it appears as if the use of accounting data when evaluating bank mergers and acquisitions should be done with great care.

Evaluating the different advantages and drawbacks of the three empirical methodologies, all have their distinct merits and benefits and it will ultimately depend on the research goal of the study which of the three approaches is the most appropriate and should therefore be used. Event studies are the primary means by which to assess the creation or destruction of shareholder wealth. Therefore, these studies are particularly useful for financial institutions that are planning to engage in an M&A transactions, since the owner, i.e. shareholders, of both firms will most likely make their decision on whether to accept or reject a merger proposal based on the effect it will have on their personal wealth. The initial market assessment, however, may be wrong at the time of the merger announcement and therefore viewing the short-term success or failure of a transaction as an indication of the long-term success or failure is questionable. Dynamic efficiency studies ought to be the preferred method if gains or deteriorations in the cost or profit efficiency of a bank following a merger are of interest. Rhoades (1994) already points out that this is the most relevant information when considering regulatory or policy changes in regard to the financial sector. Performance studies appear to be a sensible method to analyze the long-term effects of M&As. Yet, due to the variability in accounting methods over time and jurisdictions, they should primarily be used as a complementary measure to assess the long-term success of a transaction and to show whether the initial capital market reaction was justified and whether the expected synergies were actually lifted.

2.2 Prior empirical research results on the success of bank mergers and acquisitions

Evidence on the success (or failure) of mergers and acquisitions in the financial industry is overall mixed. The majority of event studies find that targets, on average, earn large, positive and statistically significant abnormal returns, while bidding banks generally do not profit from an M&A transaction. In fact, it appears as if acquirers actually destroy shareholder wealth. Only more recent research on the United States (US), Europe, and several emerging economies suggests that M&As are not detrimental to the shareholders of the bidding bank. Similarly, the results of performance and dynamic efficiency studies indicate that bank M&As are a mixed blessing at best. There are only very few differences between the results of studies focusing on the US or Europe. It appears that most US banking M&As lead to an increase in the profit efficiency of the involved institutions. The evidence for European institutions, on the other hand, remains contradictory.

Yet, overall this line of empirical research indicates that at least the owners of the acquiring institution benefit from a merger transaction.

2.2.1 Evidence from United States event studies

Table 2-1 gives an overview of more than 50 event studies on bank mergers published between 1985 and 2013 which focus exclusively on the United States. The vast majority of the research focuses on the M&As conducted during the 1990s, with only relatively few studies including transactions that took place since the year 2000.

The majority of studies on the United States suggests that bidding banks destroy rather than create shareholder value when they undertake an M&A transaction (e.g. Baradwaj, Fraser, & Furtado, 1990; Cornett, Hovakimian, Palia, & Tehranian, 2003; Cornett & Tehranian, 1992; Gupta & Misra, 2007; Hankir, Rauch, & Umber, 2011; Hannan & Wolken, 1989; Houston & Ryngaert, 1994, 1997; Kane, 2000). Table 2-2 presents a detailed overview of the cumulative average abnormal returns of US event studies. Since the year 2000, multiple studies document that bank mergers during the 1990s led to better results for the bidder than those conducted during the 1980s (Al-Sharkas & Hassan, 2010; Becher, 2000; Houston et al., 2001). Possible explanations for these observations include improved access to information of the target for bidders and better market assessment of the actual value of a merger transactions than in previous decades (Houston et al., 2001).

Table 2-1: Descriptive overview of US event studies

				Results[a]		
Author (Year)	Sample size	Period	Region	Bidding bank	Target bank	Combined institution
Desai and Stover (1985)	18	1976–1982	USA	positive	n/a	n/a
Pettway and Trifts (1985)	11	1972–1981	USA	negative	n/a	n/a
James and Wier (1987a)	19	1973–1983	USA	positive	n/a	n/a
James and Wier (1987b)	60	1972–1983	USA	positive	n/a	n/a
Neely (1987)	26	1979–1985	USA	negative	positive	n/a
Trifts and Scanlon (1987)	12	1982–1985	USA	negative	positive	n/a
Sushka and Bendeck (1988)	41	1972–1985	USA	negative	n/a	n/a

Table 2-1 (continued)

Author (Year)	Sample size	Period	Region	Results[a]		
				Bidding bank	Target bank	Combined institution
Bertin, Ghazanfari, and Torabzadeh (1989)	33	1982–1987	USA	positive	n/a	n/a
Dubofsky and Fraser (1989)	101	1973–1983	USA	negative	n/a	n/a
Hannan and Wolken (1989)	43/69[b]	1982–1987	USA	negative	positive	negative
Kaen and Tehranian (1989)	31	1979–1987	USA	negative	n/a	n/a
Wall and Gup (1989)	23	1981–1983	USA	negative	n/a	n/a
Baradwaj et al. (1990)	23/24[b]	1980–1987	USA	positive	negative	n/a
Baradwaj, Dubofsky, and Fraser (1991)	108	1981–1987	USA	negative	n/a	n/a
Cornett and De (1991)	132/36[b]	1982–1986	USA	mixed	positive	n/a
Cornett and Tehranian (1992)	30	1982–1987	USA	negative	positive	n/a
Houston and Ryngaert (1994)	131/22[c]	1985–1991	USA	negative	positive	mixed
Madura and Wiant (1994)	152	1983–1987	USA	negative	n/a	n/a
Seidel (1995)	105	1989–1991	USA	positive	n/a	n/a
Waheed and Mathur (1995)	259	1963–1989	USA	mixed	n/a	n/a
Zhang (1995)	107	1980–1990	USA	positive	positive	positive
Hudgins and Seifert (1996)	160	1970–1989	USA	negative	positive	n/a
Pilloff (1996)	48	1982–1991	USA	n/a	n/a	mixed
Houston and Ryngaert (1997)	209	1985–1992	USA	negative	positive	n/a
Subrahmanyam, Rangan, and Rosenstein (1997)	225	1982–1989	USA	negative	n/a	n/a
Frame and Lastrapes (1998)	54/19[b]	1990–1993	USA	negative	positive	n/a

Table 2-1 (continued)

Author (Year)	Sample size	Period	Region	Results[a] Bidding bank	Target bank	Combined institution
Gleason and Mathur (1998)	135	1963–1996	USA	negative	n/a	n/a
Toyne and Tripp (1998)	68	1991–1995	USA	negative	positive	negative
Chavaltanpipat, Kholdy, and Sohrabian (1999)	30	1994–1995	USA	negative	positive	n/a
Kwan and Eisenbeis (1999)	94	1989–1996	USA	n/a	n/a	positive
Becher (2000)	558	1980–1997	USA	mixed	positive	positive
Kane (2000)	110	1991–1998	USA	negative	positive	mixed
Zollo and Leshchinkskii (2000)	579	1977–1998	USA	n/a	n/a	n/a
DeLong (2001)	280	1988–1995	USA	negative	positive	mixed
Houston et al. (2001)	64	1985–1996	USA	negative	positive	positive
Cyree and DeGennaro (2002)	123	1989–1995	USA	mixed	n/a	n/a
Hart and Apilado (2002)	22	1994–1997	USA	negative	positive	positive
Cornett et al. (2003)	423	1988–1995	USA	negative	n/a	n/a
DeLong (2003)	438	1988–1998	USA	negative	positive	mixed
Anderson, Becher, and Campbell (2004)	97	1990–1997	USA	negative	positive	positive
Kiymaz (2004)	207/70[b]	1989–1999	USA	positive	positive	n/a
Scholtens and de Wit (2004)	61	1990–2000	USA	negative	positive	n/a
Becher and Campbell (2005)	443	1990–1999	USA	negative	positive	positive
DeLong and DeYoung (2007)	216	1987–1999	USA	negative	positive	negative
Gupta and Misra (2007)	503	1981–2004	USA	negative	positive	mixed
Hagendorff, Collins, and Keasey (2008)	204	1996–2004	USA / Europe	negative	n/a	n/a

Table 2-1 (continued)

Author (Year)	Sample size	Period	Region	Results[a] Bidding bank	Target bank	Combined institution
Kim and Finkelstein (2009)	2,204	1989–2001	USA	negative	n/a	n/a
Al-Sharkas and Hassan (2010)	785	1980–2000	USA	negative	positive	positive
Hankir et al. (2011)	450[d]	1990–2008	USA	negative	positive	n/a
Hagendorff and Keasey (2012)	148	1996–2004	USA	negative	n/a	n/a
Brewer and Jagtiani (2013)	8	1991–2000	USA	negative	positive	positive
Kiymaz (2013)	250	1989–2003	USA	positive	n/a	n/a

[a] Shows the general overall result or trend, independent of the significance of the results. [b] Sample is split between acquirers/targets. [c] Sample is split between completed/aborted mergers. [d] Only announcement day returns. Table similar to Kolaric and Schiereck (2014).

The results of James and Wier (1987a, 1987b) document positive abnormal returns for acquirers during the 1970s, especially if the acquirer bids for a failed bank in an Federal Deposit Insurance Corporation (FDIC) auction. Dubofsky and Fraser (1989) and Bertin et al. (1989) arrive at similar results for FDIC assisted acquisitions using data from the 1980s. In addition, Seidel (1995) reports positive abnormal returns for acquirers between the years 1989 and 1991 as well. This result is also mainly driven by government-assisted bank mergers. Targets always achieve positive and generally statistically highly significant results. These results, however, show large variations and range between 1.18% (Frame & Lastrapes 1998) and 33.58% (Neely, 1987). Nevertheless, the data overall suggests that target shareholders can expect to earn average abnormal returns between 10% and 15%. The more recent study by Hankir et al. (2011) shows that the overall trend of large and significant positive abnormal returns for target institutions still persists, while bidding banks in US bank mergers are likely to incur significant losses in shareholder wealth upon an M&A announcement.

Among the studies which also examine the effect of merger transactions on the combined entity of target and bidder, only one documents a significant decline in shareholder wealth (Toyne & Tripp, 1998), while the remaining studies either show a significant positive return for the combined unit (e.g. Al-Sharkas & Hassan, 2010; Anderson et al., 2004; Becher, 2000; Becher & Campbell, 2005; Zhang, 1995) or insignificant returns (e.g. Houston & Ryngaert, 1994; Pilloff, 1996).

Table 2-2: Average cumulative abnormal returns for US event studies

Author (year)	Sample size	Period	Event window[a]	Average CAR: Bidding bank	Average CAR: Target bank	Average CAR: Combined institution
Desai and Stover (1985)	18	1976–1982	[0;1]	0.96%**	n/a	n/a
James and Wier (1987a)	19	1973–1983	[−1;0]	2.36%***	n/a	n/a
James and Wier (1987b)	60	1972–1983	[−1;0]	1.07%***	n/a	n/a
Neely (1987)	26	1979–1985	[+1;5][c]	2.82%**	33.6%***	n/a
Trifts and Scanlon (1987)	12	1982–1985	[−40;20][b]	−3.25%	21.37%**	n/a
Sushka and Bendeck (1988)	39[d]	1972–1985	[−4;0]	−0.74%	n/a	n/a
Bertin et al. (1989)	33	1982–1987	[−4;0]	2.03%***	n/a	n/a
Dubofsky and Fraser (1989)	56[g]	1973–1983	[−1;0]	−0.46%**	n/a	n/a
Hannan and Wolken (1989)	43/69[e]	1982–1987	[−1;0]	−3.78%***	11.1%***	−0.99%[f]
Kaen and Tehranian (1989)	31	1979–1987	[−1;0]	−0.58%**	n/a	n/a
Wall and Gup (1989)	23	1981–1983	[0;3][b]	−0.349%**	n/a	n/a
Baradwaj et al. (1990)	23/24[e]	1980–1987	[−2;2]	−2.07%***	18.8%***	n/a
Baradwaj et al. (1991)	108	1981–1987	[−5;5]	−2.09%***	n/a	n/a
Cornett and De (1991)	132/36[e]	1982–1986	[−1;0]	0.85%***	9.96%***	n/a
Cornett and Tehranian (1992)	30	1982–1987	[−1;0]	−0.8%**	8.0%***	n/a
Houston and Ryngaert (1994)	131/22[i]	1985–1991	[−2;2][j]	−2.32%***	14.4%***	0.38%
Madura and Wiant (1994)	152	1983–1987	[0;36][h]	−27.1%***	n/a	n/a
Seidel (1995)	105	1989–1991	[−20;20]	1.84%***	n/a	n/a
Waheed and Mathur (1995)	259	1963–1989	[0]	−0.17%*	n/a	n/a
Zhang (1995)	107	1980–1990	[−5;5]	0.4	6.96%***	3.50%***
Hudgins and Seifert (1996)	160	1970–1989	[−1;1]	−0.25%	7.53%***	n/a

Table 2-2 (continued)

Author (year)	Sample size	Period	Event window[a]	Average CAR: Bidding bank	Average CAR: Target bank	Average CAR: Combined institution
Pilloff (1996)	48	1982–1991	[−10;0]	n/a	n/a	1.44*
Houston and Ryngaert (1997)	209	1985–1992	[−4;1][j]	−2.4%	20.4%	n/a
Subrahmanyam et al. (1997)	225	1982–1989	[−1;1]	−0.9%***	n/a	n/a
Frame and Lastrapes (1998)	54/19[e]	1990–1993	[−5;5]	−0.30%**	1.183%**	n/a
Gleason and Mathur (1998)	135	1963–1996	[−1;0]	−0.29%*	n/a	n/a
Toyne and Tripp (1998)	68	1991–1995	[−1;0]	−2.24%	10.97%	−0.7%
Kwan and Eisenbeis (1999)	94	1989–1996	[−1;0]	n/a	n/a	0.77%*
Becher (2000)	558	1980–1997	[−5;5]	−1.08%***	17.1%***	1.8%***
Kane (2000)	110	1991–1998	[0]	−1.5%[k]	11.14%[k]	0.83%[k]
DeLong (2001)	280	1988–1995	[−10;1]	−1.68%***	16.6%***	0.04%
Houston et al. (2001)	64	1985–1996	[−4;1][j]	−3.47%[k]	20.8%[k]	1.86%[k]
Cyree and DeGennaro (2002)	123	1989–1995	[−5;5]	0.28%	n/a	n/a
Hart and Apilado (2002)	22	1994–1997	[0]	−0.415%	6.02%***	0.68%***
Cornett et al. (2003)	423	1988–1995	[−1;1]	−0.74%**	n/a	n/a
DeLong (2003)	438	1988–1998	[−10;1]	−1.89%***	14.8%***	0.12%
Anderson et al. (2004)	97	1990–1997	[−5;1]	−1.12%**	15.5%***	1.7%***
Kiymaz (2004)	207/70[e]	1989–1999	[−10;2]	0.83%*	4.26%***	n/a
Scholtens and de Wit (2004)	61	1990–2000	[−3;31]	−1.86%	12.7%***	n/a
Becher and Campbell (2005)	443	1990–1999	[−5;1]	−1.29%***	16.7%***	0.93%***
DeLong and DeYoung (2007)	216	1987–1999	[−10;10]	−3.09%***	14.9%***	0.26%
Gupta and Misra (2007)	503	1981–2004	[−1;1]	−1.84%***	16.1%***	0.29%**

Table 2-2 (continued)

Author (year)	Sample size	Period	Event window[a]	Average CAR Bidding bank	Target bank	Combined institution
Kim and Finkelstein (2009)	2,204	1989–2001	[-5;5]	-0.3%[k]	n/a	n/a
Al-Sharkas and Hassan (2010)	785	1980–2000	[-5;5]	-0.09%**	7.59%***	2.26%**
Hankir et al. (2011)	450[l]	1990–2008	[-3;3]	-1.19%***	18.0%***	n/a
Hagendorff and Keasey (2012)	148	1996–2004	[0]	-1.40%***	n/a	n/a
Brewer and Jagtiani (2013)	8[m]	1991–2000	[-1;1]	-0.23%	14.9%***	5.6%***
Kiymaz (2013)	250	1989–2003	[-1;1]	0.29%*	n/a	n/a

*,**,*** denotes statistical significance at the 10%, 5% and 1% level. [a] Only the event window in which the average cumulative abnormal return exhibits the most significant CAR is selected. [b] In weeks. [c] Event window for acquirers [+1;+2], targets [+1;+5]. [d] Only non-emergency mergers are considered here. [e] Sample is split between acquirers/targets. [f] The combined unit has a sample size of 43 only and the event window is [-15;+15]. [g] Only the announcements post July 1981 are displayed here. [h] In months. [i] Sample is split between completed/aborted mergers. [j] 0 equals the leakage date. [k] All values significant, but the level of significance is not mentioned. [l] Only announcement day returns. [m] Only mergers in which the combined unit became "Too-Big-to-Fail". Table similar to Kolaric and Schiereck (2014).

2.2.2 Evidence from European and worldwide event studies

Table 2-3 gives an overview of more than 25 event studies on bank mergers published between 1999 and 2013 which focus on either Europe as a whole, another nation other than the US, or are worldwide in scope. The results for European and worldwide banking M&As differ from those of the US. European and worldwide studies document, similar to US studies, that targets on average obtain large, positive, and statistically significant abnormal returns. Acquirers, on the other hand, gain significant negative abnormal returns only in a few cases, while the combined entity of target and acquirer on average receives positive abnormal returns. DeLong (2003) finds that the positive returns observed for European bidders lack significance, but they still perform better than their US counterparts. Scholtens and de Wit (2004) directly compare the returns on European and US bank mergers. They are likewise not able to find significant gains for European bidders. European targets, on the other hand, earn lower abnormal returns than their US peers (see also Table 2-4). The more recent study by Hankir et al. (2011) underscores this conclusion again. Their results show that targets of European M&As earn on average an abnormal return of 8.8%, while their US counterparts earn on average 18.0%. US bidders, on the other hand, destroy shareholder value, while European bidders do not.

The results of Ekkayokkaya, Holmes, and Paudyal (2009) show that acquirers in European bank mergers earned slightly positive returns prior to the introduction of the Euro in 1999. Later M&A transactions in the Eurozone, however, led to no statistically significant gains for the bidding bank. Yet, acquirers engaging in transactions outside of the Eurozone still achieved significant positive returns. The results of Ismail and Davidson (2005, 2007) and Lensink and Maslennikova (2008) likewise exhibit positive, albeit small, significant returns for the acquiring bank. In line with US event studies, targets in European bank mergers and acquisitons always obtain significant and positive abnormal returns, which vary in a broad range as well. The data overall suggest that target shareholders can expect to earn 10% abnormal return on average due to an M&A annoucement. In addition, most studies which also evaluate the impact of a merger on the combined entity, find that the newly formed institution obtains significant positive returns. The results of Cybo-Ottone and Murgia (2000), Beitel et al. (2004), Lepetit et al. (2004), Ismail and Davidson (2005), and Lorenz, Beitel, and Schiereck (2006) document that the combined entity receives positive returns. This suggests that European bank mergers create rather than destroy shareholder value.

Table 2-3: Descriptive overview of European and worldwide event studies

				Results[a]		
Author (Year)	Sample size	Period	Region	Bidding bank	Target bank	Combined institution
Tourani Rad and Van Beek (1999)	56/17[b]	1989–1996	Europe	mixed	positive	n/a
Cybo-Ottone and Murgia (2000)	54	1988–1997	Europe	positive	positive	positive
Schiereck and Strauss (2000)	1	1998	Europe	negative	positive	negative
Amihud et al. (2002)	214	1985–1998	Worldwide	negative	n/a	n/a
Bessler and Murtagh (2002)	43	1998–2001	Canada	mixed	n/a	n/a
Beitel et al. (2004)[c]	98	1985–2000	Europe	mixed	positive	positive
Lepetit et al. (2004)	180	1991–2001	Europe	positive	positive	positive
Scholtens and de Wit (2004)	20/17[b]	1990–2000	Europe	positive	positive	n/a
Ismail and Davidson (2005)	76	1987–1999	Europe	positive	positive	positive

Table 2-3 (continued)

Author (Year)	Sample size	Period	Region	Results[a] Bidding bank	Target bank	Combined institution
Bohl, Havrylchyk, and Schiereck (2006)	51	1996–2002	Poland	n/a	positive	n/a
Campa and Hernando (2006)	172	1998–2002	Europe	negative	positive	n/a
Lorenz et al. (2006)[d]	71	1990–2002	Europe	mixed	positive	positive
Soussa and Wheeler (2006)	215	1990–2003	Worldwide	negative	n/a	n/a
Ismail and Davidson (2007)	67	1987–2000	Europe	positive	positive	positive
Mußhoff (2007)	96	1994–2004	Europe	negative	positive	positive
Mußhoff et al. (2007a, 2007b)	1	1999	Europe	negative	positive	n/a
Weese (2007)	117	1999–2005	Europe	mixed	n/a	n/a
Crouzille et al. (2008)	73	1997–2003	Asia	mixed	mixed	mixed
Hagendorff et al. (2008)	204	1996–2004	USA / Europe	negative	n/a	n/a
Lensink and Maslennikova (2008)	75	1996–2004	Europe	positive	n/a	n/a
Singh Mann and Kohli (2008)	8	1991–1995	India	mixed	n/a	n/a
Ekkayokkaya et al. (2009)	963	1990–2004	Europe	mixed	n/a	n/a
Choi et al. (2010)	140	1995–2002	Worldwide	positive	n/a	n/a
Dontis-Charitos, Molyneux, and Staikouras (2011)	120	1990–2006	Worldwide	n/a	n/a	mixed
Hankir et al. (2011)	150[e]	1990–2008	Europe	mixed	positive	n/a
Goddard, Molyneux, and Zhou (2012)	132	1998–2009	Asia / Latin America	positive	positive	n/a
Ma, Pagan, and Chu (2012)	83	1998–2005	Asia	positive	n/a	n/a
Kolaric and Schiereck (2013)	94/24[b]	1995–2011	Latin America	positive	positive	n/a

[a] Shows the general overall result or trend, independent of the significance of the results. [b] Sample is split between acquirers/targets. [c] See also Beitel (2002). [d] See also Lorenz (2006). [e] Only announcement day returns. Table similar to Kolaric and Schiereck (2014).

Soussa and Wheeler (2006) examine the gains of European and other bidding banks from developed countries when they undertake M&A transactions with financial institutions from emerging markets. The results show that bidders earn, on average, negative returns in such takeovers. The analysis of multiple subsamples indicates that the overall negative results are largely driven by transactions undertaken during the 1997 Asian Financial Crisis. Prior to this crisis, the returns to the bidding are not statistically different from zero. Kolaric and Schiereck (2013) investigate M&As of financial institutions that took place in Latin America. Their results show that target banks obtain significant positive returns, while bidders also receive significant positive returns on the official announcement day of a transaction. Therefore, bank mergers in Latin America appear to be successful from the viewpoint of the shareholders of the merging institutions.

Table 2-4: Average cumulative abnormal returns for European and worldwide event studies

				Average CAR		
Author (year)	Sample size	Period	Event window[a]	Bidding bank	Target bank	Combined institution
Tourani Rad and Van Beek (1999)	56/17[b]	1989–1996	[–1;1]	–0.33%	4.65%**	n/a
Cybo-Ottone and Murgia (2000)	54	1988–1997	[–10;10]	1.16%	14.2%***	3.07%***
Schiereck and Strauss (2000)	1	1998	[–20;20]	–9.6%	33.1%***	n/a
Amihud et al. (2002)	214	1985–1998	[–10;1]	–0.91%***	n/a	n/a
Bessler and Murtagh (2002)	43	1998–2001	[–5;5]	0.9%***,c	n/a	n/a
Beitel et al. (2004)[e]	98	1985–2000	[–10;10]	0.24%	14.4%***	1.35%**
Lepetit et al. (2004)	180	1991–2001	[–7;7]	1.57%[c]	2.00%**,c	2.41%**,d
Scholtens and de Wit (2004)	20/17[b]	1990–2000	[–3;31]	2.56%	9.28%**	n/a
Ismail and Davidson (2005)	76	1987–1999	[–1;1]	0.03%***	2.3%***	0.49%**
Bohl et al. (2006)	51	1996–2002	[–1;1]	n/a	2.84%***	n/a
Campa and Hernando (2006)	172	1998–2002	[–30;30]	–2.37%**	5.43%**	n/a
Lorenz et al. (2006)[f]	71	1990–2002	[–10;10]	–1.2%	14.7%***	0.7%**
Soussa and Wheeler (2006)	215	1990–2003	[–1;7]	–0.41%*	n/a	n/a
Ismail and Davidson (2007)	67	1987–2000	[–20;0]	0.1%***	3.31%***	0.3%

Table 2-3 (continued)

Author (year)	Sample size	Period	Event window[a]	Average CAR: Bidding bank	Target bank	Combined institution
Mußhoff (2007)	96	1994–2004	[−10;10]	−0.3%*	17.1%***	1.01%*
Mußhoff et al. (2007a, 2007b)	1	1999	[−20;20]	−10.9%	13.9%	n/a
Weese (2007)	117	1999–2005	[−20;20]	−0.37%	n/a	n/a
Crouzille et al. (2008)	73	1997–2003	[−7;7]	−0.99%[d]	−1.63%[d]	−1.89%*,d
Hagendorff et al. (2008)	204	1996–2004	[−1;1]	−0.5%***	n/a	n/a
Lensink and Maslennikova (2008)	75	1996–2004	[0;1]	0.03%***	n/a	n/a
Singh Mann and Kohli (2008)	8	1991–1995	[0;5]	6.8%	n/a	n/a
Ekkayokkaya et al. (2009)	963	1990–2004	[−1;1]	0.03%	n/a	n/a
Choi et al. (2010)	140	1995–2002	[−5;0]	0.57%**	n/a	n/a
Dontis-Charitos et al. (2011)	120	1990–2006	[−1;1]	n/a	n/a	0.68%**
Hankir et al. (2011)	150[g]	1990–2008	[−3;3]	0.01%	8.8%***	n/a
Goddard et al. (2012)	132	1998–2009	[−5;5]	0.08%	1.60%***	n/a
Ma et al. (2012)	83	1998–2005	[−2;+2]	0.80%	n/a	n/a
Kolaric and Schiereck (2013)	94/24[b]	1995–2011	[−20;20]	1.40%	8.14%***	n/a

*,**,*** denotes statistical significance at the 10%, 5% and 1% level.[a] only the event window with most significant CAR is selected. [b] sample is split between acquirers/targets. [c] foreign acquisitions only, domestic ones receive a CAR of −0.1%, but are insignificant. [d] standardized CAR. [e] See also Beitel (2002). [f] See also Lorenz (2006). [g] Only announcement day returns. Table similar to Kolaric and Schiereck (2014).

2.2.3 Research findings of dynamic efficiency studies

Static efficiency studies in the United States commonly show that there are large opportunities for improvement for the majority of banks' cost and profit efficiency (Berger & DeYoung, 2001; Berger & Mester, 1997). As a matter of fact, Berger and Mester (1997) document that even the banks in their sample, who are considered to have the best practices, only achieve levels of standard and alternative profit efficiency of 54.9% and 46.3%, respectively. However, Berger and Humphrey (1994) and Berger (2000) highlight that research on bank mergers using efficiency studies frequently fails to find the anticipated efficiency improvements.

The vast majority of dynamic efficiency studies focuses on cost efficiency. On average, they document mixed results at best in regard to improvements in cost efficiency following an M&A transaction. In line with expectations, cost efficiency improvements are more easily achieved if the acquirer has a higher level of efficiency than the target and is therefore able to increase the target's cost efficiency (e.g Fried, Lovell, & Yaisawarng, 1999; Peristiani, 1997; Rhoades, 1998).[10] Fixler and Zieschang (1993) are the only ones to document an outright deterioration of efficiency levels due to M&A transactions.[11] Shaffer (1993) shows in her simulation study of more than 20,000 hypothetical bank mergers that especially M&As among smaller institutions should lead to significant improvements in their cost efficiency. This is most likely due to the newly formed larger institutions being able to achieve economies of scale. In addition, DeYoung (1997) shows that government assisted mergers lead to large efficiency gains for the combined entity. Berger and Mester (1997), Berger (1998), Berger and DeYoung (2001), as well as Al-Sharkas, Hassan, and Lawrence (2008) consider profit and cost efficiency. They all find significant gains in profit efficiency for the merged banks vis-à-vis their non-merging counterparts. Technological advances appear to be the main drivers of the observed improvements in the cost efficiency (Al-Sharkas et al., 2008; Berger & Mester, 1997).

The two US studies that focus exclusively on profit efficiency (Akhavein, Berger, & Humphrey, 1997; Hughes, Lang, Mester, Moon, & Pagano, 2003) are also able to show significant improvements in efficiency levels. Akhavein et al. (1997) find that the observed gains are largely achieved by the ability of banks to shift their outputs from securities to higher yielding loans.

Dynamic efficiency studies in Europe concentrate on one particular country in general, such as the United Kingdom (UK) or Germany, rather than Europe as a whole. Research by Altunbaş and Molyneux (1996) and Altunbaş, Gardener, and Moore (2001) shows that for the majority of European banks large economies of scale and scope exist. In this context, M&As appear to be an appropriate tool to lift this potential. Small European banks in particular stand to gain the most from improvements in economies of scale (Altunbaş et al., 2001).

10 It should be noted, however, that the results of DeYoung (1997) suggest that cost efficiency improvements are more frequently achieved if the target was more efficient than the acquirer.

11 The difference in the results of Fixler and Zieschang (1993) may be due to their choice of methodology. Unlike other researchers, they employ Törnquist productivity indices to describe the results of M&A operations.

Table 2-5: Overview of efficiency study results

Author (year)	Sample size	Period	Region	Results[a]		
				Overall	Cost efficiency	Profit efficiency
Fixler and Zieschang (1993)	160	1986	USA	negative	negative	n/a
Rhoades (1993)	898	1981–1986	USA	mixed	mixed	n/a
Shaffer (1993)[b]	20,503	1984–1989	USA	mixed	mixed	n/a
Vander Vennet (1996)	492	1988–1993	Europe	mixed	mixed	n/a
Altunbaş et al. (1997)[b]	7,626	1988	Europe	mixed	mixed	n/a
Akhavein et al. (1997)	57	1981–1989	USA	positive	n/a	positive
Berger and Mester (1997)	n/a[c]	1990–1995	USA	positive	positive	positive
DeYoung (1997)	348	1987–1988	USA	mixed	mixed	n/a
Peristiani (1997)	2,045	1980–1990	USA	mixed	mixed	n/a
Rhoades (1998)	9	n/a[d]	USA	mixed	mixed	n/a
Fried et al. (1999)	1,654	1989–1994	USA	mixed	mixed	n/a
Haynes and Thompson (1999)	79	1981–1993	United Kingdom	positive	n/a	positive
Lang and Welzel (1999)	283	1989–1997	Germany	mixed	mixed	n/a
Berger (2000)	639	1991–1994	USA	positive	mixed	positive[e]
Berger and DeYoung (2001)	n/a[c]	1993–1998	USA	positive	mixed	positive
Huizinga, Nelissen, and Vander Vennet (2001)	52	1994–1998	Europe	mixed	positive	mixed
Focarelli, Panetta, and Salleo (2002)	201	1984–1996	Italy	negative	negative	n/a
McIntosh (2002)[b]	2	1996–1996	Canada	positive	positive	n/a
Wutz (2002)	174	1993–1998	Germany	negative	negative	n/a
Hughes et al. (2003)[b]	441[f]	1992–1994	USA	positive	n/a	positive
Carbo-Valverde and Humphrey (2004)	22	1986–2000	Spain	positive	positive	n/a
Peng and Wang (2004)	16	1997–1999	Taiwan	positive	n/a	positive

Table 2-5 (continued)

Author (year)	Sample size	Period	Region	Results[a] Overall	Cost efficiency	Profit efficiency
Lin (2005)	23	1997–1999	Taiwan	mixed	mixed	n/a
Hosono, Sakai, and Tsuru (2006)	84	1984–2002	Japan	mixed	positive	mixed
Bresler (2007)	35	1997–2000	Germany	negative	n/a	negative
Sufian and Majid (2007)	2	2001	Singapore	positive	positive	n/a
Al-Sharkas et al. (2008)	440	1985–1999	USA	positive	positive	positive
Koetter (2008)	1,517	1993–2005	Germany	positive	positive	positive
Radomski (2008)	168	1994–2003	Germany	negative	negative	n/a
Rezitis (2008)	14	1993–2004	Greece	negative	negative	n/a
Beccalli and Frantz (2009)	714	1991–2005	Europe	mixed	positive	mixed
Figueira and Nellis (2009)	80	2001–2001	Europe	positive	positive	n/a
Lin and Huang (2009)	19[g]	2003–2005[h]	Taiwan	positive	positive	n/a
Bernad, Fuentelsaz, and Gómez (2010)	17	1986–2004	Spain	mixed	mixed	n/a

[a] Positive if the authors see an overall improvement in the performance due to the M&A transaction. [b] Simulation study. [c] Number of mergers not given, only an efficiency increase is observed for merged banks. [d] All mergers took place in the 1990s, specific years are not mentioned. [e] For the standard profit efficiency the sample size is 546. [f] Number of BHCs in the sample, the actual number of simulated mergers is not mentioned. [g] Number of mergers that should be conducted based on a hypothetical 2142 possible mergers. [h] Years used to approximate the efficiency function. Table similar to Kolaric and Schiereck (2014).

There is a large body of research using dynamic efficiency studies, which focuses exclusively on Germany. However, they exhibit a large variation in results, depending on the groups of financial institutions under scrutiny. Lang and Welzel (1996, 1998) show that the consolidation among German cooperative and universal banks ought to lead to large gains in profit efficiency through the realization of economies of scale. Yet, they are not able to validate that these expected gains are actually realized for cooperative banks (Lang & Welzel, 1999). Wutz (2002) largely confirms these results and in some cases even documents a decrease in cost efficiency following a merger. The results of mergers among German savings banks are not much more encouraging. Neither Radomski (2008) nor Bresler (2007) are able to detect and improvements in cost or profit efficiency, respectively. Yet, at least one subsample of savings bank mergers with up to six years of data available following the M&A transaction, leaves some room for speculation that profit efficiency gains of these institutions may take longer to realize than anticipated (Bresler, 2007). Koetter (2008) arrives at remarkably different results. He documents for more than 1,500 acquisitions between 1993 and 2005 that more than half of all M&A transactions in Germany were successful in achieving improvement in the level of cost and profit efficiency following the merger. The observed improvements in profit efficiency can reach up to 2% compared to those of non-merging institutions.

The research findings for other European countries report similarly mixed results. The improvements in cost efficiency after bank mergers in Spain are mixed (Bernad et al., 2010) to slightly positive (Carbo-Valverde & Humphrey, 2004), while bank mergers in Greece led to a deterioration in the cost efficiency of the involved institutions (Rezitis, 2008). In contrast, mergers among building societies in the United Kingdom led to an increase in the profit efficiency of the involved institutions. Focarelli et al. (2002) investigate the effects of bank mergers and acquisitions in Italy between 1984 and 1996. Their study is the only one to explicitly distinguish between mergers and acquisitions and they consequently show that, at least in Italy, these two types of transaction have decidedly different motivations. Italian banks undertake mergers primarily to expand their customer base. Acquisitions, on the other hand, are undertaken to enhance the value of the newly acquired banks and therefore the overall value of the newly formed institution.

2.2.4 Insights from performance studies

The first performance studies were published at the end of the 1980s and initially focused exclusively on US bank mergers. Since the year 2000, however, numerous performance studies on European bank mergers were conducted, the majority of those studies focusing only on Germany. More than 20 different performance studies are evaluated here (see also Table 2-6).

The results documented by US performance studies range from negative (Linder & Crane, 1993), to mixed (e.g. Chamberlain, 1998; Rose, 1987), to positive (e.g Boyd & Graham, 1998). In particular, Linder and Crane (1993) and Knapp et al. (2005) observe a deterioration in the performance following the merger of banks in New England and of bank holding companies (BHC), respectively. Nonetheless, Kwan and Wilcox (1999) find that the average operating costs of merged institutions are significantly lower than the one of their counterparts, which did not engage in an M&A transaction. Mergers conducted during the 1990s generally lead to a better cost performance of the involved institutions (Cornett et al., 2006).

The majority of research on Europe centers on Germany, with the exception of Vander Vennet (1996), who examines mergers throughout Europe. The research results for Europe are mixed and appear sensitive to the time period investigated in the study. Vander Vennet (1996) finds that M&As among European banks, on average, do not generate any significant performance improvements. Yet, in a subsample of mergers among institutions of similar size (e.g. mergers of equals), he is able to document significant performance improvements for the combined entity.

Table 2-6: Overview of performance study results

Author (year)	Sample Size	Period	Region	Result[a]
Rose (1987)	138	1970–1980	USA	mixed
Boyd and Graham (1988)[b]	1,000	1971–1984	USA	mixed
Boyd et al. (1993)[b]	1,000	1971–1987	USA	mixed
Linder and Crane (1993)	47	1982–1987	USA	negative
Tebroke (1993)	154	1983–1985	Germany	mixed/
Baxmann (1995)	24	1979–1988	Germany	negative
Gold (1997)	31	1972–1979	Germany	mixed
Haun (1996)	17	1990–1991	Germany	mixed
Vander Vennet (1996)	492	1988–1993	Europe	mixed
Boyd and Graham (1998)	157	1989–1991	USA	positive
Chamberlain (1998)	180	1981–1987	USA	mixed
Kwan and Wilcox (1999)	1,134	1987–1995	USA	mixed
Hoshino and Turnbull (2002)	25	1990–1994	Japan	mixed
Laudi (2003)	37	1990–1999	Germany	negative
Knapp et al. (2005)	80	1987–1998	USA	negative
Cornett et al. (2006)	134	1990–2000	USA	positive
Drees et al. (2006)	4	1996–2000	Germany	positive
Elsas (2007)	1,484	1993–2001	Germany	mixed
Kondova Georgiev and Burghof (2007)	132	1993–2004	Germany	positive
Mußhoff et al. (2007a, 2007b)	1	1999	France	mixed
Auerbach (2009)	1,682	1993–2006	Germany	positive
Correa (2009)	220	1996–2003	Worldwide	negative
Egger and Hahn (2010)	n/a	1996–2002	Austria	positive
Behr and Heid (2011)	119	2000	Germany	mixed

[a] positive if the authors see an overall improvement in the performance due to the M&A transactions.
[b] Simulation study. Table similar to Kolaric and Schiereck (2014).

In an early study, Tebroke (1993) finds improvements in the performance in approximately 40% of the 154 M&A transactions among German cooperative banks. Extensive research has been carried out on the merger performance of German savings banks. Almost the entire period from 1972 to 2004 is covered by multiple studies.[12] The trend during this time period is one of overall increasing merger performance. Gold (1997) finds no evidence of performance improvements during the 1970s, while the results of the 1980s even suggest that the performance deteriorated during the post-merger years (Haun, 1996). At the beginning of the 1990s, mixed post-merger performance is again observed (Baxmann, 1995). Kondova Georgiev and Burghof (2007) also document that the results are mixed, but highly sensitive to the investigated time period. Savings bank mergers between 1993 and 1998 led, on average, to a decline in the cost performance of the involved institutions. However, between 1999 and 2004 takeovers led to large and significance improvements in the cost as well as the profit performance of savings banks. In a comprehensive study of 1,682 M&As among German financial institutions, Auerbach (2009) finds evidence of significant improvements in the cost performance three and four years after the takeover. The profit performance, on the other hand, is nevertheless lagging behind that of institutions that did not engage in a merger.

2.2.5 The effects of bank mergers and acquisitions: Evidence from Asia

Research on bank mergers and acquisitions in Asia is still scarce. In total, only nine research papers center on Asia or a particular country from that region. Of these studies, four are event studies (see Table 2-3 and Table 2-4 for more detailed results), four are efficiency studies (see also Table 2-5) and only one is a performance study (see also Table 2-6). The overall results indicate mixed to positive reactions to bank mergers. However, owing to the generally small sample sizes, these findings need to be interpreted carefully. It is noteworthy that all empirical studies focusing on Asia in this section were published after the year 2000.

Crouzille et al. (2008) conduct an event study to analyze the return patterns following bank M&As in Asia between 1998 and 2003. They are not able to document significant abnormal returns to neither bidder nor target, but their results indicate that the combined unit experiences significant negative abnormal returns. Their

12 Gold (1997) examines the time period from 1972 to 1979, Haun (1996) covers the time period from 1979 to 1988. The two years 1990 and 1991 are investigated by Baxmann (1995) and Kondova Georgiev and Burghof (2007) analyze the time period from 1993 to 2004. In addition, Drees et al. (2006) examine four mergers between 1996 and 2000.

results from the examination of the period of the 1997 Asian Financial Crisis and the post crises period reveals that the overall significant negative returns for the combined institution are entirely driven by mergers during the crisis period. Following the crisis, the abnormal returns cease to be significant. This result is in line with those achieved for similar subperiods by Soussa and Wheeler (2006). Singh Mann and Kohli (2008) compare the returns of government versus market driven mergers in India. Their results show that market driven mergers perform better than those that are initiated by the government. The more recent study by Goddard et al. (2012) shows that targets of bank mergers in Asia earn positive returns. Bidders, on the other hand, do not appear to destroy shareholder wealth when acquiring banks in Asia (Goddard et al., 2012; Ma et al., 2012).

Dynamic efficiency studies focusing on Asia center on three countries: Taiwan, Singapore, and Japan. The results for Taiwanese mergers are largely positive. Peng and Wang (2004) document significant improvements in the cost efficiency following a takeover, whereas Lin (2005) is not able to confirm this result for all M&As. In their simulation study of more than 2,000 mergers between Taiwanese financial institutions, Lin and Huang (2009) find 19 mergers which these financial companies should undertake in order to raise their cost efficiency. M&As between banks and insurance companies appear to be particularly well suited to improve the cost efficiency while reducing the overall risk of the combined entity at the same time. Hosono et al. (2006) examine Japanese cooperative banks ("Shinkin"), and show that mergers among these banks lead to an improvement in the cost efficiency of the involved institutions. Yet, they are only able to document improvements in the profit efficiency for mergers during the 1990s. Generally, mergers during the 1990s resulted in higher efficiency gains than those conducted during the 1980s.

The one performance study that focuses on Asia centers on Japan. Hoshino and Turnbull (2002) investigate takeovers among Japanese credit institutions and find that M&As improved the cost and profit performance of the merging institutions. Nonetheless, when compared to their non-merging counterparts, these banks actually exhibit an inferior performance. Yet, Hoshino and Turnbull (2002) argue that mergers among Japanese credit institutions should be encouraged, as they appear to be an appropriate tool to enhance the performance of the involved banks.

2.3 Evaluation of the empirical findings

At a first glance, the empirical results appear to be rather heterogeneous. The Joint Hypothesis problem, which is endogenous to the event study methodology, plays a minor role only. The event windows are usually comparatively short and the results are therefore robust. The probably largest factor contributing to the apparent heterogeneity in the event study results is the different sample selection process of the various studies. US studies usually define bank mergers along relatively narrow lines and only include institutions in their sample starting with the SIC codes 60 (banks) and 671 (holding companies), the latter category generally subject to a more thorough examination to exclude non-bank holding companies (e.g. Al-Sharkas & Hassan, 2010; Becher, 2000). Research focusing on European bank mergers, on the other hand, generally takes a broader perspective and only requires the bidder to be a bank, whereas the takeover target can either be a bank, financial services firm, or insurance company (e.g. Beitel et al., 2004; Cybo-Ottone & Murgia, 2000). The use of accounting data from different time periods and jurisdiction is most likely the main reason for the observed heterogeneity of the results of performance and efficiency studies. Accounting rules can be subject to considerable variability between different countries and time periods. Therefore, it is not particularly surprising that the results of the various empirical studies reflect this to a certain degree.

The overriding theme in the majority of event studies appears to be one of shrinking abnormal returns as the banking sector continues to mature. The research suggests that takeovers among US banks were more successful during the 1970s and early 1980s. The analysis of later time periods largely documents negative abnormal returns to bidders. The research on European bank mergers offers a similar picture, albeit the results lagging by approximately a decade. The introduction of the Euro as a single currency, for example, and increased harmonization of European financial markets led to a deeper integration among the different EU countries. Ekkayokkaya et al. (2009) point out that bank takeovers were associated with significant positive returns for bidders prior to the introduction of the Euro. After 1999, however, acquirer returns cease to be significant. More recent research centering on bank mergers in emerging economies, such as the ones of Latin America, still shows positive abnormal returns to bidders and targets. In this case, the consolidation process may be a boon to these banking markets, as less efficient institutions disappear from the market, resulting in more mature banking sectors. Yet, as the emerging market banking sectors undergo further consolidation, the returns to bidders will likely follow those already observed for the more mature markets of the US and Europe. Increased competition among banks for the few remaining targets will potentially lead to higher target premiums. This, in turn, will lead to a more critical reception of the M&A announcement by capital markets, as the high acquisition costs will probably be a drag on the financial performance of the acquirer in the years following the takeover.

2.4 Determinants of successful merger transactions in the financial sector

The drivers of successful mergers and acquisitions among financial institutions are manifold. The majority of the empirical literature uses various forms of regression analysis to identify the factors that have either a positive or negative influence on the outcome of a takeover. Beitel (2002) roughly divides these factors into three distinct categories: (i) characteristics related to the acquirer or target, (ii) characteristics specific to the particular transaction, and (iii) characteristics in regard to the current regulatory and economic environment. Table 2-7 Panel A through C lists the most important factors and their qualitative impact in the last column.

Table 2-7: Summary of the main success factors for bank mergers and acquisitions

Success factor	Effect[a]
Panel A: Characteristics related to the acquirer or target	
▪ High acquirer growth	–
▪ High target growth/market performance	+
▪ Higher efficiency/performance of the acquirer	+
▪ Low target performance	+
▪ Absolute size targets	+/–
▪ Large overall transaction size	+/–
▪ Prior acquisition experience	+
▪ High frequency of M&A engagement	+/–
▪ High degree of strategic similarities	+
▪ High management ownership	+
▪ High overlap of operations	+
Panel B: Characteristics specific to the transaction	
▪ Geographic focus	+/–
▪ Geographic diversification	+/–
▪ Product focus	+/–
▪ Product diversification	+/–
▪ Stock payment	–
▪ Combination of stock and cash or cash only payment	+
▪ High number of potential bidders	+/–
▪ High number of potential targets	+
▪ Insurance company	+
▪ Hostile takeover	+
Panel C: Characteristics in regard to the current regulatory and economic environment	
▪ Deregulation	–
▪ High regulatory efficiency and/or standard	+

Table 2-7 (continued)

Success factor	Effect[a]
▪ M&A approval by the regulator	+
▪ Low level of investor protection	+
▪ High M&A activity	+/–

[a] indicates an average increase (+) or decrease (–) in the CAR, and/or an improvement in efficiency and/or an improvement in financial performance. Table style following Kolaric and Schiereck (2014).

2.4.1 Characteristics related to the acquirer or target

The particular characteristics of the acquiring and target institution generally have a significant effect on the overall success of a takeover transaction (see Table 2-7 Panel A). A high target growth rate, which can be measured either by the target's asset growth rate or its stock market performance over a predetermined time period, leads to a significantly better M&A outcome (Beitel et al., 2004; Ismail & Davidson, 2007; Lorenz et al., 2006). Among others, Akhavein et al. (1997), Beitel et al. (2004), and Beccalli and Frantz (2009), observe that large efficiency differentials between the target and acquiring bank also lead to a better performance of the combined entity following the merger transaction. These results can be interpreted as evidence for the Inefficient Management Hypothesis: The management of the acquiring bank will transfer its superior skills or more advanced technology upon the target. Consequently, this will raise the target's efficiency level and overall performance (e.g. Beitel et al., 2004; Hernando, Nieto, & Wall, 2009).

The evidence of the influence of absolute target and/or transaction size on the impact of mergers among financial institutions is still unclear. There are multiple studies which find that either absolute target or transaction size are beneficial to the overall success of an M&A transaction (Campa & Hernando, 2006; DeLong, 2001; Gupta & Misra, 2007; Kane, 2000). Nevertheless, there is also ample evidence that larger transactions are detrimental to takeover success. This holds for US (Hagendorff & Keasey, 2012), as well as European bank mergers (Cybo-Ottone & Murgia, 2000; Mititelu & Hunger, 2009; Mußhoff, 2007). If the acquiring bank frequently engages in M&A transactions, it usually performs better than its peers, who do so less frequently (e.g. DeYoung, 1997; Haleblian, Kim, & Rajagopalan, 2006; Kolaric & Schiereck, 2013; Zollo & Singh, 2004).Wheelock and Wilson (2004) and Haleblian et al. (2006) show that banks with greater acquisition experience appear to be more likely to engage in additional takeovers. This will especially be the case if the previous acquisition was successful. Furthermore, the greater the strategic similarities between acquirer and target, the more likely the merger will become successful (Altunbaş & Marqués, 2008; Kim & Finkelstein, 2009).

Additionally, a high overlap of operations (e.g. Houston et al., 2001; Houston & Ryngaert, 1994; Pilloff, 1996) and larger management ownership appear to lead to more successful M&As (Anderson et al., 2004). It also appears as if American and European banks follow different post-merger strategies. Hagendorff and Keasey (2009) show that American banks pursue a strategy of revenue enhancement following a merger. European banks, on the other hand, appear to mainly engage in a cost cutting strategy, which allows them to improve the cost efficiency of the combined institution.

2.4.2 Characteristics specific to the transaction

There are a multitude of transaction specific factors that can potentially affect the outcome of a merger transaction (see Table 2-7 Panel B). One of the most frequently examined transaction specific factors on the success of bank M&As are geographic focus versus geographic diversification. Yet, the empirical evidence overall is not clear. Several studies show that cross-border bank mergers in Europe have an overall positive effect on the performance of M&A transactions (e.g Hagendorff et al., 2008; Ismail & Davidson, 2005, 2007; Vander Vennet, 1996). There are, however, a few studies that are not able to document this positive effect (e.g. Cybo-Ottone & Murgia, 2000; Lorenz et al., 2006). The picture is similar for research on bank mergers in the US. There is some evidence that intra-state mergers have a positive effect (Berger, 1998; Trifts & Scanlon, 1987; Zhang, 1995), but not all research concurs (e.g. Al-Sharkas & Hassan, 2010; Chavaltanpipat et al., 1999; Madura & Wiant, 1994). Trifts and Scanlon (1987) and Toyne and Tripp (1998) specifically find that interstate mergers in the US are associated with negative stock market returns for the acquiring bank, while Gleason and Mathur (1998) show that the foreign expansion by US institutes lead to this outcome. The research on whether product focus or product diversification leads to better M&A results is similarly mixed. Beitel et al. (2004) and Becher and Campbell (2005) show that product focus has a positive effect on merger performance, while DeLong (2001), Cornett et al. (2006) and Mußhoff (2007) find evidence that a combination of product and geographical focus is best for the acquiring bank. However, there are numerous studies whose results suggest that diversifying mergers lead to more desirable outcomes than non-diversifying ones (e.g. Baele, De Jonghe, & Vander Vennet, 2007; Berger, 1998; Elsas, Hackethal, & Holzhäuser, 2010; Hagendorff & Keasey, 2009).

For obvious reasons the financing method of an M&A transaction can play an important role in determining overall M&A success. From a shareholder's perspective, cash only payments or a combination of cash and stock payments are preferable to stock payments, as they are associated with positive wealth effects for the acquiring institution (e.g Al-Sharkas & Hassan, 2010; Baradwaj et al., 1991; Becher, 2000; Ismail & Davidson, 2007). Several studies actually show that mergers purely paid in stock lead to significant negative stock returns for the acquiring bank (Cornett et al., 2003; Gupta & Misra, 2007; Houston et al., 2001). Choi et al. (2010), on the other hand, observe that the bond market reaction to acquisitions paid in cash is negative. They document a marked rise in the yield-spreads of the acquiring institution. This appears to be directly linked to cash payments reducing a bank's liquidity and therefore actually being risk-increasing events for bondholders. Shareholders, on the other hand, profit from cash payments, as neither their voting rights nor the share price is diluted, as could be the case if new shares were issued to finance the acquisition.

The findings of simulation studies of mergers in the financial sector regularly show that the acquisition of an insurance company will have positive impact on the acquiring bank's performance (Boyd & Graham, 1988; Boyd et al., 1993; Lin & Huang, 2009). The empirical studies by Cybo-Ottone and Murgia (2000) and Dontis-Charitos et al. (2011) largely support the results of the simulation studies. The results of James and Wier (1987b) suggest that the availability of a larger pool of potential targets will lead to higher returns for the acquiring bank. Becher (2000), on the other hand, shows that in case bidding banks are competing for a fixed pool of targets, the acquirer is able to obtain better returns. Baradwaj et al. (1990) are the only ones who analyze the difference between hostile and friendly mergers in the banking sector. They observe that the acquiring bank of a successful hostile takeover receives higher negative returns than their counterparts, who engage in friendly takeover bids. Conversely, the targets of hostile takeovers earn significantly larger returns than those in friendly M&A deals.

2.4.3 Characteristics in regard to the regulatory and economic environment

There are a multitude of external environmental factors that can exert a significant influence on the success of an M&A transaction (see also Table 2-7 Panel C). Sushka and Bendeck (1988) and Hudgins and Seifert (1996) find that the final regulatory approval of a bank merger has a significant positive effect on the acquirer and target stock returns. This is probably due to regulatory approval removing any remaining uncertainties as to whether the transaction will actually occur. The impact of financial sector deregulation is a topic of recurrent contention and there is no clear evidence whether its effects are positive or not. The research findings of Dubofsky and Fraser (1989) as well as Becher and

Campbell (2005) suggest that deregulation may be one of the drivers behind the frequently observed negative returns to the bidding bank. On the other hand, Kwan and Wilcox (1999) find evidence that, after the full implementation of the Riegle-Neal Act, improvements in cost and profit performance of the merging institutions were higher than before the law was passed. Cornett et al. (2006) argue that although capital markets might have reacted negatively, the overall performance of US commercial banks improved significantly after the passage of the Riegle-Neal Act. Moreover, Jeon and Miller (2007) observe that US states with less restrictive branching and banking regulations register higher merger activity. The results of Hagendorff et al. (2008) indicate that in international bank M&As, US acquirers achieve better results when they choose targets from countries in which the level of investor protection is lower compared to the one in the US. At the same time, a high level of government efficiency is associated positively to the acquiring bank's returns (Kiymaz, 2004). Likewise, the results of Buch and DeLong (2004) even suggest that targets located in jurisdictions with well-developed transparency laws and higher levels of supervisory power are more attractive for international mergers. Similarly, M&As that are conducted in markets with higher levels of regulatory quality are related to better merger performance (Beccalli & Frantz, 2009). Whether banks profit from undertaking mergers during an "M&A wave" is not clear. DeLong and DeYoung (2007) suggest that acquirers can learn by observing, while Mußhoff (2007) finds that acquirers tend to overpay for targets during an "M&A wave".

2.4.4 The influence of managers on the outcome of bank mergers

A firm's executive officers, its board of directors, and the other members of the top management team have significant influence on a company's decision to engage in M&A activity. However, most empirical evidence suggest that not all mergers are truly value enhancing, especially from the perspective of the bidding firm's shareholders. Therefore, some researchers argue that instead of firm value, the personal motivations of the top management team, such as empire building, may drive the decision of entering into an M&A (e.g. Bliss & Rosen, 2001; Hughes et al., 2003).[13]

Milbourn, Boot, and Thakor (1999) develop a model grounded in agency theory and derive two reasons as to why chief executive officers (CEOs) decide to engage in mergers. Anticipated reputational gains, higher levels of compensation, and herd behavior may be among the main motivations for CEOs to enter into

13 Hagendorff, Collins, and Keasey (2007) offer a comprehensive review on the influence of bank governance on the acquisition performance of bank in the US.

an M&A transaction. This kind of behavior will generally be at the expense of the shareholders' wealth. However, a situation may also arise in which a CEO's decision to engage in a merger can be highly beneficial for the bank's shareholders. In the case of a moderate level of competition and significant uncertainty about future opportunities, the decision to expand the company through mergers may allow firms to exploit upcoming opportunities before its competitors. This will give the bank a competitive advantage, which will eventually generate additional shareholder value.

Cohen and Reid (1966) were one of the first to analyze the influence that managers exert on US commercial banks to enter into mergers and acquisitions. Their results suggest that managers largely base their decision on their desire to control additional economic resources and the reputational gains they anticipate. Bliss and Rosen (2001) and Anderson et al. (2004) later document that the growth in a banks' assets is accompanied by a similar growth in CEO compensation levels. In addition, both studies show that the compensation structure of a CEO (cash versus equity based) is a determining factor in a CEO's decision to engage in M&As. Higher levels of cash compensation are associated with an increased propensity to engage in a merger, whereas higher levels of equity compensation decrease this tendency. Bliss and Rosen (2001) find that the cash compensation of CEOs who frequently engage in acquisitions is seven percentage points higher than for those CEOs who do so less often (69% versus 62% cash compensations). They interpret this result as a comparatively high ratio of equity compensation serving as a disincentive to engage in M&As. This may be desirable from the shareholder perspective, as the large majority of empirical studies shows that the stock price of the acquiring bank will drop upon an M&A announcement. A higher level of equity compensation signifies that a higher proportion of the management's wealth is connected to the overall success of a merger and therefore the management is more likely to undertake value increasing mergers. Anderson et al. (2004) document a strong relationship between the performance of the combined entity of acquiring and target bank and the management's level of equity compensation. In this case, higher amounts of equity based compensation are associated with a better performance of the combined institution. Anderson et al. (2004) interpret this as evidence that managers do not only engage in empire building and try to increase their compensation. They point out that equity compensation is a powerful mechanism by which the interests of the management and the shareholders can be aligned. Palia (1993) analyzes the acquisition premiums managers are willing to pay. His results suggest that there is a U-shaped relationship between merger premiums and management ownership of a bank. If managers have a stake of up to 5.9% in their institution, they tend to pay lower premiums. This supports the notion that equity ownership aligns the interest of shareholder and managers. On the other hand, Palia (1993) documents that ownership in excess of 5.9% will again increase the management's willingness to pay higher merger premiums. In this case, large equity ownership may act as an incentive for managers to attempt to diversify their previously undiversified financial portfolios through M&As.

The results of Cornett et al. (2003) document that focusing as well as diversifying mergers are more successful if the CEO of the acquiring bank has a greater stake in the firm. This can be either through stock options or outright equity holdings. Hughes et al. (2003), on the other hand, show that large equity holdings by the management can lead to entrenchment. As a consequence, the management is likely to block potential takeover attempts by other banks, even though this would probably lead to significant increases to the wealth of the bank's shareholders. The results of Hadlock, Houston, and Ryngaert (1999) point in a similar direction. Using a sample of matched acquired and non-acquired banks, they find that higher levels of management ownership are associated with a decreased acquisition probability. As a consequence, they interpret this outcome as evidence for the existence of management entrenchment and view this as the main reason for the high rate of management turnover following a successful merger.

Overall, the empirical evidence indicates that the form of management compensation is one of the driving forces behind successful bank mergers (Hagendorff et al., 2007). A higher ratio of equity compared to cash compensation of the top management has a positive impact on M&A performance. It appears to be an appropriate mechanism through which the interest of shareholders and the management can be aligned and therefore ought to be an important part of management compensation packets. Yet, the decision on how to set the equity to cash ratio is important, as large amounts of equity compensation potentially lead to undesirable outcomes.

2.4.5 Evidence on regulatory arbitrage and "Too-Big-to-Fail" bank mergers

In the wake of the 2007 Financial Crisis, interest on the issues of "Too-Big-to-Fail" (TBTF) banks, regulatory arbitrage, and the potential implicit abuse of safety net subsidies by banks through large takeovers, started to increase dramatically. Since then, a growing body of empirical research began to emerge on these topics as well. The origins of TBTF go back to 1984 and are based on a statement by the Comptroller of the Currency when he testified in front of Congress in regard to the bailout of Continental Illinois in May 1984. In order to avoid a bank run and the eventual failure of Continental Illinois, the FDIC decided at that time to fully insure all of Continental Illinois's deposits and non-deposit liabilities. This was, fundamentally, a comprehensive government guarantee. Indirectly, the Comptroller of the Currency also acknowledged that the 11 largest banks in America would not be allowed to fail because of their systemic importance to the US financial system. As a consequence of this statement the Wall Street Journal on September 20th 1984 published an article listing the 11 largest US banks.

O'Hara and Shaw (1990) were one of the first to analyze the effect that the acknowledgement and subsequent listing of TBTF banks had on the institutions that benefited from it. The event study they conduct documents that 9 of the 11 banks listed by the Wall Street Journal received positive abnormal returns.[14] O'Hara and Shaw (1990) conclude that the capital market is assigning those banks a premium, which are implicitly considered to be TBTF and therefore likely to receive a government bailout. Morgan and Stiroh (2005) examine the bond ratings of the 11 TBTF banks and find that these institutions were able to issue new bonds at significantly lower interest rates than their non-TBTF peers. This suggests that market participants view these banks as considerably less risky, a development that continued throughout the 1990s. The research by Penas and Unal (2004) indicates that TBTF considerations are one of the main reasons why bondholders regard M&As among banks as overall default-risk reducing events. Brewer and Jagtiani (2013) are able to confirm this result. Gropp, Gruendl, and Guettler (2014) find evidence that German savings banks undertook riskier activities when their entire deposits were effectively guaranteed by the German government.

Brewer and Jagtiani (2013) examine the premiums that banks were willing to pay in order to obtain TBTF status. There is no explicit definition in regard to what constitutes a TBTF bank and therefore this definition is a conceptual matter. Brewer and Jagtiani (2013) therefore arrive at multiple definitions that lift a bank into TBTF status according to market participants. First, the total assets of a bank must be a minimum of 100 billion US$ (either with or without inflation adjustment. Second, the bank must rank among the largest 11 US banks according to asset size in any given year. Third, the market capitalization of the bank must exceed 20 billion US$. Brewer and Jagtiani (2013) actually show that the threshold of 100 billion US$ without inflation adjustment was perceived by the market as an important indication of a bank to be classified as TBTF during the 1990s and early 2000s. Their event study results document that bank mergers

---

14 Continental Illinois did not obtain a significant return, presumably because capital market participants were already aware of its TBTF status following the bailout by the FDIC in May 1984. For Security Pacific, on the other hand, slightly negative abnormal returns are observed.

that resulted in TBTF banks led to highly significant positive returns to the target and insignificant losses to the acquirer. Additionally, the combined unit also obtained significant positive returns as a result of the merger announcements. Overall, the results of Brewer and Jagtiani (2013) suggest that the eight acquiring banks that engaged in mergers that led to the creation of new TBTF institutions were willing to pay a combined 15.3 billion US$ in order to obtain the TBTF status. This kind of behavior by banks should clearly be of concern to policy makers and regulators alike.

Hagendorff, Hernando, Nieto, and Wall (2012) find evidence that the strength of the regulatory regime and of the deposit insurance scheme appear to play a dominant role in the takeover premiums financial institutions are willing to pay to their targets. Similar to the results of Buch and DeLong (2004), they show that target banks located in jurisdictions with a stricter regulatory environment are more attractive in cross-border M&As. In this case, the bidder is less likely to unknowingly purchase a target in financial difficulty. The more stringet disclosure requirements usually associated with stricter regulatory regimes seem to increase the confidence of the acquirer in their investment. Nevertheless, apart from cross-border mergers, stricter regulatory requirements lead to lower overall target premiums. Hagendorff et al. (2012) mainly attribute this finding to higher compliance costs. This result, however, is driven by domestic and not cross-border M&As. Therefore, Hagendorff et al. (2012) argue that there is no conclusive evidence of banks paying significantly higher premiums to exploit potential safety net benefits. In addition, there is no evidence that the acquiring banks pay higher premiums for financial institutions located in jurisdiction with lower regulatory regrimes or for becoming TBTF through cross-border takeovers.

Yet, there is also research pointing towards the existence of regulator arbitrage in regard to cross-border bank mergers and acquisitions. In stark contrast to the results presented by Buch and DeLong (2004) and Hagendorff et al. (2012), Dong, Song, and Tao (2011) find evidence that banks tend to expand from more heavily regulated markets into less regulated ones. In particular, takeover premiums appear to rise for targets that are located in countries with less stringent capital requirements, lower disclosure standards, and a more independent supervisory authority. Houston, Lin, and Ma (2012) largely arrive at similar results, but also see some advantages in this pattern, as this may lead to innovation as a result of regulation. However, they concede that this may eventually lead to a "race to the bottom", in which the country with the lowest regulatory requirements is able to attract the highest capital inflows. In addition, Carbo-Valverde, Kane, and Rodriguez-Fernandez (2012) find evidence that is consistent with European banks shifting risk onto EU safety nets by engaging in cross-border takeovers. They view this as evidence that European banks actively engaged in regulatory arbitrage, as banks appear to have increased their overall risk exposure at the cost of safety net subsidies. Using the event study methodology, Hagendorff et al. (2008) show that acquirers purchasing targets in jurisdictions with lower investor protection are able to obtain higher abnormal returns. Schaeck, Zhou, and Molyneux (2010) find evidence that banks in some cases were willing to pay significant premiums in order to become TBTF. In addition, it appears as if the overall systematic risk in European financial markets amplified in recent years. Yet, Schaeck et al. (2010) still maintain that mergers among European financial institutions did not have an adverse effect on the overall stability of European financial markets.

The research results on the impact of bank mergers and acquisitions on TBTF, regulatory arbitrage, and its effect on systematic risk, are still mixed. The majorty of studies finds at least some evidence that points towards the existence of regulatory arbitrage considerations when banks engage in cross-border mergers, but not all studies are able to confirm this. Nevertheless, it appears as if stock as well as bond markets reward bank mergers that potentially lead to TBTF institutions. Stock markets react more favorably to M&A announcements that may ultimately result in a TBTF bank, while these banks also pay lower interest rates on their outstanding bonds. This may give large banks a competitive advantage over their smaller rivals and potentially force small banks to engage in takeover as well to obtain the same benefits.

2.5 The wealth effects of mergers and acquisitions on industry rivals

The actions of one company can have significant effects beyond the company itself and may also impact other companies within the same industry. In particular, major corporate events, such as M&As, have the ability to change the competitive landscape of an entire industry and will therefore likely affect the rivals of the merging firms as well. Therefore, in order to properly measure the total effect of the consolidation process within a particular industry, these external effects ought to be included in the analysis (Berger et al., 1999). Starting with the work of Eckbo (1983) and Stillman (1983), a large body of research has emerged on the effects that M&As have on the share price of the rival companies within the same industry sector (Eckbo, 1985, 1992; Hankir et al., 2011; Keisers, 2009; Otchere & Ip, 2006; Song & Walkling, 2000). Overall, M&As appear to be beneficial to an industry, as the large majority of these studies find that rivals on average experience positive wealth effects when a competitor is acquired. This led to the development of three competing, but not mutually exclusive, hypotheses to explain the observed effects: the Market Power Hypothesis, the Efficiency Hypothesis, and the Acquisition Probability Hypothesis.

2.5.1 The Market Power Hypothesis

The Market Power Hypothesis is based on the assumption that mergers will lead to an increase in the market power for the remaining firms and may therefore lead to subsequent anticompetitive behavior by the remaining firms. Particularly in the banking industry, the possibility of such behavior leads to extensive scrutiny by antitrust authorities of mergers, as M&As may, among other things, lead to more restrictive lending behavior by banks (see e.g Berger, Goldberg, & White, 2001). Eckbo (1983) and Stillman (1983) pioneered the application of the event study methodology to investigate the Market Power Hypothesis and its effect on shareholder wealth. They argue that horizontal mergers should not only lead to positive wealth effects for the bidding firm, but also for its rivals, as all companies within a given industry should profit from an increase in its concentration level. However, even though market power considerations are frequently cited as a plausible reason for the observed positive rival effects, the majority of studies argue that it is not the main driver behind M&As (e.g. Eckbo, 1983, 1985, 1992; Stillman, 1983). Therefore, the reason behind the overall positive rival effects remains unclear. In addition, this research does not offer an explanation as to why only 50–60% of all rivals exhibit positive returns upon a merger announcement (Song & Walkling, 2000). It should be noted though that other studies, which do not use stock returns as measure, find evidence of increased market power in the wake of large horizontal mergers (e.g. Prager & Hannan, 1998; Singal, 1996).

There are only very few studies that analyze the rival effects of bank mergers. Keisers (2009) documents significant positive rival effects for European bank mergers. These positive effects are stronger, the closer the rival bank is to the target. However, Keisers (2009) also rejects that market power considerations play an important role in regard to bank mergers, and rather interprets his findings as being the result of anticipated future efficiency spill overs. In their more recent study, Hankir et al. (2011) also examine the rival effects to US and European bank mergers. In contrast to Keisers (2009), they find evidence that, among the investigated hypotheses, market power considerations play an important role when market participants evaluate bank mergers. In particular, return patterns, which are in line with those expected by the Market Power Hypothesis, are significantly related to intra-industry mergers, increasing market concentration, and large relative target size. This result suggests that bank M&As lead to a significant reduction in competition.

2.5.2 The Efficiency Hypothesis

The literature on bank mergers frequently shows that M&As are more successful if the efficiency differential between acquiring and target institution is high (e.g Akhavein et al., 1997; Beccalli & Frantz, 2009; Beitel et al., 2004). The Efficiency Hypothesis suggests that, if the combined entity is able to increase its overall efficiency levels following a merger, this could potentially result in heightened levels of competition within an industry and may ultimately make it more challenging for rivals to maintain their current performance and market share. Therefore, the rival effects are not necessarily positive, as suggested by the Market Power Hypothesis, but could also be negative.

Yet, the relationship is not one-directional. Rivals have, by definition, similar operations and production technologies. As a result, the announcement of a merger may be perceived by the market as a signal that rival companies have a similar potential to increase their efficiency levels (Eckbo, 1983). Claessens, Demirgüç-Kunt, and Huizinga (2001) even document efficiency improvements of domestic banks following the market entry of foreign banks through M&As. This can be interpreted as evidence that rival firms are able to benefit from efficiency spillover effects that arise from the existence of more efficient peer companies. Therefore, rivals may also obtain positive stock returns upon an M&A announcement (Eckbo, 1983). However, as the Market Power Hypothesis and the Efficiency Hypothesis are not mutually exclusive, the observed rival returns may reflect the combined effect of both hypotheses.

Eckbo (1983) shows that the rival effects for horizontal as well as vertical mergers are positive and therefore concludes that the observed rival gains are more likely to stem from anticipated future cost saving rather than increased market power. He thereby implies that any negative effects that may result from increased competition are outweighed by the anticipated future gains in efficiency. In his study on European bank mergers, Keisers (2009) similarly argues that the observed positive rival gains are more likely to originate from expected future efficiency spillover effects rather than from market power considerations. Hence, M&As in the banking sector are overall beneficial and should be encouraged rather than blocked.

2.5.3 The Acquisition Probability Hypothesis

The fundamental idea behind the Acquisition Probability Hypothesis is that the target of an acquisition as well as its rivals will earn positive abnormal returns surrounding the announcement of an M&A transaction, as this will increase their probability of becoming a target in the future (Song & Walkling, 2000). Eckbo (1992) is the first to point out that an increase in the acquisition probability of the remaining institutions may be an additional driver for the observed positive rival returns upon a merger announcement. He arrives at this conclusion because he observes positive rival effects for 89 non-horizontal Canadian mergers, which by definition do not have anticompetitive effects. It can rather be viewed as a signal that some production factors become more valuable and that consolidation within an industry is likely to be beneficial. Song and Walkling (2000) conduct a comprehensive empirical investigation of the Acquisition Probability Hypothesis. They also find evidence in support of this hypothesis, as rivals earn significant abnormal returns on the announcement day of an acquisition, regardless of the ultimate outcome of the takeover. Moreover, they also show that the cross-sectional variation of the rival returns are largely linked to variables that indicate the likelihood of an acquisition. Akhigbe and Madura (1999) obtain similar results. They find that the positive valuation effects they observe for target rivals are largely due to industry-specific and firms-specific characteristics, which indicate the rival's likelihood to become the target of a future merger transaction.

Akhigbe and Martin (2000) document that the returns patterns predicted by the Acquisition Probability Hypothesis are particularly noticeable for the target rivals of cross-border M&As. Foreign entry into a market may increase the competition in that market, but the positive signal that foreign takeovers send to capital markets in regard to growth opportunities and favorable asset valuations appear to offset these concerns. Yet, foreign market entry can also be viewed as evidence of anticipated future efficiency gains to firms in the same industry, as documented by Claessens et al. (2001) and therefore does not preclude the Efficiency Hypothesis. Similar to Akhigbe and Martin (2000), Otchere and Ip (2006) show for a sample of completed and aborted cross-border acquisitions in Australia that the Acquisition Probability Hypothesis and the associated return patterns are especially pronounced for the targets of cross-border takeovers. On the other hand, Keisers (2009) finds for European bank M&As that the positive rival effects associated with an M&A announcement are more distinct for domestic than for cross-border mergers. Bohl et al. (2006) also document positive wealth effects for the domestic rivals of Polish targets.

2.6 Assessment of the empirical findings on bank mergers and acquisitions

Chapter 2 summarizes the main findings of more than 135 empirical studies that examine the success of bank mergers and acquisition in the US and Europe and other worldwide markets. The three most commonly used methodologies to investigate bank mergers are, in order of frequency, event studies, dynamic efficiency studies and performance studies. The event study methodology is the by far the most frequently used of the three methodologies. Since the year 2000 a steady shift in the geographic focus of bank M&A research from the US to Europe can be observed. Until the year 2000, empirical investigation nearly exclusively centered on the US. However, since then a vast body of research has emerged that focuses on European bank M&As, with a few more recent studies investigating the emerging markets of Latin America and Asia.

Even though the results of the three different methodologies vary from each other in several aspects, they are overall not as heterogeneous as they may appear at first. The results of the research employing the event study methodology suggests that there are certain trends over different time periods and geographical regions. Bank mergers among US financial institutions were more successful for the bidding banks' shareholders during the 1970s and early 1980s. They subsequently became more detrimental during the late 1980s and the later years. The research on European bank mergers shows a similar trend over time, albeit the results seem to lag by approximately one decade. This suggests that, as a national banking industry matures over time, it is becoming gradually more difficult for banks to obtain gains in shareholder wealth through takeovers. More recent studies that center on the emerging economies in Latin America and Asia give further support to this conclusion. In these nations, bidding banks are, on average, more successful and can even expect to earn positive returns upon takeover announcements. However, it seems reasonable to assume that the banking markets in these emerging economies will likely follow the trend of the more mature banking markets in the US and Europe, where bidders cease to earn positive returns upon merger announcements. The evidence from dynamic efficiency and performance studies, on the other hand, are more diverse. Yet, as these methods heavily rely on accounting data, which is subject to different rules and regulations in different jurisdictions and over time, this is not particularly surprising. Nonetheless, dynamic efficiency studies point towards an increase in profit efficiency of the merging institutions following a takeover.

The main factors influencing M&A transactions among financial institutions can be divided into three different categories: (i) acquirer and target specific characteristics, (ii) transaction specific characteristics, and (iii) environmental characteristics, such as the regulatory environment or the economic climate. Large efficiency and performance differentials between acquirer and target, prior acquisition experience, financing a takeover with cash rather than stock, and higher regulatory efficiency and quality rank among the key drivers of successful bank M&As. Large transactions, on the other hand, appear to be more detrimental.

There is no clear empirical evidence on whether geographic or product focus or diversification is more beneficial for bank mergers.

Finally, the 2007 Financial Crisis made evident that M&As among financial institutions can have a major effect on the overall stability of global financial markets, especially if banks become large enough through mergers that they become systemically important so that their default would lead to severe economic repercussions beyond the financial sector. Large banks frequently receive implicit "Too-Big-to-Fail" subsidies, which can cause moral hazard issues and questionable merger motivations, such as regulatory arbitrage considerations through the exploitation of national safety net benefits.

So far, little attention has been paid to bank mergers in either Asia or Latin America and research on those regions is still comparatively scarce. The results so far however indicate that there may be substantial differences to prior research, which centers on the more consolidated and mature banking markets of the US and Europe. In addition, in light of the 2007 Financial Crisis and the ensuing market upheavals, it appears to be important to conduct further research on the impact of bank mergers on the financial system and its global stability. In particular, the effect of TBTF mergers, their consequences for regulatory policy, and the resulting behavior of banks and their market perception undoubtedly merit deeper analyses. The existence of explicit or implicit TBTF mechanisms is widely acknowledged, yet their effect is hardly examined and the research results so far point to the existence of regulatory arbitrage, which ought to be reason of concern to regulators and policy makers alike. Therefore, this line of research can potentially provide valuable insights for regulators and policy makers and may help design international banking regulation which may lead to overall greater stability of global financial markets.

3. The shareholder value effects of the financial sector consolidation in the Asia-Pacific region

In recent years the worldwide trend for further consolidation in the financial sector has continued almost unabated. This might be surprising, as a large body of empirical research on the shareholder wealth effects of bank M&As actually shows that only target shareholders can expect to earn large positive stock returns. Bidding banks, on the other hand, are likely to realize non-significant or slightly negative returns. If shareholders of acquiring banks do not gain in such transactions, the question arises why consolidation in the financial sector still continues, even though the rewards appear to be limited at best, at least from the bidding bank's shareholders' perspective. It is, however, not clear whether the empirical results obtained for the well-developed financial markets of the US and Europe also hold for emerging financial markets, in which avenues of significant growth are still accessible to financial institutions.

Emerging economies, especially in Asia, have been the growth engine of the world economy for some time now. Regional financial hubs, such as Hong Kong and Singapore, continuously gain in global importance, while Tokyo is still one of the major financial centers in the world, even though the Japanese economy has been struggling for more than two decades now. Furthermore, increasing harmonization of international financial markets, for example through the Basel Accords, ought to make it easier for international banks to engage in cross-border M&A transactions, as increased transparency requirements allow bidders to more easily obtain information on potential targets.

Yet, the extant literature on bank mergers and acquisitions suggests that cross-border M&As are usually less successful than domestic transactions, at least for the acquiring institution. Gleason and Mathur (1998) even show that US bidding banks destroy shareholder wealth when engaging in foreign transactions. The results of Campa and Hernando (2004) indicate that especially cross-border M&A transactions in heavily regulated industries, and the financial sector in particular, lead to a destruction of shareholder wealth. In contrast, in a majority of cases a combination of geographic and product focus leads to better results for the bidding bank, not only in the US (DeLong, 2001), but also in Europe (Beitel et al., 2004). The results for foreign M&As in the emerging economies of Central and Eastern Europe suggest that foreign firms can profit, as they acquire better performing targets. This is especially the case if the target's home country sees this as a way to attract foreign direct investment and to gain international know-how (Uhlenbruck & De Castro, 2000). Moreover, Asian markets offer growth opportunities, and hence significant profit prospects, to banks from the US and Western Europe, which their largely consolidated domestic markets cannot offer.

This chapter is motivated by the question whether international bidding banks are able to profit from acquisitions in the Asia-Pacific region and what the industry wide implications of the consolidation process in the region are. Foreign banks usually lack detailed knowledge of the local market and differences in language and corporate culture are likely to make it more difficult to integrate the new acquisition into the firm and to realize the full potential of the existing growth opportunities. Asian institutions are much more likely to have a deeper understanding of their home market, giving them a significant advantage when deciding which targets to bid for. This makes it potentially harder for foreign banks to compete for attractive targets and likely forces them to pay higher premiums to outbid their local rivals. Nevertheless, the rapid economic development of the Asian economies makes them ostensibly attractive markets for international financial institutions to participate in. This is especially the case for banks from mature and largely consolidated markets.

This study sheds light on the overall success of bank M&As in the Asia-Pacific region, not only for the institutions directly involved in the transaction, but also for their closest rivals. It sets out to answer the question whether Asian banks are able to outperform their non-Asian counterparts and if so, what the drivers of this performance are. Non-Asian bidders largely engage in cross-continental takeovers, which may make it more difficult for them to benefit from these mergers. In addition, the impact of the consolidation process in the Asia-Pacific region on its financial sector is examined in detail through an analysis of the reaction of a bank's closest rivals to merger announcements.

3.1 Related literature on wealth effects of the financial sector consolidation

The focus of empirical evidence on mergers and acquisitions among financial institutions, and banks in particular, lies largely on the advanced economies of the US and Europe. Especially the shareholder wealth effects of the acquiring and target institutions are frequently investigated in order to examine which factors influence the success or failure of such transactions. Comprehensive reviews of the recent research are given by DeYoung, Evanoff, and Molyneux (2009) and Kolaric and Schiereck (2014). Yet, the wealth effects bank shareholder experience in emerging economies are less often investigated and the results so far differ from those achieved in advanced economies. Moreover, very few studies exist in regard to the industry-wide wealth effects of M&As, particularly for the financial sector.

3.1.1 Bank mergers in advanced economies

In general, most studies find that the acquiring institution earns slightly negative stock returns, in many cases at least weakly significant. Targets, on the other hand, earn large, positive and statistically significant returns. The combined institution of target and acquirer frequently earns slightly positive returns as well. However, there appear to be some differences in regard to the overall success of bank M&As in the US and Europe.

Becher (2000) shows that the shareholders of bidding banks in the US achieve highly significant negative returns during the eleven days surrounding the official announcements day. Targets, on the other hand, earn highly significant positive returns. The combined institution also earns positive abnormal returns, indicating that the overall wealth effect was positive and hence M&As do not merely constitute a wealth transfer from bidding bank shareholders to target bank shareholders. Synergetic reasons appear to be the main force behind bank M&As, explaining why returns to the combined institution are positive on average (Becher, 2000). Analogous results are also achieved by Houston and Ryngaert (1994), albeit the combined institution only achieving non-significant returns. Nevertheless, synergetic reasons appear to be one of the drivers of the observed gains. The findings of DeLong (2001) are similar, but also show that geographic and activity focus in particular lead to better results for bidding banks.

The first comprehensive study on European bank mergers by Cybo-Ottone and Murgia (2000) shows that target institutions can expect to earn large, positive abnormal returns during the days surrounding the official announcement day. However, in contrast to US studies, acquirers do not appear to destroy shareholder wealth when engaging in M&As. On the contrary, domestic deals and deals diversifying a bank's operations into the insurance business even lead to positive shareholder wealth effects for bidding banks. The deviation of these results to prior US findings is explained by differences in the regulatory regimes in Europe and the US (Cybo-Ottone & Murgia, 2000). Beitel et al. (2004) more closely investigate the drivers of success in European bank M&As and find that acquiring banks are most successful when they purchase a relatively well-managed and efficient target, as opposed to turnaround candidates. More recent studies, such as Hankir et al. (2011), show that the return patterns observed for US and European target and bidding banks still hold. It should be noted though, that European targets earn lower returns on average than their US peers.

Irrespective of the region, M&As among financial institutions in advanced economies do not appear beneficial for the shareholders of the acquiring institution, with very few and specific exceptions (see e.g. Cybo-Ottone & Murgia, 2000). The potential for synergies is a frequently cited motivation for takeovers in the financial sector, yet these gains are seldom observed or are much smaller than originally anticipated (Berger, 2000). Hankir et al. (2011) likewise show that the return patterns for a portion of their investigated M&As are in line with those expected by synergy reasons. Nevertheless, they find that market power considerations appear to be a more prevalent reason for mergers among financial institutions in Europe and the US. In addition, mergers with targets that are financially distressed (i.e. targets having refinancing problems due to weak operating performance) are also more frequently observed than mergers for synergetic reasons. Overall, the consolidation in the financial sector in the US and Europe has largely been successful from the viewpoint of the target institution's shareholders. The success of the consolidation process is much less clear from the perspective of the bidding banks' shareholders. There is some evidence that M&As due to synergetic reasons are more successful, while some transactions appear to be successful largely due to market power considerations.

3.1.2 Bank mergers in emerging economies

Research on bank mergers and acquisitions outside of the US and European market is still rather scarce and very few studies exclusively look at the emerging economies of Asia and Latin America. This is somewhat surprising as these countries continuously gain in importance to the global economy and potentially offer attractive investment opportunities, especially for foreign banks operating in mostly consolidated markets that offer fewer avenues for future growth. Moreover, banking regulation is increasingly harmonized, which should make it easier for foreign banks to enter and succeed in these markets, as a more level playing field is created. In addition, integration of Asian financial markets, especially equity markets, is well underway (Yu et al., 2010). Waheed and Mathur (1995) are one of the first to investigate whether the mode of entry determines the success of US banks when they expand into foreign markets. They show that it does matter and that the opening of branches is perceived as preferable to other modes of market entry, as this leads to significant and positive returns on average. On the other hand, entry via subsidiaries, joint ventures or outright acquisitions leads to significant negative returns, possibly due to the costs associated with those forms of entry being relatively high in the past.

Kiymaz (2004) examines the wealth effects of US bidders engaging in foreign acquisitions. He shows that especially acquisitions in Latin America enhance the shareholder value of the bidding institutions. A large part of these gains can be explained by macroeconomic variables, such as the economic development status of the target country and the level of government efficiency. Kolaric and Schiereck (2013) later also point out that bidding banks in Latin America earn, on average, significant and positive returns on the announcement day. The results of Goddard et al. (2012) likewise show that mergers among Latin American banks lead to small and positive, albeit non-significant returns for acquiring institutions.

M&As in Asia are likewise not well documented. The evidence so far suggests that financial institutions do not destroy shareholder wealth when acquiring other financial institutions in Asia (Kiymaz, 2004), a result similar to that observed in Europe. In particular, Kiymaz (2004) documents for a subsample of US bidding banks that they earn insignificant returns in Asia. In contrast, the results of Crouzille et al. (2008) show that bank M&As in Asia have a negative effect on the share price of the acquiring institution. However, this result is largely driven by M&As during and directly following the 1997 Asian Financial Crisis and by transactions in less mature economies. Goddard et al. (2012) again find non-significant returns for Asian bidding banks that acquire targets in other emerging Asian economies. It should be noted though, that their sample also includes minority acquisitions, which ought to have a lower effect on shareholder wealth, for both target and acquirer.

Overall, evidence on the success of the consolidation process in the financial sector in the emerging economies of Latin America and Asia is still scarce. Nonetheless, for Latin America the research shows a trend towards significant positive shareholder wealth effects for domestic and foreign bidding banks. This is in stark contrast to the M&A research for the more advanced economies of Europe and the US. For bank M&As in Asia, no clear picture emerges so far.

3.1.3 The rival effects of mergers and acquisitions

Looking at industry wide effects of M&A transactions, there are currently three main hypotheses to explain different return patterns among the bidder and target firm and their closest rivals: The Acquisition Probability Hypothesis, the Efficiency Hypothesis, and the Market Power Hypothesis. All hypotheses suggest somewhat different return patterns for bidders and targets and their closest rivals, but they are not mutually exclusive.

The Acquisition Probability Hypothesis assumes that not only the acquisition target, but also the rivals will earn positive abnormal returns surrounding an M&A transaction, as this will increase their likelihood of being an acquisition target later (Song & Walkling, 2000). In this case an acquisition announcement will not only lead to higher target valuations, but also higher valuations of its closest rivals, as the announcement can be seen as a signal that consolidation within the industry is beneficial and imminent. Akhigbe and Martin (2000) show that this effect is potentially more pronounced for targets of cross-border acquisitions. Even though foreign entry into a market possibly changes the competitive landscape of the market, the overall positive signal that foreign acquisitions imply in regard to growth opportunities and favorable industry climate appear to offset these concerns. This in turn will also increase the likelihood of the target's rivals becoming future acquisition targets. Taking this to the extreme, the Acquisition Probability Hypothesis may ultimately result in a merger wave and consolidation of an industry (Hankir et al., 2011). This in turn implies that even though target rival stock market valuation rises, the effect on the bidding firm and its rivals will be negative. Bidders need to pay higher premiums to obtain desirable targets, in all likelihood overpaying for them. Bidder rivals, on the other hand, will have a smaller pool of targets to choose from and may consequently be left with a smaller market share, fewer profit opportunities and fewer growth options. Besides Akhigbe and Martin (2000), Otchere and Ip (2006) also show that the Acquisition Probability Theory and the associated return patterns are especially pronounced for targets of cross-border M&A transactions.

The Efficiency Hypothesis argues that, if it is possible for the newly combined entity raise its efficiency levels after the takeover, this may lead to a more challenging market environment for the rival firms, leading to negative shareholder wealth effect. On the other hand, this relationship may not be one-directional. By definition, rival firms have comparable operations and production technologies and as a result the announcement of a merger may be perceived by the market as a signal that rival companies have a similar potential to increase their efficiency levels (Eckbo, 1983). Hence, it is possible that rivals may also achieve positive stock returns following an M&A announcement (Eckbo, 1983). The return patterns predicted by the Efficiency Hypothesis and Market Power Hypothesis are not mutually exclusive and therefore the rival returns potentially reflect the joint effect of both hypotheses.

The Market Power Hypothesis, in contrast, argues that M&As within an industry can be beneficial for all companies, leading to higher market-wide stock valuations (Hankir et al., 2011). This hypothesis goes back to competition theory and argues that takeovers will result in lower levels of competition and increased market prices (see e.g. Werden, 2008). This allows for collusion among the remaining firms, ultimately permitting them to use their larger market power to set higher prices. Hence, all companies are poised to gain from M&As within an industry.

As these hypotheses are not mutually exclusive, it is difficult to determine, which one is more relevant. In Asia, however, one might be more dominant than the others, depending on whether the bidding bank originates from an Asian or non-Asian country. The Acquisition Probability Hypothesis may be more relevant for transactions undertaken by non-Asian institutions. Targets of non-Asian bidders are poised to gain large returns, while their rivals can expect to gain positive returns, as acquisitions by non-Asian financial institutions may indicate favorable industry conditions and growth opportunities. At the same time it raises the probability of the remaining firms to become a takeover target in the future. Non-Asian bidders, however, can be expected to earn negative returns, as their choice of target might be limited and expansion into different regulatory regimes and cultural regions can be more risky. Non-Asian bidder rivals can also be expected to earn negative returns, as another bank's decision to engage in a foreign transaction can be interpreted as a negative signal of the conditions in its domestic market. On the one hand, the market may be largely consolidated, offering fewer targets without raising regulatory concerns, signaling a lack of domestic growth opportunities.

The Market Power Hypothesis is likely to be more relevant for takeovers among Asian institutions. In this case not only the bidder, but also the bidder's closest rivals stand to gain from further consolidation. Asian financial markets still offer more room for consolidation than those of the US and Europe. At the same time targets and their rivals also gain from further consolidation, as this may result in a decrease in competition and an increase in market power, making it possible for the remaining firms to raise prices and as a result increase their profits. However, this does not preclude that efficiency gains could also be a driver of the observed returns.

This chapter of the thesis gives first tacit evidence that industry-wide wealth effects in the financial sector may differ, depending on the origin of the acquirer and the signals a takeover sends to capital markets. At the same time, it closes a gap in the research on M&As among financial institutions and offers comprehensive analysis on the success of the consolidation process in one of the most dynamic regions in the world. This is achieved by examining the wealth effects of the bidding and target institutions in conjunction with those of their closest peers.

3.2 Data set and methodology

In this section, first the data selection process for the bidding and target bank sample is explained and several descriptive statistics are provided. Second, the rival bank selection process is presented in detail and multiple descriptive statistics are given to illustrate the rival sample composition. Third, the specific empirical methodology is explained and the employed tests of statistical significance are presented in great detail.

3.2.1 Bidder and target bank data selection and sample description

The primary source for M&As among financial institutions in this study is the Thomson Financial Securities Data Company (SDC) Mergers and Acquisition database. For an event to be considered, the target of the transaction has to be from the Asia-Pacific region, whereas no restriction is placed on the nationality of the acquiring institution. The countries in the Asia-Pacific region are defined following the regional member list of the Asian Development Bank. The official announcement date has to be between January 1995 and December 2013 and the target and bidder has to be a financial institution (primary SIC codes from 6000 to 6289 and SIC codes 6712 and 6733). Therefore, all insurance carriers, real estate companies, non-bank holding companies and miscellaneous investment companies, such as oil royalty traders and patent owners and lessors are explicitly excluded. Additionally, it is required that the transaction is completed and that a transaction value is explicitly recorded. Furthermore, only majority acquisitions are considered, i.e. acquisitions in which the bidding institution held less than 50% of the target prior to the announcement and obtained a controlling stake through the M&A transaction. Thus, subsequent increases in ownership of the bidding bank and minority acquisitions are disregarded. It is also required that at least the bidding bank is listed on a stock exchange and that stock price data is available in sufficient quality.

Table 3-1: Geographic distribution of acquiring and target nation

Target	Acquirer nation																						
nation	AU	AT	CH	CN	DE	FR	HK	ID	IN	JP	KR	MY	NL	NZ	PH	PK	RU	SG	TH	TW	UK	US	ZA	Total
Panel A. Acquirer sample																								
AU	19																				2	2		23
BD																					1			1
CN				1		1					1											1		4
FJ	2																							2
HK	1		1	1			5											3		1	1		1	14
ID	1				1			2	2															6
IN									10												2			12
JP										26										1				27
KH											1													1
KR											17										2	1		20
KZ		1							1								1							3
MY												4												4
NZ	1													1							1			3
PH										1					1			1			1	1		5
PK													1			1					1			3
SG																		2						2
TH				1						1			1					1	1		1			6
TW	1								1				1							9	2			14
Total	25	1	1	3	1	1	5	2	14	28	19	4	3	1	1	1	1	7	1	11	14	5	1	150
Panel B: Target sample																								
AU	6																							6
HK			1															1						2
IN									4															4
JP										8														8
KR											1													1
MY												1												1
NZ	1																							1
PK													1			1					1			3
TH													1											1
TW																				3	1			4
Total	7	0	1	0	0	0	0	0	4	8	1	1	2	0	0	1	0	1	0	3	2	0	0	31

AU=Australia, AT=Austria, BD=Bangladesh, CH=Switzerland, CN=China, DE=Germany, FJ=Fiji, FR=France, HK=Hong Kong, ID=Indonesia, IN=India, JP=Japan, KH=Cambodia, KR=South Korea, KZ=Kazakhstan, MY=Malaysia, NL=Netherlands, NZ=New Zealand, PH=Philippines, PK=Pakistan, RU=Russia, SG=Singapore, TH=Thailand, TW=Taiwan, UK=United Kingdom, US=United States, ZA=South Africa

In the next step, it is verified that the official announcement day recorded in the SDC Mergers and Acquisition database is correct by checking them with official company announcements and the Nexis database. Any discrepancies are resolved by using the first official announcement date that could be identified. Furthermore, using the Nexis database, it is ensured that no major confounding events occur during the [–5;5] day event window, such as other M&A announcements or CEO change.

Table 3-2: Bidding bank sample description

	Number of deals	Percentage of deals	Deal value (million US$)	Percentage of total deal value
Panel A: Origin of acquirer				
Asia	96	64.00%	206,901.50	80.08%
Non-Asia	54	36.00%	51,470.27	19.92%
Total	150	100.00%	258,371.77	100.00%
Panel B: Geographic focus				
National	99	66.00%	223,486.18	86.50%
Cross-border	51	34.00%	34,885.59	13.50%
Total	150	100.00%	258,371.77	100.00%
Panel C: Frequency by years				
1995	4	2.67%	35,493.53	13.74%
1996	3	2.00%	3,325.59	1.29%
1997	1	0.67%	1,129.54	0.44%
1998	4	2.67%	1,314.09	0.51%
1999	12	8.00%	47,563.92	18.41%
2000	12	8.00%	32,708.08	12.66%
2001	9	6.00%	10,546.70	4.08%
2002	6	4.00%	5,245.03	2.03%
2003	9	6.00%	8,134.89	3.15%
2004	8	5.33%	4,110.86	1.59%
2005	10	6.67%	46,197.41	17.88%
2006	10	6.67%	2,489.65	0.96%
2007	11	7.33%	5,920.53	2.29%
2008	12	8.00%	27,845.07	10.78%
2009	14	9.33%	12,530.52	4.85%
2010	7	4.67%	4,401.02	1.70%
2011	4	2.67%	865.93	0.34%
2012	7	4.67%	1,129.34	0.44%
2013	7	4.67%	7,420.08	2.87%
Total	150	100.00%	258,371.77	100.00%

Using the above criteria, a total of 150 events for bidding banks from 23 different nations with a total deal value in excess of 258 billion U$ are identified. However, due to the majority of targets being private and the data quality for the publicly listed targets being rather poor, only 31 exchange-listed targets can be analyzed out of the original sample of 150 announcements. For this reason the target sample is not described in great detail here, but merely some trends are pointed out. Table 3-1 shows the distribution of acquiring and target nations for the entire sample. The most frequent acquiring nation is Japan with a total of 28 transactions, 26 national takeovers and two cross-border deals. This is followed by M&As of Australian banks, 19 being national and six cross-border. The third most M&As are recorded for South Korean financial institutions, consisting of 17 national deals and two cross-border ones.

Table 3-2 and Table 3-3 show the distribution of the deals of the acquirer and target sample and their value by origin of acquirer, geographic focus of the transaction and distribution over the investigation period. Approximately two thirds of acquirers are from Asia, the rest being from non-Asian countries, such as the US, the Western European nations, and Australia.[15] The value of acquisitions by Asian acquirers far exceeds those by non-Asian acquirers with more than 200 billion US$. Similar numbers can be obtained when looking at the geographic focus of the events (Table 2 Panel B). The majority of events are national M&As, led by Japanese and Australian national transactions, while cross-border deals are relatively few and make up less than a third of all events. In addition, cross-border deals account for only 13.50% of the total deal value, or less than 35 billion US$. This indicates that cross-border deals are, on average, smaller than national ones.

The distribution of deals through time also offers some insights. The number of M&A deals is roughly evenly distributed between the first half of the investigation period from 1995 to 2004 and the second half of the investigation period from 2005 to 2013. However, the deal value for the latter half of the investigation period is 108.80 billion US$ only, or about 40% of the total transaction volume. This suggests that the average deal size has decreased over time. Most transactions during a single year occur during 2009 (14), followed by the years 1999, 2000 and 2008 with 12 transactions each. The largest total deal values can be observed for the years 1999 and 2005 with approximately 47.6 billion US$ and 46.2 billion US$, respectively. That these years have such high transaction values can be explained by megamergers among Japanese banks. In particular, in 1999 Sumitomo Bank

15 Asia is defined in this case along the classical geographic demarcation of Asia and does not include countries in the Pacific region. The following countries in our sample are identified as Asian: China, Hong Kong, India, Indonesia, Japan, Malaysia, Pakistan, Philippines, Singapore, South Korea, Taiwan and Thailand. The following countries in our sample are considered non-Asian: Australia, Austria, France, Germany, the Netherlands, New Zealand, Russia, South Africa, Switzerland, the United Kingdom and the United States.

announced the acquisitions of a majority stake in Sakura Bank, a deal valued at 45.5 billion US$ at the time. In 2005 Mitsubishi Tokyo Financial Group announced the acquisition of UFJ Holdings for more than 41 billion US$.

Table 3-3: Target bank sample description

	Number of deals	Percentage of deals	Deal value (million US$)	Percentage of total deal value
Panel A: Origin of acquirer				
Asia	20	64.52%	26,777.86	16.18%
Non-Asia	11	35.48%	138,678.97	83.82%
Total	31	100.00%	165,456.83	100.00%
Panel B: Geographic focus				
National	24	77.42%	152,367.52	92.09%
Cross-border	7	22.58%	13,089.31	7.91%
Total	31	100.00%	165,456.83	100.00%
Panel C: Frequency by years				
1995	1	3.23%	503.23	0.30%
1996	2	6.45%	3,098.67	1.87%
1997	1	3.23%	1,129.54	0.68%
1998	1	3.23%	181.50	0.11%
1999	2	6.45%	45,823.36	27.70%
2000	2	6.45%	19,356.13	11.70%
2001	2	6.45%	5,947.43	3.59%
2002	2	6.45%	3,626.51	2.19%
2003	1	3.23%	1,729.16	1.05%
2004	–	–	–	–
2005	2	6.45%	41,511.54	25.09%
2006	3	9.68%	1,582.18	0.96%
2007	4	12.90%	2,437.10	1.47%
2008	3	9.68%	24,874.85	15.03%
2009	2	6.45%	9,519.64	5.75%
2010	3	9.68%	4,135.99	2.50%
2011	–	–	–	–
2012	–	–	–	–
2013	–	–	–	–
Total	31	100.00%	165,456.83	100.00%

The exchange-listed targets in the sample are mainly from Japan (8), followed by Australia (6) and India (4). Nevertheless, even though the target sample consists of only 31 M&A events, the overall deal value is approximately 165.5 billion US$, which is approximately 64% of the total transaction volume. This is not surprising, as only the largest deals, such as the ones between Sumitomo Bank and Sakura Bank and Mitsubishi Tokyo Financial Group and UFJ Holdings, have targets that are publicly listed and stock data available in sufficient quality as to allow for an analysis of the returns surrounding the announcement day.

3.2.2 Rival bank data selection and sample description

In order to select the appropriate rivals for each exchange-listed bidding and target bank, an approach similar to Hankir et al. (2011) with some modifications is followed. In a first step all financial institutions in the country of origin of each bidding and target bank are determined via Datastream. The definition of a financial institution is the same as for the bidding and target bank sample, including all firms with a primary SIC code ranging from 6000 to 6289 and primary codes 6712 and 6733. Next, in order to arrive at the closest rival firm for each bidding and target institution, the following selection process is used: First, the bidding and target bank rivals need to be domiciled in the same country as the bidder and target. In addition, they also need to be listed on a stock exchange. Second, the first two digits of the primary SIC code of bidder and target firm need to match with those of the rival firm. Third, the three closest rival firms, as measured by market capitalization, are selected. All observations that did not yield at least three rivals are dropped. Additionally, the stock price data of the rival company must be available in sufficient quality from 272 trading days prior to the official announcement day to five days after it.

The first requirement is rather restrictive, especially for smaller markets with lower data quality, such as Malaysia or the Philippines, and for largely consolidated markets, such as many of the European ones, with few exchange listed financial institutions remaining. Nevertheless, the use of country-specific rivals is preferable, as the capital markets in the Asia-Pacific region were rather heterogeneous during most of the investigation period and just recently started to converge. Some markets, such as the ones of Australia and Japan, are very similar to those of the developed economies in the US and Europe, while others are still in the process of developing more mature capital markets, such as Thailand and Malaysia. Additionally, some countries, for example South Korea, Hong Kong, and Taiwan, appear to be in a transitional stage between developing and developed capital markets. Therefore, choosing national rivals rather than regional ones is more appropriate. Furthermore, by requiring a match for the two digit SIC code rather than the four digit SIC code, it is ensured that the rivals are in a similar line of business. Four digit SIC codes frequently lead to some misclassifications for non-US financial institutions.[16]

Following the selection process described above, it is possible to determine three suitable rivals for 140 bidders out of the sample of 150 bidding banks, giving a total of 420 rival observation. From the 31 firms of the exchange-listed target sample, three rivals are identified for 28 institutions, giving a total of 84 observations. Table 3-4 gives a brief overview of the market capitalization of the rival sample in relation to the bidding and target institutions and the frequency of observations for their respective two digit SIC codes.

Table 3-4: Rival bank sample description

	All bidder rivals	Non-Asian bidder rivals	Asian bidder rivals
Panel A: Bidding bank rivals			
Ø difference in rival market capitalization to bidder	34.92%	47.62%	27.42%
Median difference in rival market capitalization to bidder	26.21%	46.70%	18.62%
Standard deviation difference in rival market capitalization to bidder	28.98%	31.24%	24.70%
n	420	156	264
n with two digit SIC code 60	390	150	240
n with two digit SIC code 61	6	0	6
n with two digit SIC code 62	24	6	18

16 A rival selection with the requirement of the same three digit primary SIC code was also conducted. This led to largely the same rivals. A match of the same four digit primary SIC code did not achieve desirable results, as the four digit primary SIC codes available on Datastream for non-US financial institutions appear to be error prone. For example, non-US commercial banks have almost exclusively a primary four digit SIC code of 6029 ("Commercial Banks, not elsewhere classified"), whereas US commercial banks generally follow a more detailed categorization.

Table 3-4 (continued)

Panel B: Target Bank rivals	All target rivals	Non-Asian bidder target rivals	Asian bidder target rivals
Ø difference in rival market capitalization to target	26.55%	39.19%	20.55%
Median difference in rival market capitalization to target	18.89%	34.43%	16.10%
Standard deviation difference in rival market capitalization to target	23.51%	27.66%	18.72%
n	84	27	57
n with two digit SIC code 60	78	27	51
n with two digit SIC code 61	3	0	3
n with two digit SIC code 62	3	0	3

The average market capitalization of a bidding bank's rival is within approximately 35% of the bidding bank. For the rivals of Asian bidding banks, this value is even lower, being closer to 27.5%. However, for non-Asian bidder rivals it is much larger, with the average difference being within 47.5%. This large difference may reflect that the overwhelming majority of non-Asian bidders originates from the advanced economies of the US and Europe, where banking markets are already largely consolidated with fewer potential exchange-listed national rivals. It is also possible that only the largest non-Asian financial institutions have the capability to undertake acquisitions in an entirely different region than their home market. Most observations are confined to the two digit SIC code 60, "Depository Institutions", with few exceptions.

The descriptive statistics for the target sample offer some valuable insights as well. For target rivals, the average rival market capitalization is within approximately 26.5%. This difference is larger for the rivals of targets by non-Asian bidders, being almost 40%. This may reflect the market entry choice of non-Asian bidders into Asia and their subsequent target selection. They can either choose to acquire a relatively small financial institution and enter a new market on a smaller scale or they can decide to engage in a larger expansion by purchasing a relatively large and well-established financial institution. The rivals of the targets of Asian bidders are much closer in market capitalization to the target bank, on average being within 20.5% of the target bank. This may indicate the option of Asian bidders to choose targets that are more in the middle of the valuation range and be more reflective of a general tendency towards market consolidation. Again, the majority of observations are for the two digit SIC code 60, "Depository Institutions".

3.2.3 Empirical methodology

The capital market reactions to M&A announcements for the bidding and target institutions and their respective rivals are analyzed using the same empirical approach. The methodology follows the market model event study, as originally defined by Dodd and Warner (1983) and Brown and Warner (1985). Prior research suggests that stock returns frequently show a considerable degree of heteroskedasticity (Schwert & Seguin, 1990). Therefore, the assumption that volatility is constant over time has to be dropped. Research by Brockett et al. (1999) suggests that abnormal returns calculated using the classical event study methodology are too high, probably due to the assumption of constant volatility. They therefore propose to use a model which also incorporates autoregressive conditional heteroskedastic effects (ARCH). This approach allows for time-varying volatility and should derive abnormal returns, which more closely reflect the abnormal returns actually achieved. Due to time-varying volatility, it is assumed that the error term follows a generalized autoregressive conditional heteroskedastic process (GARCH) with a lag of one in the conditional variance and squared error (GARCH(1,1)).

Notwithstanding the advantages of the GARCH model, it still cannot properly capture the asymmetry of returns frequently observed in stock price return time series. Engle and Ng (1993) show that asymmetric models, such as the Exponential GARCH (EGARCH) model, first introduced by Nelson (1991), are one of the best methods for forecasting volatility. Bekaerta and Harvey (1997) provide evidence that this kind of approach is especially suitable when modeling volatility and stock returns in emerging equity markets. In addition, EGARCH is also less sensitive to market shocks and volatilities estimated using EGARCH are not bound to the same constrains that ordinary GARCH volatilities are subject to.

The use of an EGARCH model over a multi-factors model, such as the Fama and French (1993, 1996) three-factor model is preferable for bank M&A studies. The factors are generally calculated by explicitly excluding financial institutions and it seems questionable, whether these factors are therefore appropriate for estimating expected returns. In addition, Daniel, Titman, and Wei (2001) document for the case of Japan that the factors introduced by Fama and French (1993, 1996) may not be suitable for all countries. In this case, a one-factor model is likely to be more appropriate, especially when modeling emerging markets (Bekaerta & Harvey, 1997). Moreover, Zollo and Leshchinkskii (2000) fail to find significant differences between the results of the classical market model and the Fama and French (1993) three-factor model and Cyree and DeGennaro (2002) show that the classical event study approach using a single-factor model is still well enough specified to achieve robust results.

The market model with EGARCH specifications is estimated using a 252 trading day period (one whole trading year) from 272 days to 21 days prior to the official merger announcement with:

$$R_{jt} = \hat{\alpha}_j + \hat{\beta}_j R_{mt} + \varepsilon_{jt} \tag{3-1}$$

where R_{jt} is defined as the return of stock *j* on day *t* during the estimation period using the Datastream total return index, R_{mt} is defined as the return of the Datastream country index on day *t* and $\hat{\alpha}_j$ and $\hat{\beta}_j$ are the regression coefficients of stock *j*, representing the slope coefficient and the sensitivity of stock *j* to the Datastream country index, respectively. The error term ε_{jt} in the EGARCH model is conditioned on the prior information set Ω_{t-1}:

$$\varepsilon_{jt} \mid \Omega_{t-1} \sim N(0, h_t) \tag{3-2}$$

where $N(0,h_t)$ stands for the conditional distribution of the error term, given all information available at time t_{-1}. The conditional distribution is assumed to have a mean of zero and a variance of h_t. According to Bollerslev (1986) and Elyasiani and Mansur (1998) financial data is best described by the lags p=1 and q=1 for the conditional and unconditional variance, respectively. The logarithm of the conditional variance, h_t in the EGARCH(1,1) model is an asymmetric function of lagged disturbances taking the form of:

$$\ln(h_t^2) = \omega + \delta \ln(h_{t-1}^2) + \psi g(z_{t-1}) \tag{3-3}$$

where h_t is the conditional variance on day *t*, ω, δ and ψ are coefficients and $g(z_{t-1})$ is an asymmetric response function, which is defined as:

$$g(z_{t-1}) = \theta z_t + \gamma[\,|z_t| - E(z_t)] \tag{3-4}$$

where θ and γ are coefficients, and z_t is a zero-mean i.i.d. sequence with a continuous distribution. The parameters defined in equations (3-3) and (3-4) are estimated using the maximum likelihood method.

The daily abnormal returns (AR) during the [−5;5] day event window surrounding the announcement day *t=0* are calculated using:

$$AR_{jt} = R_{jt} - (\hat{\alpha}_j + \hat{\beta}_j R_{mt}) \tag{3-5}$$

where $t\epsilon[-5,\dots,5]$. Average ARs (AAR) are in turn calculated as:

$$AAR_t = \frac{1}{N}\sum_{j=1}^{N} AR_{jt} \tag{3-6}$$

where AAR_t is the average abnormal return for all N M&A events in the sample on day t. The cumulative abnormal return (CAR) for stock j during the event window $[\tau_1;\tau_2]$ with $\tau_1,\tau_2 \epsilon[-5,\ldots,5]$ is calculated as:

$$CAR_{j,[\tau_1;\tau_2]} = \sum_{t=\tau_1}^{\tau_2} AR_{jt} \tag{3-7}$$

For a sample of N M&A events, the average CARs (ACARs) are calculated as:

$$ACAR_{[\tau_1;\tau_2]} = \frac{1}{N}\sum_{j=1}^{N} CAR_{j,[\tau_1;\tau_2]} \tag{3-8}$$

A 15 day gap between the last day of the estimation period and the first day of the event period is included to ensure the estimation of the parameters is not influenced by the event itself.

3.2.4 Significance tests

Multiple significance tests are used to determine whether the observed AARs and ACARs are statistically different from zero. Besides the standard parametric t-test, the variance-change corrected standardized cross-section test introduced by Boehmer, Musumeci, and Poulson (1991) is also employed. Furthermore, it is tested for significance using the nonparametric rank test first introduced by Corrado (1989).

For the parametric test by Boehmer et al. (1991), the BMP-test, the correction for serial dependence that can occur when summing up successive abnormal returns that are estimated using the same parameters are also included. This correction was first introduced by Mikkelson and Partch (1988) and incorporated into the Boehmer et al. (1991) test statistic by Cowan (1993). In a first step the standardized cumulative abnormal returns are calculated according to:

$$SCAR_{j[\tau_1;\tau_2]} = \frac{CAR_{j,[\tau_1;\tau_2]}}{s_{CAR_{j[\tau_1;\tau_2]}}} \tag{3-9}$$

where $SCAR_{j[\tau_1;\tau_2]}$ is the standardized CAR during the event period $[\tau_1;\tau_2]$ and the estimated standard deviation for each $CAR_{j,[\tau_1;\tau_2]}$, $s_{CAR_{j,[\tau_1;\tau_2]}}$ is calculated by:

$$s_{CAR_{j,[\tau_1;\tau_2]}} = \sqrt{s_{A_j}^2\left[T + \frac{T^2}{252} + \frac{\left(\sum_{t=\tau_1}^{\tau_2} R_{mt} - T\bar{R}_m\right)^2}{\sum_{t=-272}^{-21}(R_{mt} - \bar{R}_m)^2}\right]} \tag{3-10}$$

where s^2_{Aj} is the residual variance of firm j's market model regression during the 252 day estimation period, T is the number of non-missing trading days for security j during the event period $[\tau_1;\tau_2]$ and $\overline{R}_m$ is the mean market return over the estimation period. The standardized cross section test-statistic for an event window is then:

$$Z_{[\tau_1;\tau_2]} = \frac{\sum_{j=1}^{N} SCAR_{j,[\tau_1;\tau_2]}}{\sqrt{\frac{1}{N(N-1)}\sum_{j=1}^{N}\left(SCAR_{j[\tau_1;\tau_2]} - \frac{1}{N}\sum_{j=1}^{N} SCAR_{j,[\tau_1;\tau_2]}\right)^2}} \quad (3\text{-}11)$$

In addition to this parametric test statistic the nonparametric rank test introduced by Corrado (1989) is also used. The rank statistic for the announcement day is defined as:

$$Z_{rank} = \frac{\left(\frac{1}{N}\sum_{j=1}^{N} k_{j0}\right) - \overline{k}}{s_k} \quad (3\text{-}12)$$

where k_{j0} is the rank of security j's announcement day abnormal return in the combined estimation, gap and event period, s_k is the standard deviation of the mean abnormal returns of the sample and $\overline{k}$ is the expected rank as defined by:

$$\overline{k} = \frac{1}{278}\sum_{t=-272}^{5}\frac{1}{N_j}\sum_{j=1}^{N_j} k_{jt} \quad (3\text{-}13)$$

which allows for missing returns as formulated by Corrado and Zivney (1992), where N_j is the number of non-missing j security returns on day t. Finally, s_k is defined as:

$$s_k = \sqrt{\frac{1}{278}\sum_{t=-272}^{5}\left[\left(\frac{1}{N_j}\sum_{j=1}^{N_j} k_{jt}\right) - \overline{k}\right]^2} \quad (3\text{-}14)$$

This form of the rank test applies only to the announcement day itself. However, the rank test is also used for event windows consisting of several days. In order to do so, the same procedure as Cowan (1992) and Campbell, Cowan, and Salotti (2010) is followed, by substituting k_{j0} with the mean rank of security j's return during the $[\tau_1;\tau_2]$ event window and dividing s_k by the square root of the number of event days during event window. With the null hypothesis of no abnormal returns, the rank statistic converges to standard normal (Corrado, 1989; Corrado & Truong, 2008). Moreover, in order to test whether statistically significant differences exist between two subsamples, the parametric two-sample t-test and the nonparametric Wilcoxon rank-sum test are used.

Campbell et al. (2010) show that the parametric BMP-test can be a very useful robustness check, but the nonparametric rank test is better specified in most cases and should therefore be preferred. Corrado and Truong (2008) show that the nonparametric rank test is particularly well specified for security data in the Asia-Pacific region. Therefore the significance of the results is interpreted according to the nonparametric test procedure, using the parametric one as a robustness test and any stark differences between the two test statistics are highlighted.

3.3 Results of the empirical investigation

In this section the event study results for bidding and target banks and their respective rivals during the eleven day period surrounding the official announcement of an M&A transaction are described separately. This provides a comprehensive picture of the wealth effects of the institutions directly involved in a transaction and their closest rivals. In this way it is possible to derive conclusions on overall success of M&A transactions in the Asia-Pacific region and the impact the takeover have had on the financial sector in the region.

3.3.1 Bidding bank performance in Asia-Pacific bank mergers and acquisitions

The results for the entire bidding bank sample are presented in Table 3-5. Overall, the results show positive returns, but with limited significance at best. Similar to studies on the early success of European bank M&As during the pre-Euro era (e.g. Beitel et al., 2004) and prior studies on M&As in emerging economies (e.g. Goddard et al., 2012; Kiymaz, 2004), the results are slightly positive with an ACAR of 0.46% on the announcement day and 0.99% during the three day event window surrounding the official announcement day. Yet, unlike prior studies on the consolidation of the financial sector in the US (e.g Becher, 2000), this indicates that bidding banks in the Asia-Pacific region do not destroy shareholder wealth.

In order to investigate whether the results for non-Asian and Asian bidding banks differ, the sample is divided into these two subgroups. This leaves results in 54 non-Asian and 96 Asian bidding banks. The results are presented in Table 3-6.

Panel A of Table 3-6 shows the results for non-Asian bidding banks. The ACAR for the entire eleven day event window is now slightly negative, but still lacks significance. However, on the announcement day [0] and during the [–1;1] day event window, non-Asian acquiring banks obtain negative ACARs, weakly significant according to the BMP-test statistic. The results for non-Asian bidding banks in the Asia-Pacific region are very similar to the ones observed for bidding banks in the US and Europe (e.g. Hankir et al., 2011) as acquirers earn negative ACARs, which are slightly significant. However, as the Corrado-test again lacks in significance for all event windows, the overall evidence for an actual destruction in shareholder wealth appears to be limited. Therefore, the results more closely reflect those of Kiymaz (2004), who reports for a subsample of US bidding banks in Asia that there are no significant ACARs during the days surrounding the announcement day. Overall, the results therefore indicate that capital markets view acquisitions by non-Asian banks in the Asia-Pacific region critically, but less so than acquisitions in the US.

Table 3-5: Event study results for entire bidding bank sample

Event window	ACAR	Median CAR	*t*-test (*t*-value)	BMP-test (Z-score)	Corrado-test (Z-score)	Sample size
[−5;5]	1.15%	0.37%	1.879*	0.534	0.841	150
[−3;3]	0.99%	0.46%	2.044**	0.538	0.881	150
[−2;2]	0.77%	0.40%	1.644	0.261	0.414	150
[−1;1]	0.99%	0.44%	2.272**	0.998	1.372	150
[0]	0.46%	−0.02%	2.127**	0.605	1.256	150
[−5;−1]	0.20%	−0.13%	0.574	0.050	0.291	150
[−3;−1]	0.15%	−0.11%	0.562	0.204	0.040	150
[−1;0]	0.65%	0.03%	2.192**	1.062	1.223	150
[0;1]	0.79%	0.15%	2.030**	0.575	1.345	150
[1;3]	0.38%	−0.04%	0.914	0.145	0.579	150
[1;5]	0.50%	0.02%	1.003	0.340	0.395	150

*,**,*** denotes statistical significance at the 10%, 5%, and 1% level

The results for Asian acquirers stand in stark contrast to those of their non-Asian peers (see Table 3-6 Panel B). Asian bidding banks achieve highly significant and positive ACARs on the announcement day [0] and during the three day event window surrounding it. Asian bidders achieve ACARs of 0.94% on the announcement day and ACARs of 1.87% during the [−1;1] day event window. There is no evidence of information leakage prior to the official announcement, as both the [−5;−1] and [−3;−1] day event windows show no significant market reaction. The same applies to the two post-announcement event windows [1;3] and [1;5].

Panel C of Table 3-6 underscores the difference in the performance between non-Asian and Asian bidding banks. The two-sample *t*-test and the Wilcoxon rank-sum test both suggest that the difference is statistically highly significant, especially on the announcement day and during the three days surrounding the official announcement. However, during the entire eleven day event window the results are not statistically different from each other. The same holds for the pre- and post-event windows.

It appears as if capital markets perceive M&A transactions by Asian bidding banks far more favorably than by non-Asian banks. It is likely that non-Asian banks acquire banks that are either undesirable for local banks or have to pay significantly more in order to outbid their Asian counterparts.

Table 3-6: Event study results for non-Asian and Asian bidding banks

Event window	ACAR	Median CAR	*t*-test (*t*-value)	BMP-test (Z-score)	Corrado-test (Z-score)	Sample size
Panel A: Non-Asian bidder						
[-5;5]	-0.03%	-0.22%	-0.038	-0.794	0.093	54
[-3;3]	-0.56%	0.14%	-1.049	-1.603	-0.765	54
[-2;2]	-0.72%	-0.49%	-1.622	-2.120**	-1.129	54
[-1;1]	-0.59%	-0.35%	-1.497	-1.849*	-1.312	54
[0]	-0.40%	-0.46%	-1.243	-1.803*	-1.606	54
[-5;-1]	-0.11%	-0.28%	-0.259	-0.300	0.022	54
[-3;-1]	-0.21%	-0.09%	-0.598	-0.585	-0.521	54
[-1;0]	-0.57%	-0.37%	-1.474	-1.642	-1.604	54
[0;1]	-0.42%	-0.06%	-1.217	-1.946*	-1.138	54
[1;3]	0.05%	0.26%	0.161	-0.305	0.280	54
[1;5]	0.48%	0.23%	0.957	0.212	0.834	54
Panel B: Asian bidder						
[-5;5]	1.82%	1.04%	2.144**	1.374	1.044	96
[-3;3]	1.85%	0.93%	2.732***	1.958*	1.774*	96
[-2;2]	1.60%	0.96%	2.381**	1.795*	1.440	96
[-1;1]	1.87%	1.13%	2.993***	2.526**	2.857***	96
[0]	0.94%	0.44%	3.401***	2.926***	2.937***	96
[-5;-1]	0.37%	-0.09%	0.768	0.261	0.369	96
[-3;-1]	0.35%	-0.24%	0.989	0.757	0.465	96
[-1;0]	1.34%	0.55%	3.369***	2.888***	2.891***	96
[0;1]	1.48%	0.79%	2.588**	2.086**	2.685***	96
[1;3]	0.56%	-0.39%	0.905	0.307	0.549	96
[1;5]	0.51%	-0.62%	0.703	0.268	-0.134	96

Table 3-6 (continued)

Panel C: Difference non-Asian and Asian bidder				
Event window	ΔACAR	ΔMedian CAR	two-sample *t*-test (*t*-value)	Wilcoxon rank-sum test (Z-score)
[-5;5]	-1.85%	-1.26%	-1.451	-1.161
[-3;3]	-2.41%	-0.80%	-2.437**	-1.999**
[-2;2]	-2.32%	-1.45%	-2.422**	-2.289**
[-1;1]	-2.46%	-1.49%	-2.778***	-3.021***
[0]	-1.34%	-0.90%	-3.041***	-2.645***
[-5;-1]	-0.48%	-0.19%	-0.669	0.072
[-3;-1]	-0.56%	0.14%	-1.039	-0.397
[-1;0]	-1.90%	-0.92%	-3.157***	-2.754***
[0;1]	-1.89%	-0.85%	-2.356**	-2.441**
[1;3]	-0.51%	0.65%	-0.588	0.225
[1;5]	-0.03%	0.85%	-0.030	0.726

*,**,*** denotes statistical significance at the 10%, 5%, and 1% level

3.3.2 Bidding bank rival performance in Asia-Pacific bank mergers and acquisitions

The wealth effects for the bidding bank rivals are presented in Table 3-7. Concurrent to the results for the bidding bank sample, none of the investigated event windows shows significant returns. The rival returns over the entire event period are very small, but mostly positive. The lack of significance suggests that the rivals of bidding banks are not influenced by the bidder's decision to engage in an M&A transaction.

Table 3-7: Event study results for all bidding bank rivals

Event window	ACAR	Median CAR	*t*-test (*t*-value)	BMP-test (Z-score)	Corrado-test (Z-score)	Sample size
[-5;5]	0.09%	-0.26%	0.302	-1.322	-0.968	420
[-3;3]	0.49%	-0.18%	1.720*	0.729	0.433	420
[-2;2]	0.20%	-0.20%	0.821	0.057	0.077	420
[-1;1]	0.21%	0.13%	1.124	0.782	0.995	420
[0]	-0.12%	-0.05%	-0.764	-0.499	-0.117	420
[-5;-1]	0.06%	-0.06%	0.242	-0.704	-1.031	420
[-3;-1]	0.24%	-0.09%	1.210	0.693	0.377	420
[-1;0]	0.11%	-0.06%	0.570	0.570	1.191	420
[0;1]	-0.02%	-0.06%	-0.107	-0.159	-0.055	420
[1;3]	0.38%	-0.19%	1.567	0.611	0.353	420
[1;5]	0.15%	-0.26%	0.596	-0.819	-0.353	420

*,**,*** denotes statistical significance at the 10%, 5%, and 1% level

Table 3-8 splits the sample of all rivals into the ones of Asian and non-Asian bidders. Similar to the results of the bidding bank sample, the capital market reactions for the two groups differ significantly from each other. The rivals of non-Asian bidding banks show almost no significant market reactions. This lack of significance is largely expected, as non-Asian acquirers overwhelmingly engage in cross-border transactions, which should have little impact on the competitive environment in their respective country of origin. Nonetheless, the weak tendency towards negative abnormal returns during the entire event window can be interpreted as a signal of deteriorating growth opportunities in the bidder's home country. Those banks engaging in acquisitions in Asia do so, as their home market offers fewer or no attractive targets and fewer growth opportunities. Therefore, this negative outlook leads to negative capital market reactions. It may also suggest that the banks that did not engage in a merger in Asia missed potential growth opportunities.

For the rivals of Asian bidders, the capital market reactions are largely positive and even significant during the [−1;0] and [−1;1] day event windows. The consolidation process among Asian financial institutions appears to be regarded as predominantly positive not only for bidding banks, but also their closest rivals. This again implies that market power considerations potentially play an important role and that the consolidation process in Asia, especially when viewed in conjunction with the positive returns that the bidding institutions earn. The consolidation among Asian banks appears to be well perceived by capital markets.

Table 3-8 Panel C highlights the difference in the results for non-Asian and Asian bidding bank rivals. Asian bidding bank rivals perform significantly better than their non-Asian peers. This can be interpreted as further evidence that market power considerations play an important role when capital markets value takeovers among Asian financial institutions. For non-Asian financial firm rivals a takeover may indicate deteriorating conditions in the home market and a missed expansion opportunity.

Table 3-8: Event study results for non-Asian and Asian bidding bank rivals

Event window	ACAR	Median CAR	*t*-test (*t*-value)	BMP-test (Z-score)	Corrado-test (Z-score)	Sample size
Panel A: Non-Asian bidder rivals						
[–5;5]	–0.91%	–0.31%	–2.112**	–2.315**	–1.561	156
[–3;3]	0.40%	–0.19%	0.948	0.347	0.031	156
[–2;2]	–0.04%	–0.31%	–0.127	–0.580	–0.680	156
[–1;1]	–0.34%	–0.29%	–1.490	–1.181	–0.822	156
[0]	–0.55%	–0.09%	–1.785*	–1.520	–1.005	156
[–5;–1]	–0.12%	–0.24%	–0.316	–0.719	–1.537	156
[–3;–1]	0.45%	–0.09%	1.519	1.173	0.493	156
[–1;0]	–0.58%	–0.22%	–1.554	–1.289	–0.842	156
[0;1]	–0.31%	–0.26%	–1.685*	–1.261	–0.875	156
[1;3]	0.50%	–0.11%	1.133	0.437	0.135	156
[1;5]	–0.24%	0.12%	–0.721	–1.409	–0.328	156
Panel B: Asian bidder rivals						
[–5;5]	0.69%	–0.26%	1.629	0.263	–0.025	264
[–3;3]	0.55%	–0.11%	1.432	0.660	0.520	264
[–2;2]	0.35%	–0.07%	1.021	0.506	0.614	264
[–1;1]	0.54%	0.40%	1.993**	1.771*	1.873*	264
[0]	0.14%	–0.04%	0.874	0.830	0.619	264
[–5;–1]	0.16%	0.17%	0.553	–0.282	–0.121	264
[–3;–1]	0.11%	–0.09%	0.429	–0.136	0.097	264
[–1;0]	0.52%	0.01%	2.314**	1.949*	2.134**	264
[0;1]	0.16%	0.14%	0.722	0.737	0.597	264
[1;3]	0.30%	–0.30%	1.083	0.428	0.339	264
[1;5]	0.39%	–0.70%	1.073	0.105	–0.193	264
Panel C: Difference non-Asian and Asian bidder rivals						
Event window	ΔACAR	ΔMedian CAR	two-sample *t*-test (*t*-value)		Wilcoxon rank-sum test (Z-score)	
[–5;5]	–1.60%	–0.05%	–2.491**		–1.262	
[–3;3]	–0.15%	–0.08%	–0.245		–0.078	
[–2;2]	–0.39%	–0.24%	–0.762		–0.366	
[–1;1]	–0.88%	–0.69%	–2.230**		–2.297**	
[0]	–0.69%	–0.05%	–2.190**		–1.555	
[–5;–1]	–0.28%	–0.41%	–0.588		–1.296	
[–3;–1]	0.34%	0.00%	0.840		0.526	
[–1;0]	–1.10%	–0.23%	–2.686***		–1.676*	
[0;1]	–0.47%	–0.40%	–1.476		–2.018**	
[1;3]	0.20%	0.19%	0.412		0.613	
[1;5]	–0.63%	0.82%	–1.173		0.895	

*,**,*** denotes statistical significance at the 10%, 5%, and 1% level

3.3.3 Target performance in Asia-Pacific bank mergers and acquisitions

The results for the entire sample of exchange-listed target banks are presented in Table 3-9. The overall results are in line with prior research on bank mergers and acquisitions in the US and Europe (e.g. Becher, 2000; Beitel et al., 2004; Hankir et al., 2011): Target banks earn large, positive and highly significant abnormal returns during the days surrounding the official announcement. During the entire eleven day event window, the average CAR is 13.58% and during the three day period surrounding the announcement day it is 10.26%, both highly statistically significant. On the announcement day itself, the average abnormal return is 5.08%, again highly significant. There appears to be some leakage, as the [–5;–1] and [–3;–1] day event windows are statistically significant, but the ACARs are small when compared to those achieved during the [–1;1] day event window.

Table 3-9: Event study results for entire exchange-listed target sample

Event window	ACAR	Median CAR	*t*-test (*t*-value)	BMP-test (Z-score)	Corrado-test (Z-score)	Sample size
[–5;5]	13.58%	6.91%	4.059***	3.955***	3.579***	31
[–3;3]	11.61%	8.74%	4.024***	4.031***	3.547***	31
[–2;2]	11.59%	7.54%	4.200***	4.078***	4.615***	31
[–1;1]	10.26%	6.99%	4.452***	4.221***	5.931***	31
[0]	5.08%	2.42%	3.812***	3.173***	4.129***	31
[–5;–1]	3.47%	2.78%	2.210**	2.414**	3.335***	31
[–3;–1]	2.06%	1.09%	1.577	1.739*	2.255**	31
[–1;0]	6.81%	4.27%	4.647***	3.693***	5.363***	31
[0;1]	8.53%	7.41%	3.669***	3.685***	4.821***	31
[1;3]	4.47%	0.58%	1.775*	1.683*	0.779	31
[1;5]	5.02%	0.01%	1.687	1.492	0.126	31

*,**,*** denotes statistical significance at the 10%, 5%, and 1% level

In order to investigate whether non-Asian bidding banks have to pay or are willing to pay significantly more than their Asian peers, the target sample is divided into institutions acquired by Asian and non-Asian bidders. Separating the sample into these two subsamples leads to very few observations, only eleven for targets by non-Asian bidding banks and 20 for targets by Asian bidding banks. The results should therefore be interpreted carefully. Nevertheless, they still offer some valuable insights.

Table 3-10: Event study results for exchange-listed targets by non-Asian and Asian bidders

Event window	ACAR	Median CAR	*t*-test (*t*-value)	BMP-test (Z-score)	Corrado-test (Z-score)	Sample size
Panel A: Targets by non-Asian bidder						
[−5;5]	17.50%	15.41%	4.525***	3.739***	3.126***	11
[−3;3]	16.60%	14.34%	5.186***	4.447***	3.438***	11
[−2;2]	15.51%	15.43%	4.776***	4.164***	3.852***	11
[−1;1]	12.77%	13.98%	4.976***	4.074***	5.388***	11
[0]	9.57%	7.90%	3.738***	3.401***	4.628***	11
[−5;−1]	5.60%	4.70%	2.258**	2.058**	2.796***	11
[−3;−1]	3.80%	1.27%	1.876*	1.621	1.810*	11
[−1;0]	10.85%	9.17%	4.287***	3.637***	5.280***	11
[0;1]	11.48%	11.65%	4.436***	3.854***	4.592***	11
[1;3]	3.23%	0.58%	1.385	1.096	0.771	11
[1;5]	2.33%	−0.99%	0.809	0.679	−0.229	11
Panel B: Target by Asian bidder						
[−5;5]	11.42%	4.60%	2.415**	2.315**	2.256**	20
[−3;3]	8.87%	3.54%	2.197**	2.052**	1.954*	20
[−2;2]	9.43%	3.30%	2.444**	2.238**	3.059***	20
[−1;1]	8.87%	5.12%	2.700**	2.473**	3.568***	20
[0]	2.62%	0.82%	2.099**	1.882*	1.757*	20
[−5;−1]	2.31%	1.69%	1.144	1.364	2.200**	20
[−3;−1]	1.09%	0.88%	0.651	0.754	1.555	20
[−1;0]	4.59%	2.32%	2.809**	2.638***	2.888***	20
[0;1]	6.91%	4.52%	2.092*	1.862*	2.725***	20
[1;3]	5.15%	0.37%	1.383	1.247	0.416	20
[1;5]	6.49%	0.79%	1.493	1.366	0.360	20

Panel C: Difference targets of non-Asian and Asian bidder

Event window	ΔACAR	ΔMedian CAR	two-sample *t*-test (*t*-value)	Wilcoxon rank-sum test (Z-score)
[−5;5]	6.08%	10.81%	0.866	1.920*
[−3;3]	7.73%	10.80%	1.297	2.291**
[−2;2]	6.08%	12.13%	1.057	1.879*
[−1;1]	3.90%	8.86%	0.805	1.755*
[0]	6.95%	7.08%	2.750**	2.663***
[−5;−1]	3.29%	3.01%	1.002	1.094
[−3;−1]	2.71%	0.39%	0.994	1.012
[−1;0]	6.27%	6.85%	2.169	2.209**
[0;1]	4.58%	7.12%	0.940	1.796*
[1;3]	−1.92%	0.21%	−0.360	0.227
[1;5]	−4.16%	−1.78%	−0.663	−0.186

*;**,*** denotes statistical significance at the 10%, 5%, and 1% level

Panel A of Table 3-10 reports the results of the eleven targets by non-Asian bidding banks. The ACARs add up to 17.50% over the eleven day event period surrounding the announcement day, which is more than the 13.58% ACAR for the entire sample (see Table 3-9). The average announcement day return is 9.57%. In addition, there is evidence of significant leakage during the pre-announcement period, as both pre-event windows exhibit statistically significant ACARs. During the post-announcement period the ACARs are not significantly different from zero.

Panel B of Table 3-10 shows the returns to the targets by Asian acquirers. The ACARs during the eleven day event window surrounding the announcement of the M&A transaction are still high with 11.42%, but significantly lower than for the entire sample. The ACARs of targets by Asian banks are about six percentage points lower than that of their peers targeted by non-Asian bidders. Additionally, leakage appears to be less pronounced than for targets of non-Asian bidding banks and returns following the official announcement are again insignificant. Table 3-10 Panel C shows the difference in the ACARs of targets of non-Asian and Asian bidding banks, which is only statistically significant on the announcement day.

Looking at the results for non-Asian and Asian bidding banks in combination with those achieved by their targets indicate that non-Asian banks indeed pay more than their Asian counterparts when engaging in M&As in the Asia-Pacific region. This might be due to non-Asian bank's lack of local knowledge and therefore their preference to acquire publicly traded targets, where detailed information is more easily available. It is, however, also probable that Asian bidding banks have more in-depth information on their targets and can therefore choose smaller listed or even non-listed ones. This potentially leads to a more advantageous negotiating position with regard to the acquisition price. However, a caveat to this interpretation is the small target sample size, but it can reasonably be expected that the overall trend is robust.

3.3.4 Target rival performance in Asia-Pacific bank mergers and acquisitions

Table 3-11 shows the capital market reactions for all rival banks. The reactions are mostly significant. For the entire eleven day event period surrounding the announcement day, target rivals achieve an ACAR of 3.67%. This result is in line with prior results on rivals' reactions (e.g. Otchere & Ip, 2006; Song & Walkling, 2000). Overall, target rivals appear to profit from further consolidation among financial institutions.

Table 3-12 presents the results for the targets of non-Asian and Asian bidder rivals separately. In line with the prior analysis, the results differ significantly, depending on the origin of the bidding bank. Even though the sample sizes are comparatively small, they offer some valuable insights as to the industry-wide return patterns following M&A transactions.

Table 3-11: Event study results for all exchange-listed target rivals

Event window	ACAR	Median CAR	*t*-test (*t*-value)	BMP-test (Z-score)	Corrado-test (Z-score)	Sample size
[−5;5]	3.67%	1.81%	3.422***	3.118***	2.128**	84
[−3;3]	2.37%	1.13%	2.882***	3.166***	1.751*	84
[−2;2]	2.07%	1.23%	2.880***	3.261***	1.900*	84
[−1;1]	1.33%	0.53%	2.325**	2.701***	1.922*	84
[0]	0.83%	0.10%	2.479**	2.600***	1.597	84
[−5;−1]	2.07%	0.86%	2.647***	2.764***	1.582	84
[−3;−1]	1.88%	0.30%	2.862***	3.183***	1.835*	84
[−1;0]	1.23%	0.18%	2.711***	2.923***	1.638	84
[0;1]	0.92%	0.33%	2.168**	2.553**	1.845*	84
[1;3]	−0.33%	−0.52%	−0.628	−0.323	−0.082	84
[1;5]	0.77%	−0.14%	1.069	0.985	0.861	84

*,**,*** denotes statistical significance at the 10%, 5%, and 1% level

The rivals of targets of non-Asian bidders perform significantly better than those of Asian bidders especially during the three day event window surrounding the takeover announcement. This result is in line with Akhigbe and Martin (2000) and Otchere and Ip (2006), who also show that target rivals, especially those of foreign acquisitions, display positive significant market reactions surrounding M&A announcements. It does appear as if acquisitions by non-Asian financial institutions are a positive signal for the remaining competitors and that capital markets believe that it will increase the likelihood of their acquisition in the future.

The returns of the rivals of targets of Asian bidders are remarkably different than those of non-Asian bidders. The previously significant abnormal returns cease to be significant and only weak significance remains for the pre-announcement event windows. This may indicate market expectation that a takeover is imminent within the financial sector, but it is not entirely clear who will be the ultimate target. The return reversals following the transaction announcement may be seen as an indication of that, but they lack significance.

Table 3-12: Event study results for non-Asian and Asian bidder target rivals

Event window	ACAR	Median CAR	*t*-test (*t*-value)	BMP-test (Z-score)	Corrado-test (Z-score)	Sample size
Panel A: Non-Asian bidder target rivals						
[-5;5]	7.58%	6.32%	3.861***	3.036***	3.526***	27
[-3;3]	5.44%	4.33%	4.108***	3.649***	3.131***	27
[-2;2]	4.39%	2.39%	4.114***	3.703***	3.217***	27
[-1;1]	3.97%	2.62%	3.965***	3.532***	3.882***	27
[0]	2.04%	1.69%	2.924***	2.936***	3.163***	27
[-5;-1]	2.52%	1.88%	2.648**	2.193**	1.438	27
[-3;-1]	1.93%	1.52%	3.080***	2.379**	1.330	27
[-1;0]	2.64%	1.64%	2.940***	2.862***	2.731***	27
[0;1]	3.37%	2.62%	4.169***	3.907***	4.260***	27
[1;3]	1.47%	1.10%	1.722*	1.178	1.626	27
[1;5]	3.02%	2.50%	2.346**	1.556	2.378**	27
Panel B: Asian bidder target rivals						
[-5;5]	1.82%	0.59%	1.497	1.367	0.392	57
[-3;3]	0.92%	-0.32%	0.934	1.055	0.193	57
[-2;2]	0.97%	-0.48%	1.079	1.167	0.312	57
[-1;1]	0.07%	0.10%	0.113	0.180	-0.042	57
[0]	0.25%	-0.27%	0.730	0.552	0.000	57
[-5;-1]	1.86%	0.57%	1.745*	1.759*	0.964	57
[-3;-1]	1.86%	0.13%	2.009**	2.217**	1.310	57
[-1;0]	0.56%	-0.14%	1.132	1.221	0.293	57
[0;1]	-0.24%	0.12%	-0.585	-0.596	-0.344	57
[1;3]	-1.19%	-1.27%	-1.831*	-1.398	-1.016	57
[1;5]	-0.29%	-0.37%	-0.348	-0.247	-0.382	57

Panel C: Difference Non-Asian bidder target rivals and Asian bidder target rivals

Event window	ΔACAR	ΔMedian CAR	two-sample *t*-test (*t*-value)	Wilcoxon rank-sum test (Z-score)
[-5;5]	5.76%	5.72%	2.595**	2.902***
[-3;3]	4.52%	4.66%	2.648***	3.458***
[-2;2]	3.42%	2.88%	2.277**	2.605***
[-1;1]	3.90%	2.51%	3.391***	2.749***
[0]	1.79%	1.96%	2.602**	2.586***
[-5;-1]	0.66%	1.31%	0.390	1.599
[-3;-1]	0.07%	1.40%	0.045	1.686*
[-1;0]	2.08%	1.78%	2.183**	2.193**
[0;1]	3.61%	2.50%	4.405***	3.592***
[1;3]	2.66%	2.37%	2.389**	2.404**
[1;5]	3.31%	2.86%	2.192**	2.126**

*,**,*** denotes statistical significance at the 10%, 5%, and 1% level

3.4 Overall effects of financial sector consolidation in the Asia-Pacific region

The capital market reactions of bidding and target banks and their respective rivals differ significantly, depending on the origin of the acquiring institution. Figure 3-1 and Figure 3-2 present a detailed overview of the return patterns during the eleven day period surrounding a takeover announcement.

Overall, bidding banks show little significance in their positive return patterns. However, splitting the sample into non-Asian and Asian bidders offers some valuable insights. The results for non-Asian bidding banks are largely in line with prior research, as they achieve slightly negative, but only very weakly significant returns (e.g. Beitel et al., 2004; Hankir et al., 2011). Asian bidders, on the other hand, perform significantly better than their non-Asian peers, achieving an average CAR of 1.87% during the [−1;1] event window. This result stands in stark contrast to the majority of prior research findings. Looking at the market reactions of the Asian bidding bank rivals, they also experience gains in shareholder wealth, albeit smaller ones than the bidding banks (see Figure 3-1 Panel B). The positive returns of Asian bidders and their rivals upon a takeover announcement can be interpreted as evidence of the Market Power Hypothesis. A takeover leads to fewer remaining firms in the market and higher market power for each firm. This in turn may allow them to use their market power to extract higher profits. The gains to the targets of Asian bidders and their rivals also display return patterns that are in line with the Market Power Hypothesis, as both experience gains during the event window. However, their abnormal returns are significantly lower than those achieved by the targets of non-Asian bidders and their peers.

The results for non-Asian bidders, their targets, and their respective rivals display overall return patterns that are more in line with those anticipated by the Acquisition Probability Hypothesis. The rivals of non-Asian acquirers show only weak reactions, with a tendency towards negative returns during the [−5;5] day event window. Non-Asian bidders largely engage in cross-border acquisitions (with the exception of Australian banks engaging in national takeovers), a decision that will have little impact on their domestic competitive environment. However, it can serve as a signal for capital markets that their domestic market lacks growth opportunities and further consolidation may not be possible due to regulatory concerns. Therefore, even though non-Asian bidders also earn negative returns, their peers perform even worse. This can be interpreted as a preemptive merger motive, as it takes the opportunity away from other banks to purchase Asian targets. The return patterns of non-Asian bidder targets and their rivals further corroborate the Acquisition Probability Hypothesis. Targets of non-Asian acquirers earn large abnormal returns surrounding the announcement day, much more so than their peers. More importantly, the target's rivals also appear to earn rather large and highly significant abnormal returns, cumulating in an ACAR of 7.58% during the [–5;5] day event window. This reevaluation of targets may suggest that the economic conditions in the target's home market are remarkably good. At the same time it may also reflect the reduction in the number of available targets, leading to subsequently higher prices for all remaining firms in the market. The target rivals of non-Asian bidders also earn much higher returns than their peers targeted by Asian rivals.

Figure 3-1: Bidding bank and bidding banks' rivals ACARs surrounding the official M&A announcement date

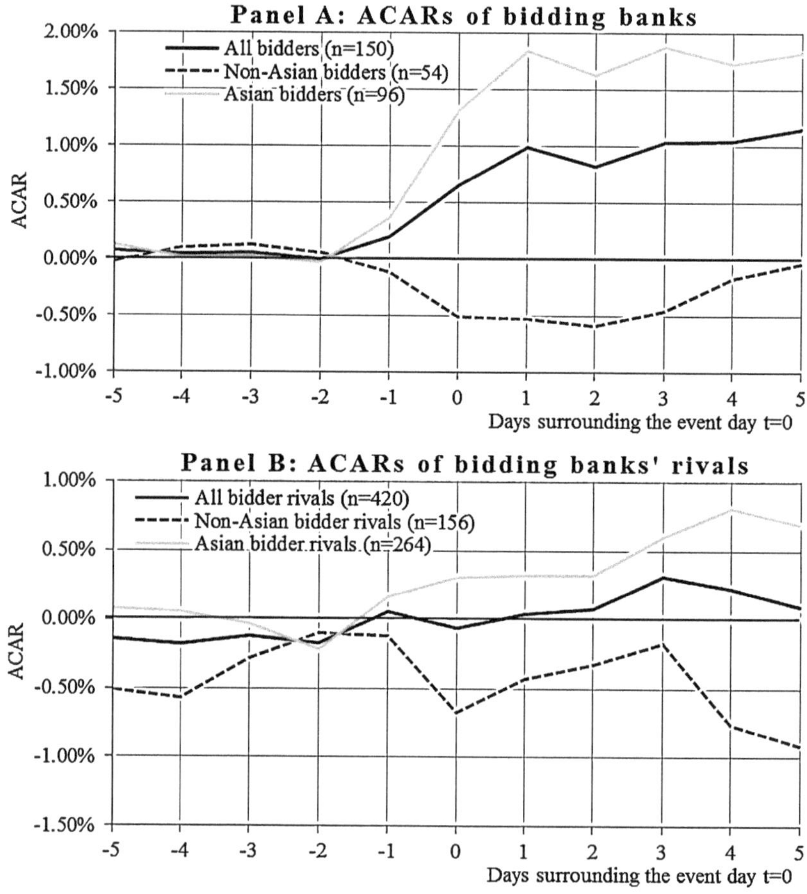

Overall, markets appear to value takeovers among Asian financial institutions in regard to market power considerations, whereas M&As of non-Asian institutions are more in line with the return patterns hypothesized by the Takeover Probability Theory. This appears to be a reasonable assumption, as regional transactions lead to more dominant players who can then use their larger market power to their advantage. Non-Asian bidders, on the other hand, send strong signals to capital markets in regard of their domestic economic environment and the potential for future growth they perceive in a different region. At the same time, foreign bidders do not decrease the competition in a country, as one competitor is replaced by a different one, albeit from another region. Foreign bank entry may even lead to increased efficiency levels of the entire banking sector (Claessens et al., 2001).

Figure 3-2: Target bank and target banks' rivals ACARs surrounding the official M&A announcement date

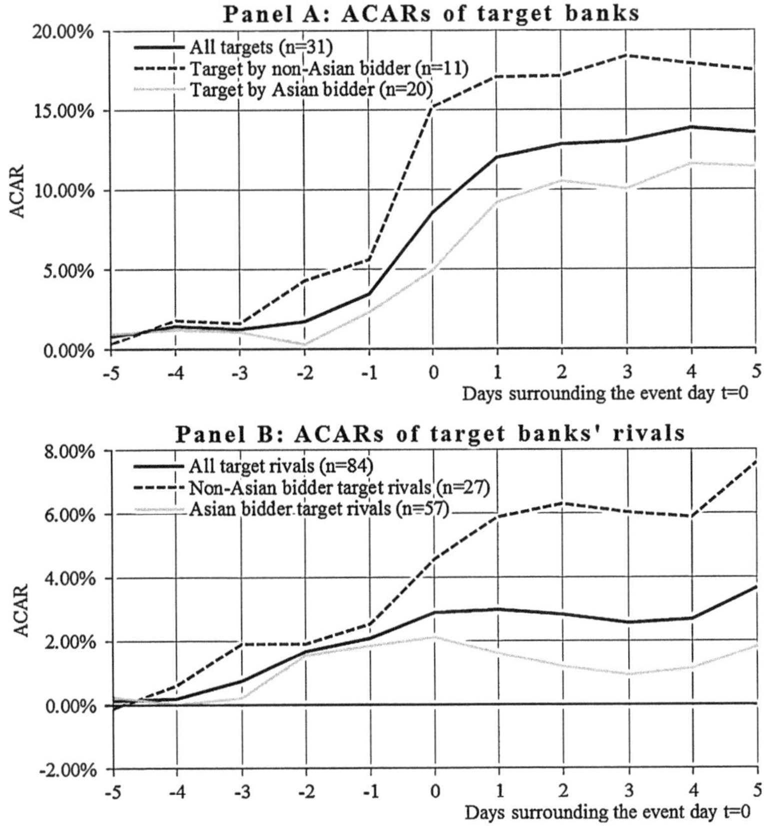

3.5 Determinants of the short-term market performance

In order to investigate and identify the drivers of the short-term stock market performance of bidding banks surrounding the announcement of an M&A transaction, a cross-sectional regression analysis is used.[17] The multivariate ordinary least squares (OLS) regression is specified as:

$$CAR_{j,[\tau_1;\tau_2]} = \delta_0 + \sum_{i=1}^{m} \delta_i VAR_i + \varepsilon \tag{3-15}$$

where the dependent variable $CAR_{j,[\tau_1;\tau_2]}$ is the cumulative abnormal return of firm $j \in [1,\ldots, N]$ during the $[\tau_1;\tau_2]$ day event window surrounding the announcement day $t=0$, VAR_i are the independent variables with $i \in [1,\ldots, m]$, m being the number of variables, δ_0 is the regression constant, δ_i are the regression coefficients for the independent variables with $i \in [1,\ldots, m]$ and ε is the error term. Multiple models are tested to offer a detailed analysis of the drivers behind successful M&A transactions in the Asia Pacific region.

3.5.1 Factors influencing the bidding bank's short-term market performance

The investigation primarily focuses on the question whether local Asian banks are more successful in the Asia-Pacific region than their non-Asian peers. In order to analyze if Asian bidding banks achieve higher CARs the variable *ASIAN* is used, which indicates whether the bidding bank is from an Asian country or not. The variable *NATIONAL* specifies domestic transactions. Prior research suggests that national M&A transactions are more likely to create shareholder value than cross-border ones (e.g. Beitel et al., 2004; Cybo-Ottone & Murgia, 2000; DeLong, 2001). The shareholders of bidding firms can also expect to receive higher returns if they bid for a private target instead of a public one (Fuller, Netter, & Stegemoller, 2002). The purchase of a private firm's assets is akin to trading in a relatively illiquid market, bidders are likely to pay lower premiums, which can be interpreted as an illiquidity discount. The variable *PRIVTAR* is used to investigate whether an acquisition of a private target leads to better stock returns to the shareholders of the bidding bank in the case of an M&A in the Asia-Pacific region. In addition, the two interaction terms *ASIAN* × *NATIONAL* and *ASIAN* × *PRIVTAR* are introduced to explicitly investigate whether Asian bidding banks perform significantly

17 Due to the small sample size of only 31 events a cross-sectional regression analysis of the target banks is forgone.

better in domestic M&As and in M&As with private targets. It can be expected that these transactions will be especially successful, as they are a sign of further consolidation where market power considerations may be a more dominant motivation.

In order to control for factors that prior empirical research identified as drivers of overall bank M&A success, several additional variables are included in the regressions. The variable *VALUE* captures the size of the deal in US dollars. Larger deals can incur significant integration costs, making smaller ones preferable (Cybo-Ottone & Murgia, 2000), at the same time, larger deals might possibly indicate a larger operational overlap and hence a larger potential for cost reductions. To analyze whether focusing mergers, i.e. M&As among institutions having the same primary SIC, we use the variable *FOCUS*. Most studies on bank M&As find that the bidding banks' shareholders can expect to earn higher stock returns in focusing mergers than in diversifying ones (e.g. Becher & Campbell, 2005; Beitel et al., 2004). In most cases a combination of geographic and product focus performs particularly well (e.g. Cornett et al., 2006; DeLong, 2001). The variables *MCAP* and *ROE* are used as a size and profitability measure in the form of the market capitalization and the return on equity for the bidding bank. Larger and more profitable bidders might be able to better integrate their new acquisitions. However, this might come at the expense of future earnings. Therefore, it is likely that shareholders of large banks and banks with high ROEs perceive acquisitions to be negative. Finally, banks in Asia are still frequently at least partially government owned. The variable *GOV* investigates the influence of government involvement on the side of the bidding bank on its stock returns. Table 3-13 gives a detailed description of all variables.

Table 3-13: Variable definition for the OLS regressions

VAR_i	Description
ASIAN	Dummy variable defined as 1 if the bidding bank is an Asian bank, zero otherwise. Asian banks are defined to be from one of the following countries: China, Hong Kong, India, Indonesia, Japan, Malaysia, Pakistan, Philippines, Singapore, South Korea, Taiwan and Thailand.
NATIONAL	Dummy variable defined as 1 if the bidding bank and target bank are from the same country, zero otherwise.
PRIVTAR	Dummy variable defined as 1 if the target bank public status is private, zero otherwise.
VALUE	Logarithm of the deal value in US dollars.
FOCUS	Dummy variable defined as 1 if the bidding and target bank have the same primary SIC code, zero otherwise.

Table 3-13 (continued)

VAR_i	Description
MCAP	Logarithm of the market capitalization of the bidding bank in US dollars on the last trading day of the year prior to the official announcement day.
ROE	Return on equity of the bidding bank as of December 31st of the year prior to the official announcement day.
GOV	Dummy variable defined as 1 if the bidding bank itself or the ultimate parent of the bidding bank is 50% or more government owned, but the stock still being publicly traded, zero otherwise.
Δ RESTRICTION	Difference in the Restriction on Banking Activity Index between bidding bank country of origin and target bank country of origin. The index is based on answers to multiple questions of the four Bank Regulation and Supervision Surveys of the World Bank (see also Barth, Caprio, & Levine, 2004, 2005, 2008, 2012). It describes the extent to which banks may undertake (i) securities underwriting, brokering, dealing and all aspects of the mutual fund industry, (ii) insurance underwriting and selling and (iii) real estate development and management. These activities could be (i) unrestricted, banks can directly conduct the full range of activities in a given category (1 point), (ii) permitted, a full range of activities but some must be undertaken by a subsidiary (2 points), (iii) prohibited, less than the full range of activities can be undertaken by the bank or a subsidiary (3 points) and (iv) prohibited, in which case neither the bank nor a subsidiary is allowed to engage in the activity (4 points). The index ranges from 0 to 12, a higher value representing more restrictions on banking activities.
Δ SUPERVISORY	Difference in the Official Supervisory Power Index between bidding bank country of origin and target bank country of origin. The index is based on answers to 16 questions in each of the four Bank Regulation and Supervision Surveys of the World Bank (see also Barth et al., 2004, 2005, 2008, 2012). It includes, among other questions, whether the supervisory authorities can meet with external auditors to discuss their reports without prior bank approval, legally require auditors to report any misconduct by managers or directors, take legal action against external auditors for negligence, force a bank to change its internal organizational structure, suspend the directors' decisions to distribute dividends, bonuses or management fees and supersede shareholder rights and declare a bank insolvent. Each time the reply to a question was positive, it is assigned a value of 1. The index therefore ranges from 0 to 16, a higher value representing higher level of supervisory power.

Table 3-13 (continued)

VAR_i	Description
Δ TRANSPARENCY	Difference in the Financial Statement Transparency Index between bidding bank country of origin and target bank country of origin. The index is based on answers to multiple questions of the four Bank Regulation and Supervision Surveys of the World Bank (see also Barth et al., 2004, 2005, 2008, 2012). It includes whether accrued though unpaid interest or principal of performing and non-performing loans enter a bank's income statement, whether financial institutions are required to produce consolidated accounts for all bank and non-bank financial subsidiaries, whether off-balance sheet items and risk management procedure are disclosed to the public and whether bank directors are liable in case the disclosed information is erroneous or misleading. The index ranges from 0 to 6, a higher value representing higher financial statement transparency requirements.
Δ MCAP	Logarithm of the absolute value of the difference in market capitalization of bidding to rival bank in in US dollars on the last trading day of the year prior to the official announcement day.
Δ ROE	Difference in the return on equity between the rival and bidding bank as of December 31st of the year prior to the official announcement day.

Recently, concerns have emerged that banks engage in regulatory arbitrage through mergers and acquisitions by purchasing targets that are located in less regulated and supervised jurisdictions. Houston et al. (2012) find evidence that banks indeed appear to move capital into less regulated markets. However, strong property and creditor rights are also important in determining these capital flows, indicating that lower regulation and supervision does not suffice to entice banks to move funds into different countries. Klomp and de Haan (2012) document that increased regulation and supervision does not have much effect on low risk banks but is more likely to have an effect on banks with higher levels of risk. Buch and DeLong (2004) show that banks in jurisdictions with higher levels of supervisory power are actually more attractive targets for international M&A transactions. Whether regulatory arbitrage is a motivation behind bank M&A transactions in Europe is not clear. The analysis of Carbo-Valverde et al. (2012) suggests that one of the drivers behind bank M&A in Europe is the possibility to shift risk onto EU safety nets. On the other hand, Hagendorff et al. (2012) find no evidence that the premiums targets receive are associated with regulatory arbitrage considerations. Even though targets in more strictly regulated countries obtain lower takeover premiums, this is most likely due to the higher compliance cost associated with such transactions.

To analyze whether differences in regulatory regimes play a role in M&A transactions in the Asia-Pacific region, proxies for regulatory and supervisory power in different countries and through time are obtained from the Bank Regulation and Supervision Survey of the World Bank. The database is created from multiple surveys and is compiled by Barth et al. (2004, 2005, 2008, 2012). It is also used by Houston et al. (2012) and Klomp and de Haan (2012) in their analyses of international bank flows and banking risk and regulation, respectively.

Since regulatory regimes can change over time, the approach of Houston et al. (2012) is followed and the investigation period is divided into four subperiods. During each subperiod the results of a different survey apply. Specifically, the first survey is used for the period from 1995 to 1999, the second survey for the period from 2000 to 2003, the third one for the period from 2004 to 2008 and the latest survey for the period from 2009 to 2013. The four surveys were conducted in 1998/1999, 2003, 2005/2006, and 2011/2012, respectively. Overall, the four surveys provide a comprehensive picture on the evolution of banking regulation and supervision during the last two decades. Three specific indices are used: the Restriction on Banking Activity Index, the Official Supervisory Power Index and the Financial Statement Transparency Index (for a more detailed description of the indices see Table 3-13). As it is of interest whether differences in regulatory and supervisory regimes drive the returns of bidding banks in M&A transactions, the difference in these indices between the acquirer and target country is calculated and captured by the following three variables: *ΔRESTRICTION*, *ΔSUPERVISORY* and *ΔTRANSPARENCY*. Therefore, including all variables of interest and control variables, the OLS regression takes the following form:

$$
\begin{aligned}
CAR_{j,[\tau_1;\tau_2]} &= \delta_0 + \delta_1 ASIAN_{j,t} + \delta_2 NATIONAL_{j,t} + \\
&\delta_3 PRIVTAR_{j,t} + \delta_4 VALUE_{j,t} + \delta_5 FOCUS_{j,t} + \\
&\delta_6 MCAP_{j,t} + \delta_7 ROE_{j,t} + \delta_8 GOV_{j,t} + \delta_9 \Delta RESTRICTION_{j,t} + \\
&\delta_{10} \Delta SUPERVISORY_{j,t} + \delta_{11} \Delta TRANSPARENCY_{j,t} + \delta_{12} ASIAN \times \\
&NATIONAL_{j,t} + \delta_{13} ASIAN \times PRIVTAR_{j,t} + \varepsilon_{j,t}
\end{aligned}
\qquad (3\text{-}16)
$$

3.5.2 Bidding bank regression results

Table 3-14 and Table 3-15 present the results of multiple OLS regressions for the bidding banks with either the [–1;1] or the [–5;5] day event window as the dependent variable. The first and basic model specification investigates whether Asian acquirers obtain higher CARs than their non-Asian peers and whether domestic transactions, the acquisition of private targets, deal value, or focusing transactions significantly contribute to the success of the bidding bank. In line with the outcome of the event study, Asian bidding banks perform significantly better than their non-Asian peers. The coefficient for *ASIAN* is positive and statistically significant. Additionally, focusing transactions also appear to positively influence bidding bank returns. This is in line with prior research results, such as DeLong (2001) and Beitel et al. (2004). However, neither domestic transactions nor the acquisition of private targets or the deal size appears to influence the overall stock market performance. Yet, the returns during the [−5;5] day event window are influenced by the transaction size (see Table 3-15). The coefficient is negative and highly significant, indicating that larger transactions are viewed more negatively by capital markets. The results for the other coefficients are largely confirmed.

Table 3-14: OLS regression results for bidding banks with $CAR_{j,[-1;1]}$ as dependent variable

	Model 1	Model 2	Model 3	Model 4	Model 5
δ_0	0.031	0.033	0.131*	0.048	0.098
	(0.744)	(0.823)	(1.662)	(0.889)	(1.173)
ASIAN	0.020**	−0.011	−0.015	−0.025	−0.026
	(2.327)	(−0.905)	(−1.179)	(−1.401)	(−1.423)
NATIONAL	0.007	−0.013*	−0.018**	−0.012*	−0.013
	(0.741)	(−1.930)	(−2.122)	(−1.664)	(−1.440)
PRIVTAR	0.022	−0.040***	−0.047***	−0.064***	−0.067***
	(1.382)	(−3.165)	(−3.291)	(−4.350)	(−3.862)
VALUE	−0.003	−0.002	−0.002	−0.003	−0.004
	(−1.344)	(−1.112)	(−1.147)	(−1.026)	(−1.510)
FOCUS	0.018**	0.016*	0.011	0.012	0.008
	(1.985)	(1.859)	(1.290)	(1.458)	(0.874)
MCAP			−0.004		−0.001
			(−1.233)		(−0.422)
ROE			0.000		0.000**
			(0.649)		(1.999)
GOV				−0.015	−0.017
				(−1.044)	(−1.124)
ΔRESTRICTION				0.004*	0.003*
				(1.769)	(1.667)
ΔSUPERVISORY				−0.002	−0.002
				(−0.710)	(−0.744)
ΔTRANSPARENCY				0.006	0.005
				(0.895)	(0.798)

Table 3-14 (continued)

	Model 1	Model 2	Model 3	Model 4	Model 5
ASIAN × *NATIONAL*		0.037**	0.037**	0.051***	0.050***
		(2.560)	(2.377)	(2.767)	(2.723)
ASIAN × *PRIVTAR*		0.076***	0.079***	0.081***	0.080***
		(3.825)	(3.563)	(4.587)	(4.064)
Observations	150	150	140	129	119
Adjusted. R^2	8.95%	14.74%	14.31%	18.57%	18.43%
F-Value	3.227***	6.291***	4.356***	8.231***	6.607***

ASIAN is defined 1 if the bidding bank is from one of the following countries: China, Hong Kong, India, Indonesia, Japan, Malaysia, Pakistan, Philippines, Singapore, South Korea, Taiwan and Thailand, zero otherwise; *NATIONAL* is defined as 1 if the bidding bank and target bank are from the same country, zero otherwise; *PRIVTAR* defined as 1 if the target bank public status is private, zero otherwise; *VALUE* is the logarithm of the deal value in US dollars; *FOCUS* is defined as 1 if the bidding and target bank have the same primary SIC code, zero otherwise; *MCAP* is the logarithm of the market capitalization of the bidding bank in US dollars on the last trading day of the year prior to the event; *ROE* is the return on equity of the bidding bank as of December 31st of the year prior to the event. *GOV* is defined as 1 if the bidding bank itself or the ultimate parent of the bidding bank is 50% or more government owned, but the stock is still being publicly traded, zero otherwise; *ΔRESTRICTION* is the difference in the Restriction on Banking Activity Index between bidding bank country of origin and target bank country of origin; *ΔSUPERVISORY* is the difference in the Official Supervisory Power Index between bidding bank country of origin and target bank country of origin; *ΔTRANSPARENCY* is the difference in the Financial Statement Transparency Index between bidding bank country of origin and target bank country of origin. The standard errors are corrected for heteroskedasticity and clustering of observations at the bidding bank level and the associated *t*-values are given in parentheses. *,**,*** denotes statistical significance at the 10%, 5%, and 1% level.

Model 2 adds two interaction terms to more closely examine whether domestic transactions by Asian bidding banks (*ASIAN* × *NATIONAL*) and the acquisition of private institutions by Asian acquirers (*ASIAN* × *PRIVTAR*) perform significantly better than other transactions. The coefficients for both transaction terms are statistically significant, strongly indicating that, on average, domestic bank M&As and bank M&As in which the target is a private institution perform significantly better. Furthermore, the coefficients for *NATIONAL* and *PRIVTAR* change from positive to negative and become significant. This indicates that especially cross-border acquisitions by non-Asian banks and acquisitions by non-Asian banks of public targets lead to a significant reduction in shareholder wealth. Focusing transactions still significantly enhance the stock returns to bidding banks and the overall model appears to be well specified.[18] Adding the two variables for bidding bank size and

18 All models were checked for collinearity with variance inflation factors. As expected, variance inflation factors are high for the interaction terms and their components, but

profitability, *MCAP* and *ROE*, does not improve the overall explanatory power of the model, as the coefficients for the *MCAP* and *ROE* are not significant.

Overall, it appears as if investors anticipate that non-Asian acquirers will not be able to overcome the difficulties associated with M&A deals in this region, such as language and cultural differences. In contrast, Asian bidding banks appear to be able to leverage their local knowledge in order to gain an edge over their non-Asian competitors. Specifically, investors appear to believe that Asian banks are able to evaluate domestic and private institutions particularly well and therefore reward such acquisitions with an increase in bidding bank's stock price. Viewed in combination with the event study results for the bidding bank rivals, it is also possible that markets reward potential gains in market power.

Model 4 introduces the three regulatory variables describing the differences in the regulatory and supervisory regimes in the acquiring and target bank country of origin. The results are largely in line with those of Model 2 and Model 3. The coefficients for the interaction terms are positive and highly significant, showing again that Asian bidders can expect to achieve higher CARs in domestic transactions and in transactions with private targets. The highly significant and negative coefficient for *PRIVTAR* underscores that non-Asian banks perform especially poorly when acquiring non-private targets. The coefficient for *GOV* is negative but not significant. The coefficient for *ΔRESTRICTION* is now positive and weakly significant, indicating that capital markets reward banks for going into jurisdictions where lower restrictions on banking activities apply. Acquiring targets in countries with less restrictive regimes on banking activities potentially offer a bank more growth opportunities and allow for better risk diversification. The signs for the coefficients of *ΔSUPERVISORY* and *ΔTRANSPARENCY* are largely in line with the findings of prior research. Buch and DeLong (2004) show that targets in jurisdictions with higher supervisory power are more attractive. Conversely, bidding banks can expect to achieve lower stock returns when acquiring targets in jurisdictions with lower levels of supervisory power than in their home country. The coefficient for *ΔTRANSPARENCY* is positive, implying that lower transparency requirements in the target country than in the bidding bank's country of origin are associated with positive stock returns. More strictly regulated countries are usually associated with higher compliance costs (Hagendorff et al., 2012). On the other hand, investors most likely expect compliance costs to be lower in countries where less stringent transparency rules apply. Nevertheless,

---

still below ten, while they are well below five for all other variables. This indicates that collinearity should not be an issue in any of the regression models.

this is merely a trend, as both variables lack significance. The final model presents the full model specification including all variables. A slight decrease in the overall explanatory power of the model is observed, but the results remain largely in line with the ones observed in the prior models. The coefficient for the variable *ROE* becomes significant, but as it is very small, the impact on the achieved CAR appears to be rather limited. The results using the CAR achieved during the [–5;5] day event window as the dependent variable largely confirm this result. However, it is noteworthy that larger transactions are associated with significant reductions in shareholder wealth, a trend that is constant for all regression specifications. In addition, domestic transactions by Asian bidding banks do not significantly influence the returns any longer. Differences in the regulatory regime have no effect on the achieved returns.

Overall, the regression analyses allow clear conclusions. Asian bidding banks are, on average, more successful than their non-Asian counterparts. This is especially the case when Asian banks acquire domestic targets and private financial institutions. Interpreting these results in combination with the ACARs achieved by the targets of Asian and non-Asian bidding banks, local Asian banks appear to have significant information advantages over their non-Asian peers. This is reasonable to expect, as they have better understanding and in-depth knowledge of their local markets, allowing them to better choose suitable targets. They seem to have a stronger negotiating position vis-à-vis the target bank, leading to lower premiums. Non-Asian bidding banks, on the other hand, appear to have to pay significantly higher premiums in order to compete against local institutions, negatively affecting their stock returns. The ACARs of the targets of Asian and non-Asian bidding banks give further support to this conclusion, as targets of non-Asian bidders enjoy larger ACARs than those of Asian bidders. On the other hand, regulatory arbitrage considerations appear to play a very minor role at best when capital markets evaluate M&A transactions.

Table 3-15: OLS regression results for bidding banks with $CAR_{j,[-5;5]}$ as dependent variable

	Model 1	Model 2	Model 3	Model 4	Model 5
δ_0	0.174***	0.176***	0.330***	0.195**	0.313**
	(2.753)	2.814	(2.696)	(2.250)	(2.114)
ASIAN	0.021**	–0.009	–0.015	–0.007	–0.010
	(2.077)	–0.594	(–0.990)	(–0.274)	(–0.395)
NATIONAL	0.000	–0.020*	–0.028**	–0.013	–0.017
	(0.003)	–1.889	(–2.531)	(–1.082)	(–1.355)
PRIVTAR	0.009	–0.042*	–0.053**	–0.074***	–0.082***
	(0.543)	–1.914	(–2.288)	(–3.177)	(–3.926)

Table 3-15 (continued)

	Model 1	Model 2	Model 3	Model 4	Model 5
VALUE	−0.010***	−0.010***	−0.010***	−0.010**	−0.012***
	(−3.018)	−2.908	(−3.533)	(−2.303)	(−3.226)
FOCUS	0.021*	0.019	0.014	0.013	0.009
	(1.792)	1.616	(1.160)	(0.950)	(0.631)
MCAP			−0.006		−0.004
			(−1.440)		(−0.789)
ROE			0.000***		0.000***
			(5.520)		(4.798)
GOV				−0.012	−0.016
				(−0.412)	(−0.605)
ΔRESTRICTION				−0.001	−0.001
				(−0.211)	(−0.250)
ΔSUPERVISORY				−0.000	−0.001
				(−0.093)	(−0.131)
ΔTRANSPARENCY				0.007	0.005
				(0.812)	(0.554)
ASIAN × NATIONAL		0.038**	0.040**	0.036	0.038
		1.991	(2.068)	(1.300)	(1.390)
ASIAN × PRIVTAR		0.063**	0.066**	0.082***	0.083***
		2.260	(2.298)	(2.664)	(2.796)
Observations	150	150	140	129	119
Adjusted. R^2	7.75%	9.29%	13.16%	6.17%	10.13%
F-Value	3.968***	5.828***	10.726***	5.774***	9.607***

ASIAN is defined 1 if the bidding bank is from one of the following countries: China, Hong Kong, India, Indonesia, Japan, Malaysia, Pakistan, Philippines, Singapore, South Korea, Taiwan and Thailand, zero otherwise; *NATIONAL* is defined as 1 if the bidding bank and target bank are from the same country, zero otherwise; *PRIVTAR* defined as 1 if the target bank public status is private, zero otherwise; *VALUE* is the logarithm of the deal value in in US dollars; *FOCUS* is defined as 1 if the bidding and target bank have the same primary SIC code, zero otherwise; *MCAP* is the logarithm of the market capitalization of the bidding bank in US dollars on the last trading day of the year prior to the event; *ROE* is the return on equity of the bidding bank as of December 31st of the year prior to the event. *GOV* is defined as 1 if the bidding bank itself or the ultimate parent of the bidding bank is 50% or more government owned, but the stock is still being publicly traded, zero otherwise; *ΔRESTRICTION* is the difference in the Restriction on Banking Activity Index between bidding bank country of origin and target bank country of origin; *ΔSUPERVISORY* is the difference in the Official Supervisory Power Index between bidding bank country of origin and target bank country of origin; *ΔTRANSPARENCY* is the difference in the Financial Statement Transparency Index between bidding bank country of origin and target bank country of origin. The standard errors are corrected for heteroskedasticity and clustering of observations at the bidding bank level and the associated *t*-values are given in parentheses. *,**,*** denotes statistical significance at the 10%, 5%, and 1% level.

It should be noted that endogeneity problems are potentially present, as non-Asian banks may not be able to choose from all available targets in Asia. This may be due to non-Asian banks only being willing to acquire targets with sufficient public information on their financial situation and business prospects. These are likely to be comparatively large and publicly listed targets, limiting their possible target options. In addition, it is also possible that governments encourage domestic mergers prior to allowing foreign institutions to enter a market. Only once the domestic banking sector has sufficiently large institutions, which are able to directly compete with foreign banks, are foreign competitors allowed to enter the market. This might leave non-Asian banks with a very small pool of available targets to choose from, possibly the least desirable ones.

3.5.3 Bidding bank rival regression results

In order to investigate the drivers of the short-term market performance of the bidding bank rivals surrounding the announcement of an M&A transaction, multiple OLS regression models are tested, using alternatively the rival banks' [−1;1] and [−5;5] day event window CARs as the dependent variable. The focus is on the same determinants as for the bidding bank sample, but the variables pertaining to regulatory arbitrage considerations are omitted, as they should not have an effect on the rival bank performance. Instead, the variables $\Delta MCAP$ and ΔROE are added to account for differences in the size and profitability between the rival and bidding bank (see Table 3-13 for a detailed description of all variables used in the regression).

Table 3-16 presents the OLS regression results for the bidding bank rivals. The coefficient for *NATIONAL* is positive and significant, indicating that the increase in the value of the bidding banks' rivals stems mostly from national takeovers within the banking sector. The coefficient for *ASIAN*, on the other hand, is only weakly significant at best, indicating that national rather than regional consolidation is the dominant driver of gains to rival banks. This can be seen as further evidence that market power considerations are an important factor when investors value Asian bank M&As. The difference between rival and bidding bank ROE appears to play a minor role as the coefficient of ΔROE is only significant when using the rival bank's [−1;1] event window CAR as the dependent variable. The coefficient is relatively small and negative, indicating that a merger has a negative impact on the rival bank's profitability.

Table 3-16: OLS regression results for bidding bank rivals

Dependent variable	$CAR_{j,[-1;1]}$				$CAR_{j,[-5;5]}$			
	Model 1	Model 2	Model 3	Model 4	Model 1	Model 2	Model 3	Model 4
δ_0	−0.027	−0.029	−0.022	−0.024	−0.088**	−0.086**	−0.082*	−0.077*
	(−0.868)	(−0.916)	(−0.753)	(−0.795)	(−2.231)	(−2.190)	(−1.885)	(−1.779)
ASIAN	0.002	−0.006	0.001	−0.004	0.013*	0.018	0.012	0.020*
	(0.365)	(−0.680)	(0.244)	(−0.464)	(1.821)	(1.563)	(1.631)	(1.673)
NATIONAL	0.013***	0.008	0.014***	0.011**	0.013*	0.021***	0.014*	0.024***
	(2.652)	(1.467)	(3.104)	(2.019)	(1.767)	(2.745)	(1.899)	(2.992)
PRIVTAR	0.004	−0.006	0.004	0.001	0.016	−0.014	0.018*	−0.007
	(0.699)	(−0.769)	(0.748)	(0.153)	(1.526)	(−0.976)	(1.673)	(−0.413)
VALUE	0.001	0.001	0.000	0.000	0.000	0.000	−0.001	−0.001
	(0.570)	(0.736)	(−0.178)	(−0.034)	(0.117)	(0.164)	(−0.282)	(−0.359)
FOCUS	−0.004	−0.004	−0.002	−0.002	−0.002	−0.004	−0.002	−0.003
	(−0.993)	(−1.104)	(−0.403)	(−0.442)	(−0.357)	(−0.590)	(−0.302)	(−0.469)
GOV	0.011	0.014	0.009	0.011	0.032**	0.031*	0.031*	0.028*
	(1.319)	(1.553)	(1.048)	(1.198)	(2.090)	(1.896)	(1.970)	(1.711)
ΔMCAP	0.000	0.000	0.001	0.001	0.003**	0.003*	0.004**	0.003**
	(0.340)	(0.328)	(0.859)	(0.862)	(2.019)	(1.915)	(2.152)	(2.061)
ΔROE			−0.000***	−0.000***			0.000	0.000
			(−3.788)	(−3.755)			(−0.509)	(−0.507)
ASIAN × *NATIONAL*		0.010		0.008		−0.017		−0.019
		(1.103)		(0.871)		(−1.289)		(−1.419)
ASIAN × *PRIVTAR*		0.012		0.004		0.036*		0.029
		(1.291)		(0.475)		(1.950)		(1.442)
Observations	420	420	381	381	420	420	381	381
Adjusted. R^2	1.78%	1.81%	4.81%	4.52%	2.66%	3.13%	2.77%	3.02%
F-Value	2.253**	2.106**	3.589***	2.911***	2.329**	2.323**	1.903*	1.918**

ASIAN is defined 1 if the bidding bank is from one of the following countries: China, Hong Kong, India, Indonesia, Japan, Malaysia, Pakistan, Philippines, Singapore, South Korea, Taiwan and Thailand, zero otherwise; *NATIONAL* is defined as 1 if the bidding bank and target bank are from the same country, zero otherwise; *PRIVTAR* defined as 1 if the target bank public status is private, zero otherwise; *VALUE* is the logarithm of the deal value in US dollars; *FOCUS* is defined as 1 if the bidding and target bank have the same primary SIC code, zero otherwise; *GOV* is defined as 1 if the bidding bank itself or the ultimate parent of the bidding bank is 50% or more government owned, but the stock is still being publicly traded, zero otherwise; *ΔMCAP* is the logarithm of the absolute value of the difference in market capitalization of bidding to rival bank in in US dollars on the last trading day of the year prior to the official announcement day; *ΔROE* is the difference in the return on equity between the rival and bidding bank as of December 31st of the year prior to the official announcement day. The standard errors are corrected for heteroskedasticity and clustering of observations at the bidding bank rival level and the associated t-values are given in parentheses. *,**,*** denotes statistical significance at the 10%, 5%, and 1% level.

Using a rival bank's [−5;5] event window CAR as the dependent variable, the coefficients for *GOV* and *ΔMCAP* are positive and significant. The significance of the coefficient for *GOV* may indicate a government's desire to further consolidate the national banking sector, which will likely benefit the remaining institutions in the market. The significance of the coefficient for *ΔMCAP*, on the other hand, indicates that rival banks, which are smaller or larger than the bidding bank, stand to gain more from M&A transactions. Similarly sized banks may have missed an opportunity to acquire another company and possibly face increased regulatory scrutiny if they wish to engage in a takeover themselves. Other variables, such as *FOCUS* and *VALUE* do not seem to determine the short-term performance of the rival banks' returns. The interaction terms *ASIAN* × *NATIONAL* and *ASIAN* × *PRIVTAR* do not help to explain much of the variation in the observed rival banks' CARs and the general overall explanatory power of the models remains modest. Overall, gains to rival banks appear to be largely driven by national rather than the regional consolidation processes. This may in part be due to the largely heterogeneous nature of the financial markets in the Asia-Pacific region during the investigation period.

3.6 Robustness checks

Three different robustness checks are conducted to test whether the results achieved so far hold for different sample periods, sample definitions and model specifications. First, it is examined whether there are major differences for the results of the bidder sample for different time periods. For this, the sample is divided into the period from 1995–2004 and from 2005–2013. Second, the rival reactions to the top five national rivals are investigated to test whether the results differ markedly from those achieved for the top three rivals. Finally, a median regression is used to identify how robust the OLS regression results are to outliers.

3.6.1 Difference in time periods

In order to check whether the results are robust for different time periods, the sample is split into the time periods from 1995–2004 and 2005–2013, leading to two almost equal time periods of ten and nine years, respectively. Dividing the sample into these two periods is particularly useful, as the first one covers the 1997 Asian Financial Crisis and its aftermath, while the second one includes the more recent 2007 Financial Crisis. This yields two comparable sample sizes where the respective number of bidding banks in each sample is 68 and 82. The results are presented in Table 3-16.

The overall results show no significance for the investigated event windows in both, the 1995–2004 and the 2005–2013 time period. This is in line with the results observed for the entire sample of bidding banks (see also Table 3-5). In addition, the results of the two time periods are not significantly different from each other. The overall results therefore appear to be robust over time.

Table 3-17: Event study results for bidding banks 1995–2004 and 2005–2013

Event window	ACAR	Median CAR	*t*-test (*t*-value)	BMP-test (Z-score)	Corrado-test (Z-score)	Sample size
Panel A: Bidding banks 1995–2004						
[−5;5]	0.57%	−0.13%	0.618	−0.151	0.326	68
[−3;3]	0.97%	0.72%	1.339	0.398	0.774	68
[−2;2]	0.48%	0.13%	0.764	−0.137	0.107	68
[−1;1]	0.78%	0.44%	1.557	0.476	1.143	68
[0]	0.53%	0.16%	1.459	0.172	1.066	68
[−5;−1]	−0.17%	−0.37%	−0.323	−0.611	−0.534	68
[−3;−1]	0.08%	−0.10%	0.184	−0.149	−0.524	68
[−1;0]	0.65%	−0.11%	1.423	0.378	0.552	68
[0;1]	0.66%	0.47%	1.431	0.273	1.602	68
[1;3]	0.36%	0.36%	0.600	0.493	1.091	68
[1;5]	0.21%	−0.09%	0.256	0.077	0.541	68
Panel B: Bidding banks 2005–2013						
[−5;5]	1.63%	0.97%	1.994**	0.816	0.833	82
[−3;3]	1.00%	0.23%	1.537	0.365	0.494	82
[−2;2]	1.01%	0.43%	1.480	0.455	0.457	82
[−1;1]	1.15%	0.44%	1.703*	0.896	0.824	82
[0]	0.40%	−0.02%	1.555	0.805	0.739	82
[−5;−1]	0.50%	−0.05%	1.116	0.583	0.852	82
[−3;−1]	0.20%	−0.20%	0.631	0.395	0.512	82
[−1;0]	0.65%	0.19%	1.663	1.155	1.144	82
[0;1]	0.91%	0.11%	1.491	0.522	0.388	82
[1;3]	0.39%	−0.39%	0.686	−0.212	−0.183	82
[1;5]	0.73%	0.02%	1.232	0.395	0.053	82

Panel C: Difference bidding banks 1995–2004 and bidding bank 2005–2013				
Event window	ΔACAR	ΔMedian CAR	two-sample *t*-test (*t*-value)	Wilcoxon rank-sum test (Z-score)
[−5;5]	−1.06%	−1.10%	−0.860	−1.066
[−3;3]	−0.02%	0.49%	−0.022	−0.047
[−2;2]	−0.53%	−0.31%	−0.564	−0.425
[−1;1]	−0.37%	−0.01%	−0.425	0.066
[0]	0.13%	0.18%	0.292	0.202
[−5;−1]	−0.67%	−0.32%	−0.975	−0.798
[−3;−1]	−0.12%	0.10%	−0.236	0.043
[−1;0]	0.00%	−0.30%	0.001	−0.345
[0;1]	−0.24%	0.36%	−0.311	0.425
[1;3]	−0.03%	0.75%	−0.030	0.489
[1;5]	−0.52%	−0.11%	−0.523	−0.602

*,**,*** denotes statistical significance at the 10%, 5%, and 1% level

Table 3-18: Event study results for non-Asian bidding banks 1995–2004 and 2005–2013

Event window	ACAR	Median CAR	*t*-test (*t*-value)	BMP-test (Z-score)	Corrado-test (Z-score)	Sample size
Panel A: Non-Asian bidding banks 1995–2004						
[–5;5]	–0.93%	–0.51%	–1.054	–1.236	–0.457	30
[–3;3]	–0.89%	0.14%	–1.232	–1.408	–0.735	30
[–2;2]	–0.91%	–0.62%	–1.501	–1.750*	–0.835	30
[–1;1]	–0.58%	–0.10%	–1.001	–1.318	–0.647	30
[0]	–0.62%	–0.59%	–1.249	–1.716*	–1.458	30
[–5;–1]	–1.02%	–0.81%	–2.023*	–1.941*	–1.278	30
[–3;–1]	–0.73%	–0.17%	–1.530	–1.481	–1.508	30
[–1;0]	–0.93%	–0.57%	–1.851*	–2.066**	–1.850*	30
[0;1]	–0.26%	0.09%	–0.488	–1.033	0.027	30
[1;3]	0.45%	0.71%	1.040	1.192	1.227	30
[1;5]	0.71%	0.46%	1.216	0.936	1.253	30
Panel B: Non-Asian bidding banks 2005–2013						
[–5;5]	1.09%	0.77%	0.810	0.108	0.652	24
[–3;3]	–0.13%	0.16%	–0.170	–0.810	–0.321	24
[–2;2]	–0.47%	–0.35%	–0.724	–1.193	–0.754	24
[–1;1]	–0.60%	–0.41%	–1.149	–1.310	–1.239	24
[0]	–0.12%	–0.02%	–0.320	–0.614	–0.770	24
[–5;–1]	1.02%	0.44%	1.567	1.379	1.470	24
[–3;–1]	0.43%	0.31%	0.822	0.559	0.913	24
[–1;0]	–0.10%	–0.12%	–0.178	–0.120	–0.326	24
[0;1]	–0.61%	–0.14%	–1.592	–2.143**	–1.736*	24
[1;3]	–0.45%	–0.65%	–0.890	–1.660*	–0.959	24
[1;5]	0.19%	–0.04%	0.217	–0.513	–0.158	24

Panel C: Difference non-Asian bidding banks 1995–2004 and bidding bank 2005–2013

Event window	ΔACAR	ΔMedian CAR	two-sample *t*-test (*t*-value)	Wilcoxon rank-sum test (Z-score)
[–5;5]	–2.02%	–1.27%	–1.299	1.018
[–3;3]	–0.76%	–0.02%	–0.711	0.601
[–2;2]	–0.44%	–0.26%	–0.491	0.444
[–1;1]	0.02%	0.32%	0.025	0.061
[0]	–0.50%	–0.56%	–0.783	0.374
[–5;–1]	–2.04%	–1.25%	–2.518**	2.115**
[–3;–1]	–1.16%	–0.48%	–1.634	1.367
[–1;0]	–0.83%	–0.46%	–1.075	0.740
[0;1]	0.35%	0.23%	0.498	–0.792
[1;3]	0.90%	1.36%	1.359	–1.715*
[1;5]	0.52%	0.50%	0.516	–0.618

*;**,*** denotes statistical significance at the 10%, 5%, and 1% level

Table 3-18 and Table 3-19 document the results when splitting the non-Asian and Asian bidding bank sample into the time periods from 1995 to 2004 and from 2005 to 2013. There is weak evidence that non-Asian bidders between 1995 and 2004 performed worse than those between 2005 and 2013. This, however, only appears to be the case for the [–5;–1] event window, suggesting that there was significant information leakage prior to the event. The results for the time period between 2005 and 2013 show almost no significance, except for the [0;1] day even window. In this case, bidders receive weakly significant negative returns.

Table 3-19: Event study results for Asian bidding banks 1995–2004 and 2005–2013

Event window	ACAR	Median CAR	*t*-test (*t*-value)	BMP-test (Z-score)	Corrado-test (Z-score)	Sample size
Panel A: Asian bidding banks 1995–2004						
[–5;5]	1.76%	0.53%	1.181	1.063	0.891	38
[–3;3]	2.45%	1.22%	2.186**	2.071**	1.783*	38
[–2;2]	1.57%	1.46%	1.604	1.415	0.942	38
[–1;1]	1.86%	1.54%	2.522**	2.216**	2.216**	38
[0]	1.44%	0.71%	3.017***	2.803***	2.878***	38
[–5;–1]	0.50%	0.15%	0.590	0.604	0.466	38
[–3;–1]	0.71%	0.34%	1.098	1.147	0.697	38
[–1;0]	1.91%	0.66%	2.905***	2.610***	2.530**	38
[0;1]	1.39%	1.45%	2.009*	1.680*	2.219**	38
[1;3]	0.29%	–0.85%	0.284	–0.088	0.364	38
[1;5]	–0.18%	–1.04%	–0.128	–0.442	–0.432	38
Panel B: Asian bidding banks 2005–2013						
[–5;5]	1.86%	1.11%	1.820*	0.926	0.599	58
[–3;3]	1.46%	0.24%	1.714*	0.952	0.812	58
[–2;2]	1.62%	0.67%	1.769*	1.193	1.044	58
[–1;1]	1.88%	0.65%	2.042**	1.615	1.807*	58
[0]	0.62%	0.07%	1.859*	1.411	1.400	58
[–5;–1]	0.28%	–0.23%	0.493	–0.150	0.096	58
[–3;–1]	0.11%	–0.42%	0.270	0.064	0.038	58
[–1;0]	0.97%	0.45%	1.948*	1.541	1.609	58
[0;1]	1.53%	0.60%	1.840*	1.415	1.593	58
[1;3]	0.73%	–0.26%	0.949	0.454	0.394	58
[1;5]	0.96%	0.15%	1.254	0.819	0.166	58

Table 3-19 (continued)

Panel C: Difference Asian bidding banks 1995–2004 and bidding bank 2005–2013				
Event window	ΔACAR	ΔMedian CAR	two-sample *t*-test (*t*-value)	Wilcoxon rank-sum test (Z-score)
[-5;5]	-0.10%	-0.58%	-0.057	-0.378
[-3;3]	0.99%	0.98%	0.710	0.633
[-2;2]	-0.05%	0.80%	-0.034	0.251
[-1;1]	-0.02%	0.89%	-0.018	0.461
[0]	0.82%	0.64%	1.454	1.105
[-5;-1]	0.22%	0.38%	0.220	0.251
[-3;-1]	0.61%	0.76%	0.842	0.985
[-1;0]	0.94%	0.21%	1.159	0.648
[0;1]	-0.14%	0.85%	-0.121	0.356
[1;3]	-0.44%	-0.58%	-0.346	-0.363
[1;5]	-1.14%	-1.19%	-0.769	-1.270

*;**,*** denotes statistical significance at the 10%, 5%, and 1% level

Table 3-19 shows the results for Asian bidding banks between 1995–2004 and 2005–2013. The significant positive effects observed for the entire time period for Asian bidders (see also Table 3-6 Panel B) appear to be more pronounced in the time period from 1995 to 2004. Especially on the announcement day and the three day period surrounding the announcement day, the results are positive and highly significant. For the time period from 2005 to 2013, the results are less significant. In particular, only the [-1;1] day event window remains weakly significant. However, the results achieved for both time periods do not differ significantly from each other (see Table 3-19 Panel C).

3.6.2 Sensitivity analysis of the rival reactions

The rival selection process for the sensitivity analysis follows the same procedure as for the regular analysis. However, instead of choosing the top three rivals by market capitalization, the top five rivals are chosen. It is possible to identify five suitable rivals for 126 bidders out of the sample of 150 bidding banks, giving a total of 630 rival observations. The reduction in sample size in comparison to the prior analysis is due to fewer firms having five rivals. This is owed to the restriction that the rivals have to have the same nationality as the bidder.[19]

19 An analysis of the targets is not conducted, as almost none of the rivals have five direct competitors from the same country, resulting in a very small sample size that would not lead to meaningful insights.

Table 3-20: Event study results for top five bidding bank rivals

Event window	ACAR	Median CAR	*t*-test (*t*-value)	BMP-test (Z-score)	Corrado-test (Z-score)	Sample size
[-5;5]	0.59%	0.04%	2.005**	0.724	0.505	630
[-3;3]	0.70%	0.07%	2.770***	2.295**	1.717*	630
[-2;2]	0.18%	0.00%	0.856	0.563	0.543	630
[-1;1]	0.12%	0.11%	0.667	1.162	1.238	630
[0]	-0.02%	0.00%	-0.163	0.407	0.958	630
[-5;-1]	0.28%	-0.02%	1.451	0.311	-0.157	630
[-3;-1]	0.37%	0.05%	2.327**	1.877*	1.153	630
[-1;0]	0.09%	-0.08%	0.492	1.066	1.458	630
[0;1]	0.01%	0.01%	0.062	0.526	0.735	630
[1;3]	0.35%	-0.05%	1.755*	1.030	0.917	630
[1;5]	0.33%	-0.12%	1.434	0.473	0.478	630

*;**,*** denotes statistical significance at the 10%, 5%, and 1% level

Table 3-20 gives the results for the entire sample of the top five rivals. The results confirm those of the top three rival analysis. The rivals experience largely insignificant gains, with an overall trend to positive ones. However, the positive reaction is only significant during the [-3;3] day event window. It therefore appears as if the overall reactions previously observed are robust, even when increasing the number of potential rivals.

Table 3-21 again splits the sample into the rivals of Asian and non-Asian bidders. This also largely confirms the results of the top three rival analysis presented in Table 3-8, albeit at generally lower levels of significance. Non-Asian bidders experience some slight losses, but these losses lack significance for all event windows. Asian bidders, on the other hand, still experience weakly significant gains during the entire [-5;5] day event window.

Overall, the results are less significant, but still support those achieved by the top three rival investigation. The lower levels of significance are most likely due to the fewer observations in regard to the M&A events, as only 126 M&A are observed, instead of 140 for the prior analysis. Moreover, the top five national rivals are a more heterogeneous group than the top three rivals, as size differentials in market capitalization in regard to the bidder are higher. The larger the size differential, the lower the competition might be between the bidder and its rivals.

Table 3-21: Event study results for non-Asian and Asian top five bidding bank rivals

Event window	ACAR	Median CAR	*t*-test (*t*-value)	BMP-test (Z-score)	Corrado-test (Z-score)	Sample size
Panel A: Top five non-Asian bidder rivals						
[−5;5]	−0.48%	0.02%	−1.015	−1.224	−0.258	215
[−3;3]	0.65%	−0.04%	1.777*	1.406	1.243	215
[−2;2]	0.19%	0.00%	0.665	0.339	0.325	215
[−1;1]	−0.17%	−0.10%	−0.665	−0.236	−0.012	215
[0]	−0.33%	0.04%	−1.100	−0.654	0.668	215
[−5;−1]	−0.12%	−0.20%	−0.383	−1.105	−1.214	215
[−3;−1]	0.42%	0.00%	1.766*	1.312	0.621	215
[−1;0]	−0.35%	−0.02%	−0.983	−0.389	0.383	215
[0;1]	−0.15%	−0.14%	−0.698	−0.456	0.075	215
[1;3]	0.56%	0.00%	1.669*	1.278	0.892	215
[1;5]	−0.04%	0.11%	−0.124	−0.280	0.532	215
Panel B: Top five Asian bidder rivals						
[−5;5]	1.14%	0.05%	3.099***	2.093**	0.790	415
[−3;3]	0.73%	0.20%	2.174**	1.811*	1.237	415
[−2;2]	0.18%	0.00%	0.620*	0.449	0.437	415
[−1;1]	0.26%	0.38%	1.158	1.620	1.512	415
[0]	0.14%	−0.05%	1.068	1.303	0.707	415
[−5;−1]	0.49%	0.12%	1.973**	1.320	0.639	415
[−3;−1]	0.35%	0.05%	1.664*	1.355	0.977	415
[−1;0]	0.31%	−0.11%	1.664*	1.843*	1.510	415
[0;1]	0.09%	0.15%	0.486	1.022	0.842	415
[1;3]	0.24%	−0.12%	0.969	0.333	0.504	415
[1;5]	0.52%	−0.30%	1.656*	0.775	0.217	415
Panel C: Difference top five non-Asian and Asian bidder rivals						
Event window	ΔACAR	ΔMedian CAR	two-sample *t*-test (*t*-value)		Wilcoxon rank-sum test (Z-score)	
[−5;5]	−1.62%	−0.03%	−2.638***		−1.408	
[−3;3]	−0.08%	−0.24%	−0.144		0.355	
[−2;2]	0.01%	0.00%	0.026		0.356	
[−1;1]	−0.43%	−0.48%	−1.185		−1.435	
[0]	−0.47%	0.09%	−1.667*		0.057	
[−5;−1]	−0.61%	−0.32%	−1.482		−1.731*	
[−3;−1]	0.07%	−0.05%	0.194		−0.094	
[−1;0]	−0.66%	0.09%	−1.812*		0.320	
[0;1]	−0.24%	−0.29%	−0.796		−1.402	
[1;3]	0.32%	0.12%	0.767		1.173	
[1;5]	−0.56%	0.41%	−1.147		0.902	

*,**,*** denotes statistical significance at the 10%, 5%, and 1% level

3.6.3 Median regression on the short-term performance of bidding banks

As a robustness check for the results of the OLS regression a nonparametric median regression is performed. The advantage of the median regression over the standard OLS regression is its robustness in regard to outliers. It is preferable to use a median regression to winsorizing the results, as this leaves more observations, allowing more detailed insights into the results and to draw clearer conclusions in regard to the overall sample. The median regression is performed using the same model specifications as for the OLS regressions conducted in section 3.5.2, but only with [−1;1] event window CAR as the dependent variable. The results are presented in Table 3-22.

Model 1 in Table 3-22 describes the results for the basic model specification. The coefficient for *ASIAN* is positive and significant, again providing evidence that Asian bidding banks perform better than their non-Asian counterparts. Instead of the coefficient for *FOCUS* the negative coefficient for *VALUE* becomes significant in the median regression. This is in line with the results of the OLS regression using the [−5;5] event window CAR as the dependent variable. The median regression therefore confirms that this result is also of importance when explaining the returns achieved during the [−1;1] day event window. Adding the interaction terms shows that the results for *ASIAN* × *PRIVTAR* are more robust than those for *ASIAN*×*NATIONAL*, again in line with the OLS regression using the [−5;5] day CAR as the dependent variable. Asian bidding banks acquiring private targets perform significantly better than their peers. National acquisitions by Asian banks, on the other hand, cease to be significant. Nevertheless, in line with expectations, the coefficient is still positive in all regression specifications.

Table 3-22: Median regression results for bidding banks

	Model 1	Model 2	Model 3	Model 4	Model 5
δ_0	0.069	0.066	0.186**	0.086	0.143
	(1.628)	(1.491)	(2.082)	(1.415)	(1.311)
ASIAN	0.020**	0.003	−0.009	−0.011	−0.018
	(2.014)	(0.151)	(−0.383)	(−0.489)	(−0.721)
NATIONAL	−0.001	−0.007	−0.012	−0.001	−0.012
	(−0.107)	(−0.652)	(−0.932)	(−0.038)	(−0.740)
PRIVTAR	0.007	−0.029*	−0.030*	−0.053*	−0.048
	(0.550)	(−1.664)	(−1.670)	(−1.750)	(−1.570)

Table 3-22 (continued)

	Model 1	Model 2	Model 3	Model 4	Model 5
VALUE	–0.004**	–0.004*	–0.005**	–0.005	–0.005*
	(–1.982)	(–1.672)	(–2.344)	(–1.653)	(–1.981)
FOCUS	0.010	0.010	0.004	0.012	0.012
	(1.229)	(1.374)	(0.422)	(1.343)	(1.189)
MCAP			–0.004		–0.002
			(–1.124)		(–0.510)
ROE			–0.000		–0.000
			(–1.160)		(–0.352)
GOV				–0.026	–0.030*
				(–1.557)	(–1.748)
ΔRESTRICTION				0.002	0.002
				(0.690)	(0.671)
ΔSUPERVISORY				–0.003	–0.003
				(–1.018)	(–1.162)
ΔTRANSPARENCY				–0.007	–0.010
				(–0.701)	(–1.014)
ASIAN × NATIONAL		0.016	0.023	0.029	0.041
		(0.783)	(0.907)	(1.134)	(1.487)
ASIAN × PRIVTAR		0.047**	0.049**	0.064*	0.056*
		(2.302)	(2.104)	(1.973)	(1.667)
Observations	150	150	140	129	119
Pseudo R^2	5.76%	8.82%	10.81%	13.60%	15.45%
Quasi-LR statistic	13.223**	21.086***	23.209***	25.179***	26.300**

ASIAN is defined 1 if the bidding bank is from one of the following countries: China, Hong Kong, India, Indonesia, Japan, Malaysia, Pakistan, Philippines, Singapore, South Korea, Taiwan and Thailand, zero otherwise; *NATIONAL* is defined as 1 if the bidding bank and target bank are from the same country, zero otherwise; *PRIVTAR* defined as 1 if the target bank public status is private, zero otherwise; *VALUE* is the logarithm of the deal value in US dollars; *FOCUS* is defined as 1 if the bidding and target bank have the same primary SIC code, zero otherwise; *MCAP* is the logarithm of the market capitalization of the bidding bank in US dollars on the last trading day of the year prior to the event; *ROE* is the return on equity of the bidding bank as of December 31st of the year prior to the event. *GOV* is defined as 1 if the bidding bank itself or the ultimate parent of the bidding bank is 50% or more government owned, but the stock is still being publicly traded, zero otherwise; *ΔRESTRICTION* is the difference in the Restriction on Banking Activity Index between bidding bank country of origin and target bank country of origin; *ΔSUPERVISORY* is the difference in the Official Supervisory Power Index between bidding bank country of origin and target bank country of origin; *ΔTRANSPARENCY* is the difference in the Financial Statement Transparency Index between bidding bank country of origin and target bank country of origin. The coefficient covariances are computed using the robust Huber Sandwich method and associated t-values are given in parentheses. *,**,*** denotes statistical significance at the 10%, 5%, and 1% level.

Models 4 and 5 again introduce the regulatory variables *ΔRESTRICTION*, *ΔSUPERVISORY* and *ΔTRANSPARENCY*. The coefficients for the variables were mostly non-significant in the OLS regression specifications and are not significant in the median regression specifications either, but still add to the overall explanatory power of the models. This indicates that if regulatory arbitrage considerations played a role for bidding banks when engaging in M&As in the Asia-Pacific region, it was of minor importance to the bidding banks' shareholders, Nonetheless, the coefficient for *GOV* is negative and weakly significant in the full model specification. This gives further support to the interpretation that government involvement on the side of the bidding banks is seen critical by shareholders, as political considerations, rather than economic ones, are possibly a dominating motivation behind the M&A transaction.

Overall, the results of the median regression have lower levels of significance than the ones of the standard OLS regression, but still largely confirm the OLS regression results, especially those using $CAR_{j,[-5;5]}$ as the dependent variable. Nonetheless, the results of the median regression reveal that regulatory arbitrage considerations are not a primary driver of stock returns surrounding the announcement day. In addition, national and focusing transactions do not necessarily lead to significantly better results for the bidding bank, even though the coefficients still have the expected sign. Nevertheless, M&A transactions by Asian bidding banks with private targets still lead to significantly better results than other transactions, a result which is robust among all model specifications. This gives support to the interpretation that market power considerations play an important role when markets value takeovers by Asian institutions. The acquisition of private targets is an important step towards market consolidation, possibly allowing the remaining banks in the market to use their larger market share to earn higher profits. Furthermore, the detrimental effect of large transactions to bidding banks' shareholders is confirmed.

3.7 Evaluation of the shareholder wealth effects of the financial sector consolidation in the Asia-Pacific region

In this chapter the industry-wide shareholder wealth effects of bidders, targets, and their closest rivals surrounding the official announcement of bank M&As in the Asia-Pacific region between 1995 and 2013 are investigated. The sample is composed of 150 international bank transactions in the region. The overall results show that, on average, bidding banks receive positive, but non-significant stock returns, while targets enjoy large, highly significant and positive returns on the announcement day and during the surrounding days. However, when the sample is divided into Asian and non-Asian bidding banks the results show that shareholders of Asian bidding banks can expect to earn significant positive abnormal returns during the three days surrounding the announcement. In contrast, shareholders of non-Asian bidding banks only realize small, negative returns. The targets of Asian and non-Asian bidding banks display different capital market reactions as well: targets of non-Asian bidders receive much higher returns than those of Asian ones. In fact, the difference amounts to approximately six percentage points during the eleven day window surrounding the M&A announcement.

The results of the rival analysis show that the rivals of Asian bidding banks can expect to earn positive returns surrounding the announcement, while the returns to rivals of non-Asian bidders remain insignificant. The positive returns of the Asian bidding banks in conjunction with the positive returns earned by their rivals suggest that market power considerations may play an important role when capital markets value these transactions. The decision by a non-Asian institution to acquire an institution in Asia, on the other hand, has little effect on the bidder's domestic market. However, the rivals of targets of non-Asian bidders receive significant and positive returns, while the rivals of targets of Asian bidders receive only slightly significant and considerably lower positive returns. This result suggests that the rivals of targets of non-Asian financial institutions profit from an increased acquisition probability.

The results of the multivariate regression analysis show that the most successful bidding banks are Asian bidders purchasing private financial institutions. Non-Asian banks, on the other hand, perform significantly worse and actually destroy shareholder value when purchasing non-private targets, most likely because they need to pay significantly higher premiums when they compete with local institutions for attractive targets. The results of the analysis of the target bank returns corroborate this interpretation. Only weak evidence at best is found that investors reward bidding banks for choosing targets in countries with a lower level of restrictions on banking activity than in their home country. Therefore, it appears as if regulatory arbitrage considerations are not a dominant factor when capital markets value an M&A transaction in the Asia-Pacific region.

Overall, the return patterns of acquiring banks and their rivals suggest that market power considerations play an important role when markets value bank mergers among Asian institutions, as both the bidding banks and its rivals achieve positive returns. The analysis of the short-term performance of the bidding banks' rivals' returns even suggest that market power considerations are more prevalent in national mergers than in Asian regional ones. The same consideration does not seem to play a role when markets evaluate bank M&As by non-Asian institutions.

In that case, the targets of non-Asian bidders and their closest rivals appear to be the major beneficiaries, as both can expect to earn large and highly significant returns surrounding the announcement of a transaction. This result is in line with the Acquisition Probability Hypothesis. There are fewer remaining acquisition targets for other potential bidders, driving up the valuation of the remaining institutions. In addition, the M&A announcement can also be seen as a strong signal to markets in regard to the positive economic situation in the industry and the presence of growth and profit opportunities. That bidding banks gain significant positive stock returns when undertaking M&A transactions is in stark contrast to prior empirical research on bank M&As. However, previous studies primarily focused on the advanced and largely consolidated financial markets of the US and Western Europe (e.g. Beitel et al., 2004; Hankir et al., 2011). In the Asia-Pacific region further consolidation by local institutions benefits bidding banks and their rivals as capital markets appear to see considerable advantages for these institutions due to an increase in their market power.

4. The impact of bank mergers in the Asia-Pacific region on the acquiring institutions cost of debt

Credit default swaps have become one of the most widely used credit derivative instruments and now play an important role in international financial markets. They are a hedging tool, which allows market participants to insure themselves against the default of a given company or sovereign. Moreover, due to their increasing popularity and an increasing number of market participants offering daily quotes, CDS spreads provide an up-to-date reflection of the market's perception of a debtor's default probability. Empirical research points to the benefits CDS have on market efficiency as a complementary instrument to the well-established stock and bond markets, since they serve as a valuable risk indicator (Hull et al., 2004; Norden & Weber, 2004; Packer & Suthiphongchai, 2003).

The availability of CDS spreads allows to assess the impact that major corporate events, such as mergers and acquisitions, rating changes, and earning announcements, have on the probability of a firm's default. An increase in CDS spread levels would indicate that the market perceives that the event increases the company's default risk. The majority of prior research focuses on the effect of rating changes on CDS spreads (e.g. Finnerty et al., 2013; Hull et al., 2004; Norden & Weber, 2004) or the effect of earnings announcements (e.g. Greatrex, 2008; Shivakumar et al., 2011). The studies focusing on rating announcements primarily find that only negative rating announcements have a significant impact on CDS spreads, leading to increased spread levels following the announcement. Positive rating announcements, on the other hand, appear to have little influence at best. Moreover, there is an inverse relationship between CDS spread changes and stock price returns: as the former rises, the latter drops, and vice versa. For earnings announcements or forecasts, the results are similar, as only negative earnings announcements have an effect on CDS spread levels. This effect is particularly pronounced for firms with lower long-term issuer ratings.

Yet, even though CDS are an established proxy to obtain current information on the expectations of international investors in regard to changes in the default probability of a given company, very little research has been carried out as to the effects of corporate mergers on CDS spreads, and bank mergers in particular. Prior research focuses primarily on the effects of takeover announcements on a bank's bond yield (e.g. Ongena & Penas, 2009; Penas & Unal, 2004). Penas and

Unal (2004) explicitly investigate the effects of bank M&As on bondholders and find that bondholders gain due to merger announcements, primarily due to these gains being associated with "Too-Big-to-Fail" considerations and diversification gains. Ongena and Penas (2009) show that especially bondholders of European banks engaging in domestic mergers experience significant gains, while those undertaking cross-border transactions do not. The gains in domestic mergers can again serve as an indication that "Too-Big-to-Fail" considerations may also play a dominant role when markets evaluate bank M&As. Yet, as the results of Ongena and Penas (2009) and Choi et al. (2010) suggest, cross-border mergers are generally perceived as risk increasing events, as bondholders stand to obtain negative returns.

CDS contracts are generally more liquid than corporate bonds and have a more standardized contract design. Therefore, using CDS spread changes offers significant advantages over the use of bond yields. Given the importance and advantages of CDS spreads for sovereigns and firms, and financial institutions in particular, it is surprising that little research has been carried out on the effect that bank mergers and acquisitions have on the CDS spreads of the involved institutions. This chapter addresses this gap in the empirical literature by explicitly focusing on the effect that mergers among financial institutions have on their CDS spreads. This allows for an examination as to whether market participants perceive M&As to be risk increasing or decreasing events. Given the prior research results, it is expected that bank mergers and acquisitions are generally considered to be risk increasing events and associated with a widening of CDS spread levels. However, if "Too-Big-to-Fail" considerations play a dominant role, it is anticipated that significant decreases in CDS spread levels will be observed.

4.1 Related literature on CDS spread changes and the effect of mergers on debtholders

The empirical research in regard to CDS event studies focuses predominantly on two fields: (i) the effect of rating announcements on the CDS spreads and (ii) the effect of earning announcements on a firm's CDS spread. In addition to these two main strands of literature other studies investigate, among other things, the industry wide reaction of CDS spreads to bankruptcy filings of companies (Jorion & Zhang, 2007) or the effect of government rescue packages on the CDS spreads of the recipient institutions (King, 2009). There is very little research on the effect of M&As on debtholders in general, and bank takeovers in particular. These studies look almost exclusively at the changes in the bond yields of the merging institutions (e.g. Choi et al., 2010; Penas & Unal, 2004).

There is little evidence on the effect of M&A transactions on the CDS spreads of the involved financial institutions.

4.1.1 CDS event studies

The large majority of prior research using CDS event studies examines the impact of credit rating announcements by one of the big three rating companies, Standard & Poor's (S&P) Moody's Investors Service (Moody's), and Fitch Ratings (Fitch), on the CDS spreads of the affected companies. Among the first and most prominent studies on this subject are Hull et al. (2004) and Norden and Weber (2004). Both show that positive rating announcements, such as an actual rating upgrade or a review for an upgrade, have no significant effect on CDS spreads of companies, even though an overall tightening of CDS spread can be observed. Negative rating announcements, such as downgrades and reviews for downgrades, on the other hand, have a very strong effect on the CDS spread of a company, resulting in significant spread increases. Yet, while Norden and Weber (2004) find that the actual downgrade as well as the review for a downgrade induces a significant market reaction, Hull et al. (2004) can only document significant reactions for reviews for downgrades. Actual downgrades and negative outlooks have no discernible effect on the CDS spread of a company. Both Hull et al. (2004) and Norden and Weber (2004) find that CDS markets anticipate negative rating announcements. Furthermore, it appears that S&P and Moody's reviews for downgrades have a stronger impact on both the stock and CDS markets than those of Fitch and that the reaction of a CDS following a negative announcement is influenced by the company's rating class prior to the announcement (Norden & Weber, 2004). Micu et al. (2004) largely arrive at similar results as Norden and Weber (2004). They also document increases in the CDS spread of a company due to rating downgrades or negative reviews. Moreover, their results suggest that CDS markets appear to anticipate impending negative announcements as well.

Daniels and Shin Jensen (2005) investigate the impact of rating changes on CDS spreads and the link between credit spreads and CDS spreads. They show that there is a link between CDS and credit spreads, but CDS spreads react more quickly and show more significant reactions. In line with Norden and Weber (2004) they find a significant widening of credit spreads in case of a rating downgrade, while rating upgrades have no discernible effect on a company's CDS spread. They also document that the strength of the reaction depends on the company's rating class and that an apparent anticipation of the CDS market exists prior to a rating downgrade. Lehnert and Neske (2006) exclusively look at CDS spreads of European companies. While they also find CDS spread increases for negative rating announcements, they are the first to document significant decreases in CDS spread levels for positive rating announcements, such as rating upgrades and positive outlook reports. This result is in contrast to prior research findings, indicating that the European CDS spread market is possibly overall more sensitive to rating announcements.

More recent studies by Galil and Soffer (2011), Finnerty et al. (2013), and Imbierowicz and Wahrenburg (2013) arrive at more nuanced results than prior research. While all three studies still show that negative rating announcements lead to stark increases in CDS spreads for the concerned companies, Finnerty et al. (2013) are, after Lehnert and Neske (2006), the only ones that show that positive rating announcements are associated with significant reduction in CDS spread levels. Galil and Soffer (2011) go beyond just the rating announcement in their investigation and also examine other news and information concerning a company on the days surrounding a rating announcement. They find that rating announcements frequently highly correlate with significant other information flows of that firm. Therefore, the residual informational contribution of a rating announcement appears to be much lower than what prior studies suggest. In particular, negative rating announcements appear to have little informational content at times, while positive rating announcements actually carry significant information more often than not. Hence, it is not easily possible to determine the actual contribution of the rating announcement on the change in the CDS spread level. Finnerty et al. (2013) are the first to find that CDS spreads contain information in regard to the probability of a negative and positive rating announcement, not only for investment grade firms, but also for non-investment grade companies. Generally, however, the CDS market appears better at anticipating negative rating announcement than positive ones. Imbierowicz and Wahrenburg (2013) not only analyze the CDS market reaction to rating announcements, but also the equity market reaction. They document significant wealth transfers from bondholders to stockholders, an effect particularly prominent for firms engaged in an M&A transactions. Stockholders experience significant gains, while bondholders suffer losses. Yet, the increase in the CDS spread level is less pronounced than in case of a negative rating change.

Instead of investigating the effect of rating announcements on companies, Ismailescu and Kazemi (2010) analyze the effect such announcements have on the CDS spreads of emerging market sovereigns. They find that both positive and negative rating announcements have an impact on the CDS spread levels of the affected countries. However, in line with prior research on companies (e.g. Hull et al., 2004) only negative rating announcements appear to be anticipated, not positive ones. Yet, positive rating announcement lead to a significant decrease in the CDS spread levels, particularly during the days surrounding the event. Moreover, there appear to be spillover effects to other emerging market countries stemming from the rating change of another emerging market sovereign.

There are far fewer studies investigating the effect of earnings announcements on CDS spreads than there are on credit rating announcements. Yet, this strand of research offers some valuable insights as well. Greatrex (2008) is among the first to examine the market reaction of a company's CDS to its earnings announcements. She observes significant increases in CDS spreads in case of a negative earnings announcements and a steady, albeit small, decrease in case of positive earnings announcements. However, the widening of the CDS spread following negative announcements is subsequently reversed, indicating that the market overreacts to negative information. She therefore concludes that earnings announcements contain valuable information for capital markets, even though the CDS market may not react efficiently. Callen et al. (2009) likewise analyze the effect of earnings announcements on CDS spreads. Their results document that CDS spreads are significantly and negatively correlated with earnings: higher earnings are associated with lower CDS spreads and lower earnings with higher ones. This correlation is more pronounced for firms in lower rating categories than for ones in higher rating classes. Shivakumar et al. (2011) look at the impact of management earnings forecasts on CDS spreads. They find that forecasts actually result in a stronger reaction than the actual earnings announcements. Similar to Callen et al. (2009), Shivakumar et al. (2011) also document that the forecast induces a more pronounced reaction for firms with lower credit ratings and in case of negative forecasts. Moreover, they show that the importance of management earnings announcements was higher during the recent credit crisis than during the pre-crisis period. This possibly indicates a management's willingness to become more transparent in regard to such announcements, particularly during times with high market uncertainty or during economic downturns.

Table 4-1: Overview of CDS event studies

Author (year)	Investigated effect	Time period	CDS benchmark model	Calculation of spread change	Data source	Results
Panel A: Effect of rating announcements on CDS spreads						
Hull, Predescu, and White (2004)	Rating announcements	1998–2002	Matched index of CDS with the same rating class as the event firm.	Absolute	GFI	Only reviews for downgrades lead to significant increases in CDS spreads. Actual downgrades or negative outlooks do not. Results for positive rating announcements generally not significant.
Micu, Remolona, and Wooldridge (2004)	Rating announcements	2001–2003	Matched index of CDS with the same rating class as the event firm.	Absolute	Markit	CDS spreads increase after negative rating announcements. Negative rating reviews and rating downgrades have the strongest effect, negative outlooks the weakest.
Norden and Weber (2004)	Rating announcements	2000–2002	Matched index of CDS with the same rating class as the event firm.	Absolute	Unnamed European bank	Rating downgrades and reviews for downgrades increase CDS spreads. Reviews for downgrades and actual downgrades are anticipated by the market. Results for positive rating announcements generally not significant.

Table 4-1 (continued)

Author (year)	Investigated effect	Time period	CDS benchmark model	Calculation of spread change	Data source	Results
Daniels and Shin Jensen (2005)	Rating announcements	2000–2002	Constant mean model	Absolute	JP Morgan Chase	Rating downgrades lead to increased CDS spreads, while upgrades show no significant reaction.
Lehnert and Neske (2006)	Rating announcements	2000–2003	Matched index of CDS with the same rating class as the event firm.	Relative	JP Morgan Chase	Rating downgrades and upgrades as well as outlook reports influence CDS spreads of European firms.
Ismailescu and Kazemi (2010)	Rating announcements	2001–2009	Equally weighted portfolio of all reference entities within the sample.	Absolute	Markit	Positive and negative rating announcements have effects on the CDS spreads of emerging market sovereigns. CDS spreads appear to anticipate negative rating announcements, while positive events lead to a reduction in CDS spreads and some spillover effects to other emerging market economies.
Galil and Soffer (2011)	Rating announcements	2002–2006	Matched index of CDS with the same rating class as the event firm.	Absolute	Markit	CDS spreads increase after negative rating announcements and decrease after positive ones. The market anticipation of negative rating announcements is higher than for positive ones.

Table 4-1 (continued)

Author (year)	Investigated effect	Time period	CDS benchmark model	Calculation of spread change	Data source	Results
Finnerty, Miller, and Chen (2013)	Rating announcements	2001–2009	Matched index of CDS with the same rating class as the event firm.	Absolute	Markit	Negative rating announcements lead to significant increases in CDS spreads, while positive rating announcements lead to significant reductions in CDS spreads. Both kinds of events are anticipated by the market, but negative rating events better than positive ones.
Panel B: Effect of earnings announcements on CDS spreads						
Greatrex (2008)	Earnings announcements	2001–2006	(i) CDS index with the same rating class as the event firm. (ii) Market model.	Absolute	Markit	CDS and stock markets show significant reactions to earnings announcements. In particular negative earnings news show signs of overreaction.
Callen, Livnat, and Segal (2009)	CDS spreads in relation to earnings	2002–2005	Comparison of two different contracts with the same contractual features for the same reference entity.	Relative	Lombard Risk	Earnings convey significant information as CDS spreads and earnings are negatively and significantly correlated with CDS spread levels.

Table 4-1 (continued)

Author (year)	Investigated effect	Time period	CDS benchmark model	Calculation of spread change	Data source	Results
Shivakumar, Urcan, Vasvari, and Zhang (2011)	Management earnings forecasts an-nouncements	2001–2008	Matched portfolio of CDS with the same rating class as the event firm.	Absolute	Markit	Management earnings forecasts have a significant impact on CDS spreads. This impact is especially significant during periods of crisis, for lower rated companies, and for bad news announcements.
Panel C: Effect of other events on CDS spreads						
Jorion and Zhang (2007)	Chapter 7 and Chapter 11 bankruptcy	2001–2004	Matched portfolio of CDS with the same rating class as the event firm.	Absolute	Markit	Chapter 11 bankruptcies lead to CDS spread increases for all firms within the same industry, whereas Chapter 7 bankruptcies lead to CDS spread decreases.
King (2009)	Banks receiving government rescue packages	2008–2009	(i) Multi-factor model (ii) Market-adjusted model with CDS index	Absolute	Markit	CDS spreads go down around the announcements of bank rescue packages, but the stock price of the banks continues to significantly underperform.

Jorion and Zhang (2007) examine the effects of companies filing for either Chapter 7 or Chapter 11 bankruptcy have on the CDS spread levels of the other firms within the same industry sector. Their results show that Chapter 11 bankruptcies lead to a rise in the CDS spreads of other firms within the same industry sector, while Chapter 7 bankruptcies lead to a significant reduction in spread levels. They interpret this finding as the restructuring allowed to companies under Chapter 11 protection in all likelihood allows these firms to reemerge in a much better financial position, leading to a more competitive industry environment. This would explain why CDS spreads of other firms within the industry increase. In contrast, Chapter 7 bankruptcies lead to the liquidation of a corporation and hence fewer firms remain within the same industry. This, in turn, allows the remaining firms to acquire the market share of the bankrupt firm, potentially improving their financial position.

King (2009) is one of the first to exclusively investigate bank CDS. He examines the impact of bank rescue packages between 2008 and 2009 in six different countries on the CDS and stock prices of the institutions that received government support. He shows that CDS spreads tightened significantly around the announcement of a rescue package; yet, stock prices continued to decline, except in the US. In particular, banks receiving government support showed a worse performance than those that did not, implying that markets regard government support as a negative signal in regard to a bank's financial stability. CDS spreads, on the other hand, decreased for all banks, including those that did not receive government support. It therefore appears as if at least CDS market participants assumed that governments were willing to support other institutions as well, should they face financing difficulties.

Overall, CDS event studies mainly examine the effect of positive and negative rating announcements on the CDS spreads of companies, with only a few studies investigating the effect of earnings announcements or other events (see Table 4-1 for a detailed overview of the most prominent CDS event studies). The large majority of research finds that only negative rating announcements have any impact, resulting in increased CDS spread levels. Particularly negative reviews appear to result in pronounced spread changes, while the effect of actual downgrades is not this clear. Positive rating announcements, on the other hand, only rarely result in a reduction of spread levels. Anticipation effects are also frequently observed, but largely for negative rating announcements. Yet, it is not entirely clear whether downgrades are actually anticipated or whether the downgrade is the result of the deteriorating debt position, as signaled by the increase in the CDS spread. In addition, CDS spread changes can also be observed during the days surrounding earnings announcements and other major events, the intensity and direction of these changes again depending on the nature of the announcement. It can therefore be stated that the analysis of CDS spread and their reactions can yield important insights into the effects of major corporate events on a firm's cost of debt. CDS spreads are an effective means of discerning the current debt position of a given company that can readily be used to examine the immediate market expectation in regard to the default probability of a company following an important event.

4.1.2 The effect of bank mergers and acquisitions on debtholders

There are only very few studies investigating the effects that bank mergers and acquisitions have on the cost of debt of the involved institutions. The majority of the literature focuses exclusively on the effect of M&As on bond holders. Research in regard to the effect of takeover announcements on CDS spreads, and CDS spreads of banks in particular, is extremely scarce.

One of the most prominent general studies on the effect of M&As on bondholders is by Billett, King, and Mauer (2004). They analyze 940 takeover announcements in multiple industries between 1997 and 1998. They are able to show that target bondholders experience significant excess gains in the months surrounding a merger announcement, while acquirers obtain significant negative excess returns. In particular, targets stand to gain the most if their rating is below that of the acquiring firm. Billett et al. (2004) interpret this finding as pointing towards the existence of a coinsurance effect for target debt, an effect that is particularly pronounced for non-investment grade target bonds. Yet, they do not find any evidence for a wealth transfer between shareholders and bondholders.

Penas and Unal (2004) are one of the first to explicitly investigate the effects of bank M&As on bondholders. Their results show that bank mergers are perceived by capital markets participants as overall risk reducing events, as bondholders gain from such transactions. Therefore, one of the advantages of mergers in the financial industry appears to be the lower cost of debt capital for banks. Penas and Unal (2004) suggest that the gains to bondholders are largely due to gains associated with "Too-Big-to-Fail" considerations, diversification gains, and, to a somewhat lesser degree, with anticipated synergies. In a later study by Ongena and Penas (2009), European national and cross-border bank mergers between 1998 and 2002 are analyzed. They find that only bondholders in domestic mergers experience positive returns, while those in cross-border mergers do not. This can be viewed as an indication that market participants expect domestic mergers to increase the probability of a government bailout in case the bank falls into financial distress. Choi et al. (2010), on the other hand, focus exclusively on the effect that cross-border transactions have on bondholders. They analyze a sample of 147 cross-border bank mergers from 1995 to 2002. Their results indicate that cross-border bank takeovers are perceived as risk increasing events by capital market participants, as the yield spread of the acquiring bank increases significantly following an M&A announcement.

The only study that looks at CDS spread changes in conjunction with M&A announcements, albeit not only for financial institutions, is by Imbierowicz and Wahrenburg (2013). Takeover announcements that occur in combination with a rating review for downgrade are associated with significant wealth transfers between shareholders and bondholders. In this case a significant increase in the stock price and CDS spread can be observed for target firms. In line with the empirical results of Billett et al. (2004), the wealth transfer appears to predominantly benefit the target shareholders. However, besides the relatively narrow case of M&A and review for downgrade announcements coinciding, Imbierowicz and Wahrenburg (2013) are not able to document any wealth transfers.

Overall, it can be expected that CDS spread levels increase for the bidding bank due to takeover announcements in the Asia-Pacific region. However, based on the results of Choi et al. (2010), it is anticipated that this widening in credit spreads will be more pronounced for acquirers from outside the region, as they engage in transactions that are akin to cross-border and in many cases cross-continental M&As.

4.2 Data and empirical methodology

This section describes the merger data set as well as the CDS data and the CDS event study methodology. First, the investigated M&A events are described and several descriptive statistics are offered to gain a deeper inside into the sample. Second, the construction of the CDS data used for the event study is given in great detail. In particular, the course of the CDS spreads for the different rating classes over time is shown and descriptive statistics are provided to obtain a better understanding of the CDS data. Third, the CDS event study methodology is explained.

4.2.1 The mergers and acquisitions data set

In order to find M&A announcements of financial institutions in the Asia-Pacific region the Thomson Financial Securities Data Company (SDC) Mergers and Acquisition database is used as the primary source for events. Countries that are part of the Asia-Pacific region are defined along the lines of the regional member list of the Asian Development Bank. Only the target is required to be from the Asia-Pacific region, whereas the acquiring institution can come from any nation.

The official announcement date of the takeover transaction has to be between January 2004 and December 2013 and the takeover needs to be completed. The starting point of the investigation period is chosen to be January 2004 primarily for data availability considerations. Data on CDS spreads is largely not available prior to this point and if data is available, it is of poor quality with many missing observations. In order to ensure that the target and bidder are financial institutions, only firms with a primary SIC code ranging from 6000 to 6289 and the codes 6712 and 6733 are considered. Insurance carriers, real estate companies, non-bank holding companies and miscellaneous investment companies, such as oil royalty traders and patent owners and lessors, are explicitly excluded to ensure that the focus is on financial institutions only. Furthermore, any takeovers for which no specific transaction value is recorded are dropped from the sample. Also, only majority acquisition, in which case the bidding institution holding less than 50% in the target prior to the M&A, but more than 50% following the transaction are considered. Therefore, minority acquisitions and subsequent increases in ownership by the bidding bank are disregarded. The requirements listed so far are similar to those described in section 3.2.1. In addition, it is required that the bidding bank has CDS spread data in sufficient quality and a long-term issuer rating by either S&P or Moody's during the days surrounding the official merger announcement.

After applying all of the above criteria, it is possible to identify a total of 33 takeover events in the Asia-Pacific region with a total deal value in excess of 38 billion US$. The bidding institutions are from ten different nations acquiring targets in twelve different countries. The most frequent transactions are inter-Australian and inter-Korean ones (4 each), followed by inter-Indian ones (3). The inter-Australian ones also have the largest total deal value with approximately 20 billion US$, or a little more than half of the total deal size of the entire sample. Most bidders are from India (6) followed by the United Kingdom and South Korea (5 each), while Australian and South Korean banks are most frequently targeted (6 each).

Table 4-2: Descriptive statistics of the bidding bank sample

	Total sample	Asian	Non-Asian
Market capitalization (million US$)			
Average	45,058.43	16,887.31	74,990.24
Median	21,923.88	11,008.22	51,665.72
Std. Dev	59,908.83	18,080.69	73,843.79
n	33	17	16
ROE (%)			
Average	13.54	11.10	16.13
Median	14.00	10.09	16.96
Std. Dev	5.74	5.61	4.79
n	33	17	16
Leverage			
Average	5.60	6.70	4.43
Median	4.06	6.09	3.64
Std. Dev	3.94	3.90	3.74
n	33	17	16
Deal value (million US$)			
Total deal value	38,287.10	11,919.86	26,367.23
Average	1,160.22	701.17	1,647.95
Median	160.30	114.10	197.26
Std. Dev	3,220.44	1,445.61	4,404.96
n	33	17	16
Rating class			
AA	9	–	9
A	16	9	7
BBB	6	6	–
BB	2	2	–

ROE is the return on equity as of December 31st of the year prior to the event; *Leverage* is the total debt to total assets ratio of company as of December 31st in the year prior to the event, *Deal Value* is the transaction value recorded in the Thomson Reuters SDC database, *Rating class* describes the long-term issuer rating that was assigned to the bidding bank by S&P or Moody's prior to the takeover announcement, described in detail in Table 4-3. Std. Dev. stands for standard deviation.

Table 4-2 gives selected descriptive statistics for the bidding bank sample, divided into statistics for the total sample and Asian and non-Asian bidders only.[20]

20 Asia is defined in this case along the classical geographic demarcation of Asia and does not include countries in the Pacific region. The following countries in the sample are

The descriptive statistics offer some valuable insights, even though the sample size is rather small and therefore interpretation of the results needs to be done carefully. The average market capitalization of a bank in the sample is approximately 45 billion US$. However, non-Asian institutions are on average more than four times larger than their Asian counterparts. In addition, the return on equity for the average Asian bank is lower than that for the average non-Asian bank, suggesting that Asian institutions are less profitable. At the same time, the leverage of an Asian institution is higher. Moreover, the deal size between these two subgroups differs drastically. Takeovers by non-Asian bidding banks in the Asia-Pacific region average approximately 1.65 billion US$, while that of Asian institutions is less than half with 700 million US$. Looking at the long-term issuer ratings, it is informative to see that non-Asian banks have higher levels of creditworthiness than Asian ones. In particular, non-Asian institutions engaging in takeover do not have a long-term rating below rating category A, while Asian ones generally have lower ratings and some are even rated non-investment grade.

The comparison of Asian and non-Asian banks in Table 4-2 suggests that overall, non-Asian financial institutions are more profitable, less leveraged, and enjoy better credit ratings than their Asian counterparts. This can be seen as an indication that only large international banks are able to engage in transactions in the Asia-Pacific region. On the other hand, the higher profitability and lower leverage levels may also suggest that these banks have to engage in a more aggressive expansion program in order to try to sustain their profits. In this case, their lower leverage position and higher credit worthiness is the reason that they are able to engage in transactions that are potentially not in the best interest of their stockholders and debtholders. Large cross-border transactions can have considerable risk implications for all stakeholders (Choi et al., 2010). Asian banks, on the other hand, appear to be more careful when engaging in transactions. The generally smaller deal sizes can be seen as an indication of this. It may also relate to these banks engaging in regional or possibly even national transactions, to further consolidate their local market. Yet, as these institutions are smaller in size, overall comparatively highly leveraged with lower levels of profitability, and lower credit worthiness, they may simply not have the opportunity to undertake larger transactions.

---

identified as Asian: China, Hong Kong, India, Indonesia, Japan, Malaysia, Pakistan, Philippines, Singapore, South Korea, Taiwan and Thailand. The following countries in the sample are considered non-Asian: Australia, Austria, France, Germany, the Netherlands, New Zealand, Russia, South Africa, Switzerland, the United Kingdom and the United States. This is in line with the definition in chapter 3.

4.2.2 The CDS data

This chapter examines the changes in CDS spread levels surrounding the announcement of bank mergers and acquisitions in the Asia-Pacific region. In a first step, all financial institutions (SIC codes 6000–6282 and 6712 and 6733) that have available CDS data are sourced from the Thomson Reuters financial database from January 2004 to December 2013. In a next step, each institution is matched with its S&P long-term issue rating or, if an S&P rating is not available, it's Moody's rating. Using this procedure, it is possible to identify 232 different financial institutions that have at least at some point during the investigation period from 2004 to 2013 a valid CDS spread and rating. Of these 232 banks, 87 are from Europe, 85 from the Asia-Pacific region, 53 from North America, six from Latin America and one from Africa.

The CDS data obtained from the Thomson Reuters financial database offers CDS spreads provided by Credit Market Analysis (CMA) until the end of the third quarter of 2010. Starting at the beginning of October 2010, only Thomson Reuters EOD data is available. CMA collects CDS quotes data from more than 40 contributors, which actively participate in the CDS market and uses a strict methodology to calculate end of day CDS spread levels for single name issuers and sovereigns. Similarly, Thomson Reuters takes different CDS quotes each day from more than 30 contributors located worldwide. It offers end of day data for single name CDS with different tenors and different restructuring types. Prior to calculating the daily composite spread, Reuters applies a rigorous screening procedure to eliminate outliers or doubtful data.[21] Mayordomo, Peña, and Schwartz (2014) compare in their study the five most popular CDS databases, CMA, Markit, Reuters EOD, Fenics, and GFI. They find that CMA and Markit data appear to contribute most to the price discovery process in the CDS market, CMA contributing the most, in the US as well as Europe. Yet, the newer Thomson Reuters EOD database is also a reliable source, especially for more recent data.[22] Therefore, in order to generate an as complete as possible time series of CDS spreads for all available financial institutions, the CMA and Thomson Reuters

21 It should be noted that Thomson Reuters EOD offers four different structuring types: (i) full restructuring (CR), (ii) modified restructuring (MR), (iii) modified-modified restructuring (MM), and (iv) no restructuring (XR). The restructuring type is based on regional preference. As set out in the guidelines by Reuters, CR is the preferred type for Asia, MM for Europe, and XR for the US.

22 Data from the Thomson Reuters EOD database is generally not available prior to mid-December 2007.

data are combined, using the splice function provided by Reuters. In this way, it is possible to generate time series of the different bank CDS starting in January 2004 and ending in December 2013.

In line with common practice in the literature (e.g. Finnerty et al., 2013; Hull et al., 2004; Norden & Weber, 2004) the CDS spreads of the firms are divided into different equally weighted indices, based on their rating class. The approach of Norden and Weber (2004) is followed and companies are separated into seven different rating classes based on their respective S&P or Moody's long-term issuer rating: AAA, AA, A, BBB, BB, B, and CCC and below. The first four rating classes are considered investment-grade and therefore comparatively safe, while the latter three rating classes are non-investment grade, with the lowest being extremely speculative and close to default (see also Table 4-3 for a detailed description of the different rating classes).

Table 4-3: Definition of rating classes

Long-term rating				
S&P	Moody's	Rating class	Rating category definition	Investment status
AAA	Aaa	AAA	Prime	Investment grade
AA+	Aa1			
AA	Aa2	AA	High	
AA-	Aa3			
A+	A1			
A	A2	A	Medium	
A-	A3			
BBB+	Baa1			
BBB	Baa2	BBB	Low	
BBB-	Baa3			
BB+	Ba1			Non-investment grade
BB	Ba2	BB	Speculative	
BB-	Ba3			
B+	B1			
B	B2	B	Highly speculative	
B-	B3			
CCC+	Caa1			
CCC	Caa2			
CCC-	Caa3	CCC and below	Extremely speculative / Default	
CC	Ca			
C	C			
D	C			

Figure 4-1 and Figure 4-2 show the time series of the different rating classes divided into investment grade (Figure 4-1) and non-investment grade rating categories (Figure 4-2). For investment grade rated banks, there is a marked peak starting the end of 2008 and ending in 2009 due to the 2007 Financial Crisis. Depending on the rating status, this peak is more pronounced the lower the rating category. A second, albeit much smaller, peak can be observed at the end of 2011, in all likelihood due to the European sovereign debt crisis. Since then, however, CDS spread levels came down again. Nevertheless, CDS spread levels overall increased since the beginning of the investigation period in January 2004 and are at generally higher levels than at the end of 2013.

Figure 4-1: Average bank CDS spread by investment grade rating class from January 2004 to December 2013

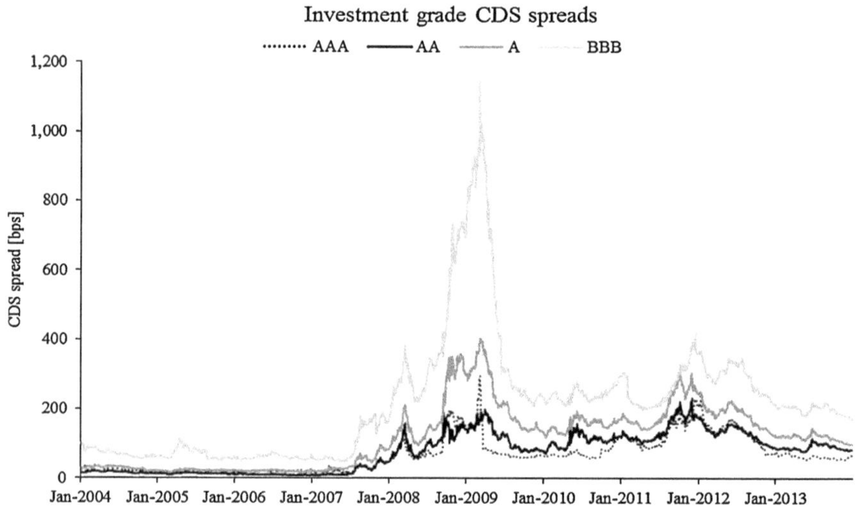

The time series of the non-investment grade class financial institutions is much more erratic than the one for the investment grade rated ones. This is not surprising, as there are generally fewer observations in those rating classes, especially the B and below CCC rating class. Moreover, these institutions are much closer to default and any new information regarding their financial situation will have a large impact on their CDS spread. For the BB rating class, the time series is considerably smoother and significantly lower than for the other two non-investment grade rating categories. This is to be expected, as financial institutions in this rating class are still relatively far away from default and may even be upgraded into investment grade status.

Figure 4-2: Average bank CDS spread by non-investment grade rating class from January 2004 to December 2013

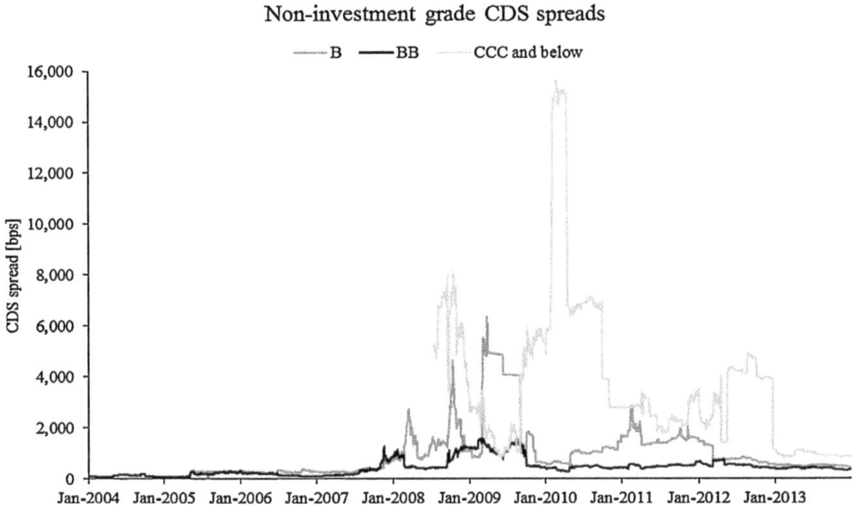

Table 4-4 gives an overview of the CDS data set of this study. It can be seen that there is an inverse relationship between the creditworthiness of a company and its average and median CDS spread level: The higher the rating of a company the lower its CDS spread. This effect is especially pronounced for firms with a non-investment grade rating. Financial institutions, which are BBB rated, the lowest investment grade, have an average CDS spread level of 259.63. In contrast, the spread level of the highest rated non-investment grade institutions is almost twice that at 494.46 bps for BB rated banks. The number of daily observations differs among the different rating classes as well. The fewest observations are for the CCC and below category, followed by the B and AAA categories. This mainly reflects the different number of banks in each index. Most institutions and daily observations are available for banks which are in the A rating category.

The average number of companies in each rating class per year is shown in Table 4-4 Panel B. Generally, most banks are in the A category, followed by the BBB category. In the CCC and below category only a few banks are available, as the majority of these institutions default eventually and exit the market. The 2007 Financial Crisis lead to a noteworthy shift in the number of companies within each rating category. Until 2008 the number of banks in the AA rated category was comparatively high. However, starting in 2009 this number has been drastically reduced, while those in the A and BBB rating class increased. It seems as if financial institutions that were rated AA prior to 2009 dropped down to A and, in turn, a number of those rated A dropped down to BBB. Since 2009, the number of banks in each category has remained approximately the same. It therefore appears as if rating agencies assign generally lower credit ratings to financial institutions following the 2007 Financial Crisis.

Table 4-4: Descriptive statistics of the CDS data by rating class

	Rating class						
	AAA	AA	A	BBB	BB	B	≤CCC
Panel A: Descriptive statistics of CDS data by rating class							
Mean CDS spread [bps]	66.82	73.25	138.57	259.63	494.46	1,088.55	3,789.09
Median CDS spread [bps]	40.48	64.13	110.10	191.00	353.02	641.02	1,977.34
Min. [bps]	2.05	1.00	1.00	5.50	31.23	31.18	400.54
Max. [bps]	948.00	775.01	2,969.40	8,698.59	6,192.99	17,351.10	27,555.72
Std. Dev. [bps]	81.47	70.99	138.09	333.71	522.29	1,753.95	4,662.07
Number of daily obs.	11,470	67,883	176,430	74,481	23,441	10,058	4,501
Panel B: Average number of companies by rating class per year							
2004	5.0	21.5	42.0	12.4	1.7	0.0	0.0
2005	4.5	23.8	46.4	14.6	3.3	0.6	0.0
2006	4.0	28.4	52.2	11.9	5.5	1.3	0.0
2007	4.3	36.2	48.9	16.4	3.7	2.3	0.0
2008	7.5	41.7	67.1	26.3	6.5	3.1	1.2
2009	6.4	25.9	84.3	36.4	8.9	3.7	3.8
2010	5.2	22.6	83.1	38.5	8.9	7.5	2.7
2011	2.9	22.1	85.2	38.0	14.0	5.6	2.5
2012	2.0	19.7	85.5	44.7	17.8	6.8	4.7
2013	2.0	18.2	81.5	46.2	19.6	7.6	2.4
2004–2013	4.4	26.0	67.6	28.5	9.0	3.9	1.7

4.2.3 Empirical methodology

The impact of takeover announcements on the CDS spreads of the bidding bank are analyzed using the CDS event study approach first used by Hull et al. (2004) and Norden and Weber (2004).[23] First, all banks and other financial institutions

23 Andres, Betzer, and Doumet (2013) introduce a more sophisticated multifactor model based on the level and slope of the risk-free yield curve and the implied equity volatility

for which CDS spreads are available in the Thomson Reuters Financial database are divided into different categories according to their S&P long-term issuer rating and, in case no S&P rating is available, according to their Moody's rating as described in section 4.2.2. Following Norden and Weber (2004) seven different rating classes are used: AAA, AA, A, BBB, BB, B, and CCC and below, disregarding the plus and minus suffix that S&P awards to allow for a more detailed evaluation of a company's overall credit worthiness.[24] Second, seven different daily CDS spread indices, one for each rating class are constructed, based on the mean CDS spread change of all firms within the same rating class. The M&A announcement is then defined as the event day $t = 0$ and the adjusted spread changes (ASC) for each day during the event window $[\tau_1, \tau_2] \epsilon [-5, \ldots, 10]$ are calculated by:

$$ASC_{i,t} = (CDS_{i,t} - CDS_{i,t-1}) - (I_{r,t} - I_{r,t-1}) \quad (4\text{-}1)$$

where $ASC_{i,t}$ is the adjusted (abnormal) spread on day t, $CDS_{i,t}$ is the observed spread change of bank i on day t, r is the letter rating class of bank i on the day of the merger announcement, and $I_{r,t}$ is the CDS spread index for rating class r on day t. The index for a given rating class must consist of at least two benchmark companies at any given time.

The cumulative adjusted spread changes (CASC) for the entire event period and different sub-periods are calculated adding the daily $ASC_{i,t}$ from event day τ_1 to event day τ_2 by:

$$CASC_{[\tau_1;\tau_2]} = \sum_{\tau_1}^{\tau_2} ASC_{i,t} \quad (4\text{-}2)$$

The CDS spread changes are tested for statistical significance using the standard parametric cross-sectional t-test, as well as the nonparametric Wilcoxon signed-rank test (Wilcoxon-test). Andres et al. (2013) suggest that for CDS event studies nonparametric significance tests are preferable. Furthermore, the number of positive and negative abnormal spread changes are reported.

---

to approximate abnormal CDS spread changes. However, they are the only ones that implement this approach and it seems not clear yet, whether this approach is robust. Therefore, in order to make the results more readily comparable to prior research the most frequently used approach in the literature introduced by Hull et al. (2004) and Norden and Weber (2004) is followed.

24 Moody's uses a different alphanumerical scale for their ratings than S&P, but the Moody's ratings are matched to their corresponding S&P ratings. See also Table 4-3.

4.3 The impact of merger announcements on bidder CDS spreads

Table 4-5 shows the bidding banks' cumulative adjusted spread changes surrounding the announcement of a bank merger. During the entire 16 day event period CDS spreads rise on average around 5.9bps. This widening of CDS spreads is also weakly significant according to the Wilcoxon-test statistic. The largest increase in CDS spreads can be observed during the [−5;5] day event window during which spreads rise and average of approximately 7.7bps. This spread widening is significant according to all test statistics. The only other weakly significant event window is the [−1;0] window, suggesting that CDS spreads somewhat anticipate imminent takeover announcements. The remaining event windows lack significance. Nevertheless, the overall trend is clear: M&As among financial institutions in the Asia-Pacific region are generally perceived as risk increasing events, at least from the perspective of debtholders.

Table 4-5: CDS spread changes surrounding M&A announcements for all bidders

Event window	CASC	Median ASC	*t*-test (*t*-value)	Wilcoxon-test (Z-score)	Pos:Neg	Sample size
[−5;10]	5.936	3.012	1.414	−1.778*	22:11	33
[−5;5]	7.686	2.360	2.001*	−2.171**	24:9	33
[−1;1]	−1.492	0.382	−0.604	−0.777	19:14	33
[−5;−1]	4.757	0.812	1.470	−1.456	22:11	33
[0;0]	1.232	0.303	1.587	−0.706	18:15	33
[−1;0]	1.049	0.802	0.775	−1.760*	20:13	33
[0;1]	−1.308	0.332	−0.793	−0.241	18:15	33
[1;5]	0.682	0.513	0.164	−0.045	17:16	33
[1;10]	1.316	1.435	1.470	−1.206	22:11	33

*;**,*** denotes statistical significance at the 10%, 5%, and 1% level

Table 4-6 divides the sample of all bidding banks into non-Asian and Asian bidders in order to investigate whether there are any differences in the impact of merger announcements on the CDS spreads of financial institutions from those two regions. Table 4-6 Panel A presents the results of non-Asian bidders. Overall, as for the entire sample, CDS spread increased significantly during the entire event period. However, in this case the significances are rather weak and concentrate on [−5;10], [−5;5], and [−1;1] day event window, during which CDS spreads widen by 6.6bps, 8.6bps and 0.5bps, respectively. For Asian banks the results are very similar, as the CDS spread levels surrounding M&A announcements generally increase. Nevertheless, none of the event windows show any statistical significance. It therefore appears as if the overall results are largely driven by the spread increases of non-Asian bidding banks.

Table 4-6: CDS spread changes surrounding M&A announcements for Non-Asian and Asian bidders

Event window	CASC	Median ASC	*t*-test (*t*-value)	Wilcoxon-test (Z-score)	Pos:Neg	Sample size
Panel A: Non-Asian bidding banks						
[-5;10]	6.606	1.658	1.789*	-1.293	10:6	16
[-5;5]	8.576	1.153	1.809*	-1.913*	12:4	16
[-1;1]	0.513	1.280	0.134	-1.758*	12:4	16
[-5;-1]	3.721	0.593	0.886	-0.776	11:5	16
[0;0]	1.883	0.172	1.417	-0.569	8:8	16
[-1;0]	2.315	0.474	1.531	-1.034	9:7	16
[0;1]	0.081	0.177	0.036	-0.259	9:7	16
[1;5]	0.810	1.366	0.112	-1.241	11:5	16
[1;10]	0.862	1.379	0.145	-0.724	11:5	16
Panel B: Asian bidding banks						
[-5;10]	5.305	6.508	0.707	-0.970	12:5	17
[-5;5]	6.849	2.551	1.121	-1.254	12:5	17
[-1;1]	-3.379	-0.437	-1.055	-0.355	7:10	17
[-5;-1]	5.732	3.671	1.147	-1.160	11:6	17
[0;0]	0.620	0.303	0.723	-0.544	10:7	17
[-1;0]	-0.143	1.665	-0.064	-1.254	11:6	17
[0;1]	-2.616	0.371	-1.088	-0.024	9:8	17
[1;5]	0.562	-2.959	0.123	-0.497	6:11	17
[1;10]	1.742	1.435	0.355	-0.828	11:6	17

*;**,*** denotes statistical significance at the 10%, 5%, and 1% level

Overall, the results strongly indicate that bank mergers in the Asia-Pacific region are risk increasing events for the bidding banks (see also Figure 4-3 for development of the CASC during the event period). This is not entirely surprising, as the literature on the effect of bank M&As on debtholders arrives at largely similar conclusions (e.g. Choi et al., 2010; Ongena & Penas, 2009). The difference between Asian and non-Asian bidding banks is also not stark, as both experience a widening in CDS spread levels, even though only the non-Asian institutions show individually significant results. Yet, non-Asian banks experience higher spread changes. This is in line with the results of Choi et al. (2010), who find that especially cross-border mergers are perceived as risk increasing events. This may, however, also reflect the nature of the transactions in which non-Asian banks engage. They are generally larger compared to those of their Asian peers, many of them not cross-border, but rather cross-continental. Yet, the results need to be interpreted with some care, as the sample size is comparatively small. Nonetheless, the findings should serve as a valuable indication for the risk dynamics surrounding bank merger announcements.

Figure 4-3: Bidding bank adjusted CDS spread changes surrounding takeover announcements

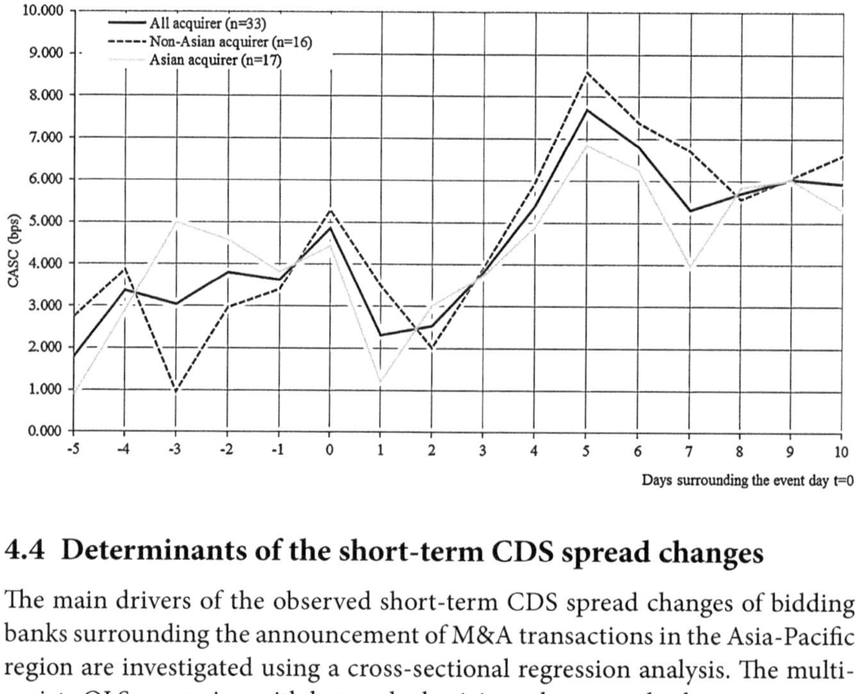

4.4 Determinants of the short-term CDS spread changes

The main drivers of the observed short-term CDS spread changes of bidding banks surrounding the announcement of M&A transactions in the Asia-Pacific region are investigated using a cross-sectional regression analysis. The multivariate OLS regression with heteroskedasticity-robust standard errors is specified as:

$$CASC_{i,[-1;0]} = \delta_0 + \sum_{j=1}^{m} \delta_j VAR_j + \varepsilon \qquad (4\text{-}3)$$

where the dependent variable $CASC_{i,[-1;0]}$ is the cumulative adjusted spread change for bank $i \in [1,\ldots,n]$ during the $[-1;0]$ day event window surrounding the takeover announcement on day $t=0$. The $CASC_{i,[-1;0]}$ is chosen as the dependent variable, as the prior results and the robustness checks (see section 4.5) indicate that the CDS and spread changes occurring during the [–1,0] day event period are significant, independent of the methodology used. VAR_j are the independent variables with $j \in [1,\dots, m]$, m being the number of variables, δ_0 is the regression constant, δ_i are the regression coefficients for each independent variable j and ε is the error term.

In light of the comparatively small sample size, it is not possible to conduct an in-depth examination of the drivers of the CASCs. Nevertheless, several factors are investigated, which in all likelihood affect spread changes in a significant way. The first variable of interest is *ASIAN*, defined as one, if a bank is from an Asian country, otherwise zero. This variable is introduced in order to see whether regional banks from Asia perform differently than their non-Asian peers. The results presented in Table 4-6 suggest that there may be differences between Asian and non-Asian bidders, albeit not large ones. The impact of a firm's rating on its CASC surrounding a takeover announcement is also examined through the variable *RATING*. Norden and Weber (2004) and Daniels and Shin Jensen (2005), among others, show that the long-term issuer rating of a company can have an impact on CDS spread changes, at least in the case of rating announcements. Imbierowicz and Wahrenburg (2013) also show that rating announcements especially in connection with M&A activity influence CDS spreads significantly. Moreover, as the results of Choi et al. (2010) indicate, M&As are perceived as risk increasing events; CDS spreads may well widen more for banks, whose rating is higher, as the additional risk stemming from the takeover may reduce their creditworthiness. Multiple studies on the stock returns surrounding bank merger announcements show that an institution's profitability can influence the short-term capital market reaction (e.g. Becher & Campbell, 2005; Beitel et al., 2004; Kolaric & Schiereck, 2013). It stands to reason that profitability will also have an effect on the debtholders of financial institutions. A bank's return on equity (*ROE*) is used as a measure of its profitability. More profitable banks may be able to better cope with the risks associated with an M&A transaction and therefore decreases in CDS spreads levels may be observed. At the same time it may also be that capital markets perceive the future profitability of a bank to be at risk and therefore a higher ROE may lead to an increase in the CDS spread, rather than a decrease. A bank's leverage is also examined, defined as the total debt divided by the total assets of a bank and captured by the variable *LEVERAGE*. More highly leveraged banks may increase their risk by undertaking a transaction than those banks with a lower leverage as they are more likely to issue more debt to finance the merger. Research on stock price reactions to bank M&A announcements also frequently suggests that the deal size can have a significant influence on the stock returns of the bidding bank. It is, however, not clear whether the effect is positive (e.g. Campa & Hernando,

2006; DeLong, 2001) or negative (e.g. Cybo-Ottone & Murgia, 2000). The impact of the takeover size is assessed using the variable *VALUE*, defined as the deal value recorded by the Thomson Reuters SDC database.

Another important factor in bank merger transaction may be the market concentration, as larger banks are more likely to achieve a "Too-Big-to-Fail" (TBTF) status, which may induce governments to bail them out should they face financial distress. Penas and Unal (2004) show that TBTF considerations appear to be a dominant consideration when debtholder value bank mergers. As a proxy for TBTF the variable *CONCENTRATION* is used in the regression analysis. This variable is constructed by dividing the market capitalization of the bidding bank by the sum of the market capitalization of the bidding bank and its three closest national rivals. The larger the size of the bidding bank compared to its rivals, the more likely it is to become a dominant bank in its home market and therefore enjoy the "Too-Big-to-Fail" status, which should lead to a reduction in borrowing costs and hence a decrease in CDS spreads. Morgan and Stiroh (2005) show that the eleven US banks originally considered TBTF in 1984 were able to issue new debt at considerably lower interest rates than their non-TBTF peers, implying that markets regard these banks as less risky than others. Besides TBTF, market power considerations may also play a role, as the newly formed institutions will be able to obtain a larger market share and potentially increase its profits, which may not only benefit stockholders but also bondholders. The rival selection process is similar to that of Hankir et al. (2011), with some modest modifications. First, all financial institutions in the country of origin of each bidding bank with a primary SIC code ranging from 6000 to 6289 and primary codes 6712 and 6733 are determined via Datastream. Rival banks are selected if they are (i) domiciled in the same country as the bidding bank and (ii) the first two digits of the primary SIC code of the acquiring and rival bank match. Then the three closest banks by market capitalization are selected. All observations that did not result in at least three appropriate rivals are dropped.

Table 4-7: OLS regression results for bidding banks

	Model 1	Model 2	Model 3	Model 4	Model 5
δ_0	2.315	-9.807	6.033***	0.559	-3.132
	(1.581)	(-1.178)	(3.678)	(0.080)	-0.295
ASIAN	-2.458				
	(-0.946)				
CONCENTRATION			-13.884***	-12.767***	-12.596***
			(-3.777)	(-3.852)	(-3.787)
RATING		4.079**		3.095*	2.806*
		(2.078)		(1.785)	(1.883)
ROE		-0.563**		-0.497**	-0.500**
		(-2.382)		(-2.196)	(-2.222)
LEVERAGE		-0.320		-0.665*	-0.676*
		(-1.628)		(-2.002)	(-2.027)
VALUE					0.274
					(0.639)
Observations	33	33	31	31	31
Adjusted. R^2	-0.57%	31.69%*	4.59%***	37.70%***	35.78%***
F-Value	0.894	2.454	14.265	6.285	5.501

ASIAN is defined 1 if the bidding bank is from one of the following countries: China, Hong Kong, India, Indonesia, Japan, Malaysia, Pakistan, Philippines, Singapore, South Korea, Taiwan and Thailand, zero otherwise; *CONCENTRATION* is the market capitalization of the bidding bank divided by the sum of the market capitalization of the bidding bank and its three closest rivals on the last trading day in the year prior to the event; *RATING* is the rating of the bidding bank on the announcement day based on 7 rating classes converted to a point scale where AAA=7; AA=6; A=5; BBB=4, BB=3, B=2 and ≤CCC=1; LEVERAGE is the total debt to total assets ratio of a bank on the last trading day in the year prior to the event; *VALUE* is the logarithm of the deal value in US dollars; The standard errors are corrected for heteroskedasticity and the associated *t*-values are given in parentheses. *,**,*** denotes statistical significance at the 10%, 5%, and 1% level.

Table 4-7 shows the results of multiple OLS regression models for the bidding bank sample.[25] The first and basic regression model investigates whether Asian bidders perform differently from their non-Asian peers. The coefficient for *ASIAN* is negative and insignificant and the regression is overall not well specified. This result strongly indicates that Asian banks do not perform differently from non-Asian ones and the variable is consequently dropped from the further regression models. The second model specification introduces the variables *RATING*, *ROE*, and

25 All models were checked for collinearity with variance inflation factors. They are all well below five for all variables in all model specification, indicating that collinearity is not an issue in any of the regression models.

LEVERAGE. This model is better specified as the first one and the coefficients for *RATING* and *ROE* are significant at the 5% level, while the one for *LEVERAGE* is not significant. In particular, the positive sign of the coefficient for *RATING* indicates that banks with higher ratings experience more pronounced increases in their CDS spread levels due to a merger announcement. This can be interpreted as a sign that debtholders are particularly concerned that higher rated banks will increase their risk substantially when engaging in takeovers and that they may not be able to maintain their creditworthiness once the merger is completed. The negative and significant coefficient for *ROE*, on the other hand, suggests that more profitable banks will likely be able to gain even more from their mergers or that the comparatively high ROE will allow them to keep serving their debts, even though the M&A transaction may be an overall risk increasing event for the bank as a whole.

Model 3 to Model 5 introduce the *CONCENTRATION* variable. The coefficient for this variable is negative and highly significant in all three regression models and the models themselves appear to be well specified, too. Model 3 tests the *CONCENTRATION* variable by itself. The coefficient is highly significant, large and negative, indicating that mergers, in which the bidding bank is one of the largest banks in its market, are substantially risk decreasing events for the bidder. Model 4 adds the previously significant variables *RATING*; *ROE*, and *LEVERAGE* to Model 3. The coefficient for *CONCENTRATION* remains negative and highly significant. The coefficient for *RATING* is also still positive and significant, albeit at a lower level of significance than in the previous model. The level of significance and the negative sign of the coefficient for *ROE* remains the same as in Model 2. Somewhat surprisingly, however, the coefficient for *LEVERAGE* is now weakly significant. This may appear somewhat counterintuitive at first glance since debtholders of more highly leveraged banks appear to profit from M&As, even though this potentially increases the leverage of the bank. Yet, when this result is viewed in conjunction with the significant coefficient for *CONCENTRATION*, it may be reasonable to assume that more highly leveraged banks in a more concentrated market are increasingly likely to receive government support in case they run into financial difficulties. Debtholders appear to anticipate a government bailout in this case and allow banks cheaper access to capital. The final model adds the transaction size variable *VALUE* as an explanatory factor. The coefficient is positive, but insignificant and actually decreases the explanatory power of the regression model compared to Model 4. Transaction size therefore does not appear to be a decisive factor for debtholders. This is in contrast to prior studies on the stock market reaction to bank merger announcements.

Overall, the results of the OLS regression strongly suggest that TBTF considerations, or at least market power considerations, play an important role when determining the influence that takeover announcements have on acquiring banks' CDS spreads in the Asia-Pacific region. The larger the bidding bank is in comparison to its national peers, the more its CDS spread declines. The rating of a financial institution is also an important factor, whereby higher ratings are associated with CDS spread increases. Capital markets seem to anticipate that the rating may not be maintained. Higher profitability of the bidding bank, on the other hand, leads to a decrease in the CDS spread level. However, due to the comparatively small sample size, the results need to be interpreted carefully. Nonetheless, the results show clear trends that offer valuable insights into the capital market reaction of debtholders to bank merger announcements.

4.5 Robustness checks

As a robustness check to the overall results, the M&A announcement effects are investigated using the constant mean model, an approach previously used by Daniels and Shin Jensen (2005). Andres et al. (2013) even suggest that the constant mean model delivers comparatively good results and is therefore a methodology well-suited to the investigation of CDS spread changes. One of the advantages of this method is its independence of other banks within the same rating class in order to form a benchmark index.

The abnormal spread change in this case is simply the realized spread change minus the expected normal spread change:

$$ASC_{i,t} = \delta_{i,t} - \mu[\delta_{i,t} \mid \Omega_T] \tag{4-4}$$

where $ASC_{i,t}$, is the abnormal CDS spread change for the CDS spread of bank i on day t, and $\delta_{i,t}$ and $\mu[\delta_{i,t}|\Omega_T]$ are the actually realized and the expected normal spread change, for bank i on day t. The expected normal spread change is the spread change based on the conditional information set Ω_T and is estimated, similar to Daniels and Shin Jensen (2005),[26] using a 63 trading day period (3 months) prior to the first day of the event window:[27]

$$\mu[\delta_{i,t} \mid \Omega_T] = \bar{\delta}_{i,t} = \frac{1}{63}\sum_{t=-6}^{-68} \delta_{i;t} \tag{4-5}$$

26 Daniels and Shin Jensen (2005) actually use a 75 day estimation period. However, a three month period is preferable, as it is a more clearly defined time frame.

27 Two of the 33 sample banks did not have enough CDS spread observations during the 63 day estimation period and consequently had to be dropped from the sample. The sample size of the robustness test therefore consists of 31 takeover announcements.

The cumulative abnormal CDS spread changes (CASC) are subsequently calculated by adding the daily ASCs during the event period ranging from $[\tau_1; \tau_2] \epsilon[-5,\ldots,10]$ using:

$$\text{CASC}_{i[\tau_1;\tau_2]} = \frac{1}{T}\sum\nolimits_{t=\tau_1}^{\tau_2} ASC_{i,t} \tag{4-6}$$

where T is the number of days in the event window. The final step is to calculate the mean cumulative abnormal spread change (MCASC) for the entire sample of N banks through:

$$MCASC_{[\tau_1;\tau_2]} = \frac{1}{N}\sum_{i=1}^{N} \text{CASC}_{i[\tau_1;\tau_2]} \tag{4-7}$$

The MCASC are tested for statistical significance using the parametric t-test as well as the nonparametric Wilcoxon signed-rank test. This methodology differs markedly from the standard approach used by other authors (e.g. Finnerty et al., 2013; Hull et al., 2004; Norden & Weber, 2004) so it is only possible to test whether merger announcements have a significant impact on the CDS spread of the bidding bank and whether this effect is overall positive or negative.

Table 4-8: Constant mean model CDS spread changes surrounding the M&A announcement day

Event window	Mean CASC	Median CASC	t-test (t-value)	Wilcoxon-test (Z-score)	Pos:Neg	Sample size
[−5;10]	−2.180	0.030	−0.377	−0.118	16:15	31
[−5;5]	−2.648	−0.165	−0.366	−0.353	15:16	31
[−1;1]	2.504	0.967	0.726	−1.117	18:13	31
[−5;−1]	1.223	0.578	0.473	−0.745	17:14	31
[0;0]	3.662	0.056	1.224	−0.705	18:13	31
[−1;0]	5.380	0.852	1.842*	−1.960*	19:12	31
[0;1]	0.787	−0.683	0.226	−0.333	12:19	31
[1;5]	−7.534	−0.066	−1.223	−0.412	15:16	31
[1;10]	−7.746	0.556	−1.225	−0.020	16:15	31

*;**,*** denotes statistical significance at the 10%, 5%, and 1% level

Table 4-8 shows the results of the abnormal CDS spread changes surrounding a bank merger announcement in the Asia-Pacific region using the constant mean model. The results suggest that the mean CASC actually decreases during the entire [−5;10] day event period, but the results are not significantly different from zero and spread increases and decreases are almost evenly distributed. In fact, all event windows lack statistical significance, except the [−1;0] day event window. During this event window a mean CASC of 5.4bps can be observed, significant at the 10%-level. This is in line with the results presented in Table 4-5 for the cumulative abnormal spread changes using the rating class benchmark model of, among others, Norden and Weber (2004). Therefore, for the day of the takeover announcement and the day immediately preceding it, robust results that M&A announcements are perceived by capital market participants as risk increasing events, are received.

Figure 4-4: Bidding bank MCASC surrounding takeover announcements

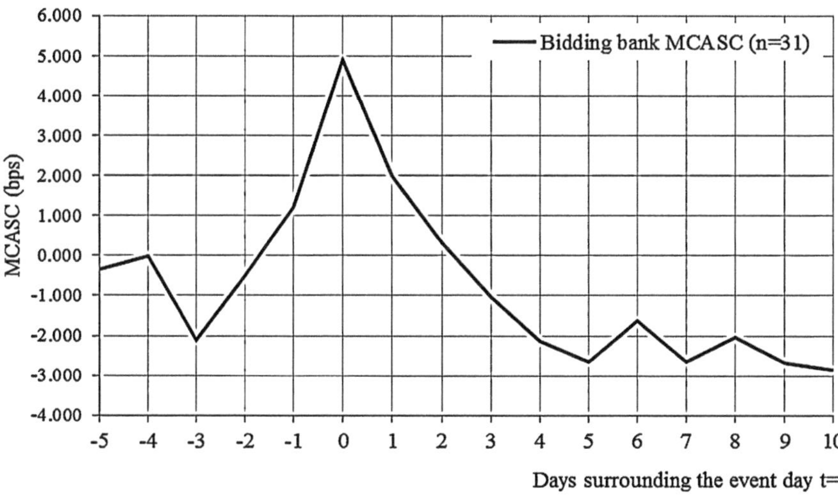

Figure 4-4 shows the development of the MCASC during the entire event period. The course of the MCASC in Figure 4-4 differs from the adjusted CDS spread changes in Figure 4-3. However, both show that takeover announcements have a clear impact on the bidding bank, especially during the immediate days surrounding the announcement. This, in conjunction with the, albeit weak, significance of the [−1;0] day event window gives consistent evidence that market participants perceive takeovers to be overall risk increasing events. Nevertheless, the sharp decline following the initial increase may also be a sign of an initial market overreaction to the merger announcement. That CDS markets can overreact to negative announcements is also shown by Greatrex (2008), in that particular case for negative earnings announcements.

4.6 Evaluation of the impact of bank mergers on the acquirer cost of debt

The bidding bank CDS spread reaction to bank merger announcements in the Asia-Pacific region is analyzed in this chapter. The sample consists of 33 international bidding banks that engaged in a transaction in this region between January 2004 and December 2013. The results show that M&As among financial institution are generally perceived as risk increasing corporate events for the bidder, as CDS spread levels widen. This widening is most pronounced during the eleven day event period surrounding the announcement day, where the average CDS spread experiences a significant increase in excess of 7.6 bps. Robust evidence of a widening of CDS spreads due to the merger announcement is also observed during the [−1;0] day event period, during which CDS spreads increase by 1bp. The analysis also shows that there are differences in the CDS spread changes of Asian and non-Asian bidding banks. The CDS spreads of non-Asian bidding banks widen approximately 2bps more than those of Asian ones during the eleven day period surrounding the announcement day. This result is in line with those of Choi et al. (2010), who show that cross-border mergers are perceived as particularly risk increasing events by market participants. The larger rise in CDS spreads for non-Asian acquirers, however, may also reflect the nature of their transactions. They usually engage in larger acquisitions than their Asian peers, many of them even cross-continental rather than cross-border.

The results of the cross-sectional regression analysis reveals that bidding banks, which are comparatively larger than their rivals, experience a highly significant reduction in their CDS spread levels due to the takeover announcement. This finding can be interpreted as evidence that TBTF considerations, or at least market power considerations, are a dominant factor in explaining the CDS spread changes of the acquiring institution surrounding the takeover announcement. Other factors that influence the CDS spread changes include a bank's creditworthiness, as expressed by its long-term issuer rating, and a bank's profitability. Higher ratings are associated with CDS spread increases as market participants may anticipate that the bank will not be able to maintain its rating following the merger. More profitable banks, on the other hand, experience significant decreases in their CDS spread levels. This suggests that more profitable banks will likely be able to continue serving their debt, despite the M&A transaction being an overall risk increasing event.

Future research should extend the geographic focus from bank mergers in the Asia-Pacific region to a global sample. In particular, as the sample size of this study is comparatively small, it does not allow for an in-depth analysis of the drivers behind the observed CDS spread changes due to M&A announcements.

Especially in light of the TBTF considerations that potentially play a dominant role in those spread changes a further analysis may yield valuable insights. The research of Penas and Unal (2004) as well as Morgan and Stiroh (2005) already shows that TBTF considerations are an important factor for bank debtholders and it certainly merits a more detailed analysis whether the same results hold for the CDS market.

5. Concluding remarks

5.1 Summary and discussion of the main results

The present thesis offers a comprehensive analysis of the shareholder wealth effects of the financial sector consolidation in the Asia-Pacific region and its impact on the acquirer's cost of debt. By not only examining the capital market reactions to the institutions directly involved in the M&A transaction, but also their closest rivals, clearer conclusions can be drawn in regard to the overall success of the financial sector consolidation in this region. In addition, by investigating the acquiring institution's CDS market reaction to merger announcements, valuable insights are offered in regard to the difference between the equity and debt market perception of bank M&As.

Chapter 2 reviews the findings of more than 135 empirical studies that examine the success of bank mergers and acquisitions in the US and Europe and several other markets. Among the three most frequently used methodologies, the event study approach is used most often, followed by dynamic efficiency studies and performance studies. The research focus has shifted from the US to Europe since 2000 and only more recently to the emerging economies of Asia and Latin America.

Despite the results of the three different methodologies exhibiting a certain degree of heterogeneity, some general overall trends can be observed in regard to international bank mergers. The event study results indicate that the success of bank M&As varies over time and geographic region. US bank mergers were more successful from a shareholder perspective during the 1970s and early 1980s, becoming gradually more detrimental for the bidding bank's shareholders in later time periods. European M&As follow similar patterns, albeit lagging by roughly a decade, suggesting that as markets harmonize and mature, it becomes increasingly difficult for shareholders to benefit from mergers. Emerging economies, such as the ones in Latin America and Asia, still seem to offer substantial room for further consolidation in the banking sector and therefore, especially bidding banks' shareholders, are still able to profit from transactions in these markets. The evidence from dynamic efficiency and performance studies, on the other hand, show a considerable degree of variation, likely due to their use of accounting data, which is subject to different rules and regulations in different jurisdictions and over time.

Pervious research suggests that large efficiency and performance differentials between the acquiring and target institutions, prior acquisition experience, financing via cash rather than stock, and higher regulatory efficiency and quality are among the main factors for successful bank mergers. However, there is no consensus in the literature as to whether geographic or product focus or diversification are more beneficial. The 2007 Financial Crisis highlighted the importance of banks and bank mergers to the overall stability of the global financial system. In the wake of this crisis, studies show that large banks implicitly receive "Too-Big-to-Fail" subsidies, which can lead to moral hazard problems and questionable merger motivations. Moreover, regulatory arbitrage considerations also appear to play a role in bank M&As.

Chapter 3 analyzes the shareholder wealth effects of bidders, targets, and their closest rivals surrounding the official announcement of bank M&As in the Asia-Pacific region between 1995 and 2013. The results show that, overall, bidders obtain positive, but insignificant stock returns, while targets achieve large and significant positive returns during the days surrounding a merger announcement day. Dividing the sample into Asian and non-Asian bidding banks reveals that Asian bidding banks can expect to earn significant positive abnormal returns during the three days surrounding the announcement, whereas non-Asian bidding banks earn small, negative returns. Targets of Asian and non-Asian bidders likewise exhibit vastly different capital market reactions, as the targets of non-Asian bidders achieve returns that are up to six percentage points higher than of those targeted by Asian bidders.

The outcome of the rival analysis shows that rivals of Asian bidders obtain positive returns upon M&A announcements, while those of the rivals of non-Asian bidders remain insignificant. The positive returns of the Asian bidding banks, in combination with those of their closest rivals, indicate that market power considerations potentially play an important role when capital markets value these transactions. The decision of a non-Asian institution to undertake a takeover in Asia does not affect their domestic peers, but, the rivals of their targets. They earn significantly higher returns that the target rivals of Asian bidders. This can be interpreted as the rivals of targets of non-Asian banks benefiting from an increased acquisition probability. The investigation into the drivers of the observed returns reveals that Asian bidders perform best when purchasing private financial institutions in Asia. The inferior performance of non-Asian bidders compared to their Asian counterparts may be due to them being more likely to purchase non-private targets. This may require them to pay significantly higher premiums to outbid local institutions for desirable targets. The target bank analysis gives further evidence to this interpretation. In addition, regulatory arbitrage considerations do not play a dominant role when capital markets value bank mergers in the Asia-Pacific regions.

In chapter 4 the CDS market reaction to bank M&A announcements between 2004 and 2013 in the Asia-Pacific region is examined. The empirical analysis shows that mergers among financial institutions are, on average, risk increasing events for bidders. A significant increase in excess of 7.6 bps can be observed during the eleven day event period surrounding the announcement day. There is also evidence that the CDS spreads of Asian and non-Asian acquirers react differently to merger announcements, as those of non-Asian institutions widen by approximately 2bps more than those of Asian ones. This is in line with prior evidence that cross-border bank mergers are perceived as more risky by market participants (Choi et al., 2010). On the other hand, this may also reflect that non-Asian banks, on average, usually engage in larger acquisitions than their Asian counterparts, which are cross-continental rather than cross-border in nature.

However, the regression analysis shows that bidders, which are relatively larger than their rivals, experience a highly significant reduction in their CDS spread levels in the wake of a takeover announcement. This can be interpreted as evidence that "Too-Big-to-Fail" considerations or market power are a key factor in explaining CDS spread changes of the acquiring institution surrounding an M&A announcement. Higher ratings are associated with CDS spread increases, as markets seem to expect that bidding banks will not be able to maintain their creditworthiness following the merger. Higher levels of profitability, however, mitigate this effect.

Overall, the results suggest that equity and debt markets consider different factors when evaluating the success of mergers. For shareholders, the origin of the bidding bank is a significant driver for successful mergers, while for debt-holders implicit TBTF expectations appear to be a major factor for successful mergers. The shareholders of bidding banks benefit most from national takeovers in Asia, as do their closest rivals. Following a merger, it appears as if investors anticipate that banks will be able to take advantage of the lower levels of competition, as fewer banks remain in the market. This strongly suggests that market power considerations play an important role when equity markets react to M&A announcements in the banking industry. Regulators should be wary of this and carefully assess whether this leads to collusion that may ultimately result in undesirable outcomes for consumers and the financial system due to lower levels of competition. Yet, for M&As by non-Asian institutions, the targets and their rivals are the main beneficiaries, as they can expect to earn large and positive returns surrounding a takeover announcement. The positive and significant returns for the acquiring institutions differ markedly from previous research findings that center on the largely consolidated banking markets of the US and Europe (e.g. Beitel et al., 2004; Hankir et al., 2011). In the Asia-Pacific region further consolidation by local institutions seems to offer considerable advantages for local institutions due to a potential increase in their market power or possibly through efficiency gains. Debtholders, on the other hand, appear to react positively to bank mergers in which the acquiring institution is already large compared to its closest competitors. This points towards the existence of implicit "Too-Big-to-Fail" expectations by debtholders, which should be of concern to regulators and policy makers alike.

5.2 Limitations and avenues for future research

The empirical investigations of bank M&As on the stock price of bidding and target banks and their respective rivals in chapter 3 has several drawbacks. Owning to the framework of the event study methodology, only exchange-listed bidding and target banks can be examined. This specifically excludes non-exchange listed institutions. Although similar valuation effects can be expected for non-exchange listed firms, they are not easily observable, as constant and consistent information in regard to the value of these banks is not available.

Furthermore, event studies only observe the short-term wealth effects. In order to obtain a more complete picture of the overall impact of mergers, future research could augment the short-term investigation with a long-term one. This could be either achieved through a buy-and-hold abnormal return analysis or through a focus on the change in accounting ratios or efficiency over several years.

Another limitation lies in the relatively small target bank sample. The small sample size is owing to the majority of targets either not being exchange-listed or suffering from poor data quality, which does not allow for the application of the event study methodology. As a consequence, the results of the target bank analysis need to be interpreted carefully. Therefore, future research should attempt to extend the target bank sample, which would allow for a joint analysis of the wealth effects for the combined institution. At the same time, the drivers of the abnormal returns to the target could be investigated in more detail. This would, for example, allow one to see whether size or efficiency differentials between target and acquirer play an important role.

A limitation of the rival analysis is its sensitivity to the rival definition. Selecting the most appropriate rivals is a challenging undertaking. The present study closely follows the approach by Hankir et al. (2011), which appears to be the most suitable selection process. However, some adjustments to their selection process are made, largely due to the differences in the size and depth of banking markets in the Asia-pacific region and the heterogeneity in national banking regulations. Therefore, national rather than regional rivals are selected. For European acquirers, on the other hand, selecting the closest regional rivals, as suggested by Hankir et al. (2011), may also be sensible.

A deeper analysis of the underlying drivers of the observed rival returns would also be fruitful. Doing so will permit clearer conclusions as to whether market power considerations play a key role in domestic mergers or whether other motives dominate a bank's decision to engage in an M&A transaction. Additionally, if domestic mergers indeed lead to increased market power, it would be interesting to see whether this translates into non-competitive behavior by banks and, if so, what the effects on borrowing and deposit rates are. In this way, research could extend beyond the capital market perspective and offer valuable insights into whether the financial sector consolidation in the Asia-Pacific region offers benefits to the financial system overall and consumers in particular. In this context, the impact of foreign market entry into a given banking sector and the associated effects on the competitive landscape are interesting subjects for further research.

The CDS event study in chapter 4 has a rather limited sample size. This is largely due to the quality of the available CDS data, but also because prior research on bank mergers did not investigate the effect of M&As on the CDS spreads of the involved banks. In order to obtain more easily generalizable results, future research should increase the geographic scope from the Asia-Pacific region to a worldwide sample. This would allow for a deeper analysis of the drivers of the observed spread changes.

Another possible way to take a deeper look at the reaction of debt markets to bank merger announcements would be to undertake a bond event study along the lines of Choi et al. (2010). This, however, will in all likelihood be very challenging, as debt markets in the Asia-Pacific region are, with few exceptions, not as well developed as those in the US or Europe. Yet, as these markets increase in size and importance and data becomes more readily available, using bond event studies may help to obtain a more comprehensive picture of the way capital markets perceive bank mergers and to see whether differences exist between shareholders and bondholders.

Moreover, the regression results indicate that for bidding banks with a comparatively large market share mergers are perceived as risk reducing events. This suggests that TBTF considerations, or at least market power considerations, play an important role in the way capital markets view bank M&As. An analysis to test whether the same results hold for a global sample of banks definitely merits a more detailed analysis, which would offer important insight to regulators and policy makers.

6. Reference list

Akhavein, J. D., Berger, A. N., & Humphrey, D. B. (1997). The effects of megamergers on efficiency and prices: evidence from a bank profit function. *Review of Industrial Organization, 12*(1), 95–139.

Akhigbe, A., & Madura, J. (1999). The industry effects regarding the probability of takeovers. *Financial Review, 34*(3), 1–17.

Akhigbe, A., & Martin, A. D. (2000). Information-signaling and competitive effects of foreign acquisitions in the US. *Journal of Banking & Finance, 24*(8), 1307–1321.

Al-Sharkas, A. A., & Hassan, M. K. (2010). New evidence on shareholder wealth effects in bank mergers during 1980–2000. *Journal of Economics and Finance, 34*(3), 326–348.

Al-Sharkas, A. A., Hassan, M. K., & Lawrence, S. (2008). The impact of mergers and acquisitions on the efficiency of the US banking industry: further evidence. *Journal of Business Finance & Accounting, 35*(1–2), 50–70.

Altunbaş, Y., Gardener, E. P. M., & Moore, B. (2001). Efficiency in European banking. *European Economic Review, 45*(10), 1931–1955.

Altunbaş, Y., & Marqués, D. (2008). Mergers and acquisitions and bank performance in Europe: the role of strategic similarities. *Journal of Economics and Business, 60*(3), 204–222.

Altunbaş, Y., & Molyneux, P. (1996). Economies of scale and scope in European banking. *Applied Financial Economics, 6*(4), 367–375.

Altunbaş, Y., Molyneux, P., & Thornton, J. (1997). Big-Bank Mergers in Europe: An Analysis of the Cost Implications. *Economica, 64*(254), 317–329.

Amihud, Y., DeLong, G. L., & Saunders, A. (2002). The effects of cross-border bank mergers on bank risk and value. *Journal of International Money and Finance, 21*(6), 857–877.

Anderson, C. W., Becher, D. A., & Campbell, T. L. (2004). Bank mergers, the market for bank CEOs, and managerial incentives. *Journal of Financial Intermediation, 13*(1), 6–27.

Andres, C., Betzer, A., & Doumet, M. (2013). *Measuring abnormal credit default swap spreads*. SSRN Working Paper Series.

Auerbach, C. M. (2009). *Fusionen deutscher Kreditinstitute: Erfolg und Erfolgsfaktoren am Beispiel von Sparkassen und Kreditgenossenschaften*. Wiesbaden: Gabler Verlag.

Baele, L., De Jonghe, O., & Vander Vennet, R. (2007). Does the stock market value bank diversification? *Journal of Banking & Finance, 31*(7), 1999–2023.

Baradwaj, B. G., Dubofsky, David A., & Fraser, D. R. (1991). Bidder returns in interstate and intrastate bank acquisitions. *Journal of Financial Services Research, 5*(3), 261–273.

Baradwaj, B. G., Fraser, D. R., & Furtado, E. P. H. (1990). Hostile bank takeover offers: Analysis and implications. *Journal of Banking & Finance, 14*(6), 1229–1242.

Barth, J. R., Caprio, G., & Levine, R. (2004). Bank regulation and supervision: what works best? *Journal of Financial Intermediation, 13*(2), 205–248.

Barth, J. R., Caprio, G., & Levine, R. (2005). *Rethinking bank regulation: till angels govern*. Cambridge: Cambridge University Press.

Barth, J. R., Caprio, G., & Levine, R. (2008). *Bank regulations are changing: for better or worse?*. World Bank Policy Research Working Paper, (4646).

Barth, J. R., Caprio, G., & Levine, R. (2012). *The evolution and impact of bank regulations*. World Bank Policy Research Working Paper, (6288).

Baxmann, U. G. (1995). *Kreditwirtschaftliche Betriebsgrößen*. Stuttgart: Deutscher Sparkassenverlag.

Beccalli, E., & Frantz, P. (2009). M&A operations and performance in banking. *Journal of Financial Services Research, 36*(2–3), 203–226.

Becher, D. A. (2000). The valuation effects of bank mergers. *Journal of Corporate Finance, 6*(2), 189–214.

Becher, D. A., & Campbell, T. L. (2005). Interstate banking deregulation and the changing nature of bank mergers. *Journal of Financial Research, 28*(1), 1–20.

Behr, A., & Heid, F. (2011). The success of bank mergers revisited. An assessment based on a matching strategy. *Journal of Empirical Finance, 18*(1), 117–135.

Beitel, P. (2002). *Akquisitionen und Zusammenschlüsse europäischer Banken. Wertsteigerung durch M&A-Transaktionen*. Wiesbaden: Deutscher Universitäts-Verlag.

Beitel, P., & Schiereck, D. (2003). Zum Erfolg von Akquisitionen und Zusammenschlüssen zwischen Banken: Eine Bestandsaufnahme der empirischen Forschung *Bank-Archiv: Zeitschrift für das gesamte Bank- und Börsenwesen, 51*(7), 501–515.

Beitel, P., Schiereck, D., & Wahrenburg, M. (2004). Explaining M&A success in European banks. *European Financial Management, 10*(1), 109–139.

Bekaerta, G., & Harvey, C. R. (1997). Emerging equity market volatility. *Journal of Financial Economics, 43*(1), 29–77.

Berger, A. N. (1998). The efficiency effects of bank mergers and acquisition: a preliminary look at the 1990s data. In Y. Amihud & G. Miller (Eds.), *Bank Mergers & Acquisitions* (pp. 79–111). Boston: Kluwer.

Berger, A. N. (2000). The integration of the financial services industry: where are the efficiencies? *North American Actuarial Journal, 4*(3), 25–45.

Berger, A. N., Demsetzc, R. S., & Strahanc, P. E. (1999). The consolidation of the financial services industry: causes, consequences, and implications for the future. *Journal of Banking & Finance, 23*(2–4), 135–194.

Berger, A. N., & DeYoung, R. (2001). The effects of geographic expansion on bank efficiency. *Journal of Financial Services Research, 19*(2–3), 163–184.

Berger, A. N., Goldberg, L. G., & White, L. J. (2001). The effects of dynamic changes in bank competition on the supply of small business credit. *European Finance Review, 5*(1–2), 115–139.

Berger, A. N., & Humphrey, D. B. (1994). *Bank scale economies, mergers, concentration, and efficiency: the U.S. experience*. Working Paper 94–25, Financial Institution Center, The Wharton School, Philadelphia.

Berger, A. N., & Humphrey, D. B. (1997). Efficiency of financial institutions: International survey and directions for future research. *European Journal of Operational Research, 98*(2), 175–212.

Berger, A. N., & Mester, L. J. (1997). Inside the black box: what explains differences in the efficiencies of financial institutions? *Journal of Banking & Finance, 21*(7), 895–947.

Bernad, C., Fuentelsaz, L., & Gómez, J. (2010). The effect of mergers and acquisitions on productivity: an empirical application to Spanish banking. *Omega, 38*(5), 289–293.

Bertin, W. J., Ghazanfari, F., & Torabzadeh, K. M. (1989). Failed bank acquisitions and successful bidders' returns. *Financial Management, 18*(2), 93–100.

Bessler, W., & Murtagh, J. P. (2002). The stock market reaction to cross-border acquisitions of financial services firms: an analysis of Canadian banks. *Journal of International Financial Markets, Institutions and Money, 12*(4–5), 419–440.

Billett, M. T., King, T.-H. D., & Mauer, D. C. (2004). Bondholder wealth effects in mergers and acquisitions: new evidence from the 1980s and 1990s. *The Journal of Finance, 59*(1), 107–135.

Bliss, R. T., & Rosen, R. J. (2001). CEO compensation and bank mergers. *Journal of Financial Economics, 61*(1), 107–138.

Boehmer, E., Musumeci, J., & Poulson, A. B. (1991). Event-study methodology under conditions of event-induced variance. *Journal of Financial Economics, 30*(2), 253–272.

Bohl, M. T., Havrylchyk, O., & Schiereck, D. (2006). Foreign acquisitions and industry wealth effects of privatization: evidence from the Polish banking industry. In M. Balling, F. Lierman, & A. Mullineux (Eds.), *Financial Markets in Central and Eastern Europe: Stability and Efficiency* (pp. 80–95). London: Routledge.

Bollerslev, T. (1986). Generalized autoregressive conditional heteroskedasticity. *Journal of Econometrics, 31*(1), 307–327.

Boyd, J. H., & Graham, S. L. (1988). The profitability and risk effects of allowing bank holding companies to merge with other financial firms: a simulation study. *Federal Reserve Bank of Minneapolis Quarterly Review, 12*(2), 3–20.

Boyd, J. H., & Graham, S. L. (1998). Consolidation in U.S. banking: implications for efficiency and risk. In Y. Amihud & G. Miller (Eds.), *Bank Mergers & Acquisitions* (pp. 113–135). Boston: Kluwer.

Boyd, J. H., Graham, S. L., & Hewitt, R. S. (1993). Bank holding company mergers with nonbank financial firms: effects on the risk of failure. *Journal of Banking & Finance, 17*(1), 43–63.

Bresler, N. (2007). *Effizienz von Sparkassen und Sparkassenfusionen: Eine empirische Untersuchung*. Hamburg: Verlag Dr. Kovač.

Brewer, E., & Jagtiani, J. (2013). How much did banks pay to become Too-Big-To-Fail and to become systemically important? *Journal of Financial Services Research, 43*(1), 1–35.

Brockett, P. L., Chen, H.-M., & Garven, J. R. (1999). A new stochastically flexible event methodology with application to Proposition 103. *Insurance: Mathematics and Economics, 25*(12), 197–217.

Brown, S. J., & Warner, J. B. (1980). Measuring security price performance. *Journal of Financial Economics, 8*(3), 205–258.

Brown, S. J., & Warner, J. B. (1985). Using daily stock returns: The case of event studies. *Journal of Financial Economics, 14*(1), 3–31.

Buch, C. M., & DeLong, G. L. (2004). Cross-border bank mergers: what lures the rare animal?. *Journal of Banking & Finance, 28*(9), 2077–2102.

Bühner, R. (1990). *Erfolg von Unternehmenszusammenschlüssen in der Bundesrepublik Deutschland*. Stuttgart: Schäffer-Poeschel Verlag.

Cable, J., & Holland, K. (1999). Modelling normal returns in event studies: a model-selection approach and pilot study. *The European Journal of Finance, 5*(4), 331–341.

Callen, J. L., Livnat, J., & Segal, D. (2009). The impact of earnings on the pricing of credit default swaps. *The Accounting Review, 84*(5), 1363–1394.

Campa, J. M., & Hernando, I. (2004). Shareholder value creation in European M&As. *European Financial Management, 10*(1), 47–81.

Campa, J. M., & Hernando, I. (2006). M&As performance in the European financial industry. *Journal of Banking & Finance, 30*(12), 3367–3392.

Campbell, C. J., Cowan, A. R., & Salotti, V. (2010). Multi-country event-study methods. *Journal of Banking & Finance, 34*(12), 3078–3090.

Carbo-Valverde, S., & Humphrey, D. B. (2004). Predicted and actual costs from individual bank mergers. *Journal of Economics and Business, 56*(2), 137–157.

Carbo-Valverde, S., Kane, E. J., & Rodriguez-Fernandez, F. (2012). Regulatory arbitrage in cross-border banking mergers within the EU. *Journal of Money, Credit and Banking, 44*(8), 1609–1629.

Carhart, M. M. (1997). On persistence in mutual fund performance. *The Journal of Finance, 52*(1), 57–82.

Chamberlain, S. L. (1998). The effect of bank ownership changes on subsidiary-level earnings. In Y. Amihud & G. Miller (Eds.), *Bank Mergers & Acquisitions* (pp. 137–172). Boston: Kluwer.

Chavaltanpipat, A., Kholdy, S., & Sohrabian, A. (1999). The wealth effects of bank acquisitions. *Applied Economics Letters, 6*(1), 5–11.

Choi, S., Francis, B. B., & Hasan, I. (2010). Cross-border bank M&As and risk: evidence from the bond market. *Journal of Money, Credit and Banking, 424*(4), 615–645.

Claessens, S., Demirgüç-Kunt, A., & Huizinga, H. P. (2001). How does foreign entry affect domestic banking markets? *Journal of Banking & Finance, 25*(5), 891–911.

Cohen, K. J., & Reid, S. R. (1966). The benefits and costs of bank mergers. *Journal of Financial and Quantitative Analysis, 1*(4), 15–57.

Cornett, M. M., & De, S. (1991). Medium of payment in corporate acquisitions: evidence from interstate bank mergers. *Journal of Money, Credit and Banking, 23*(4), 767–776.

Cornett, M. M., Hovakimian, G., Palia, D., & Tehranian, H. (2003). The impact of the manager–shareholder conflict on acquiring bank returns. *Journal of Banking & Finance, 27*(1), 103–131.

Cornett, M. M., McNutt, J. J., & Tehranian, H. (2006). Performance changes around bank mergers: revenue enhancements versus cost reductions. *Journal of Money, Credit and Banking, 38*(4), 1013–1050.

Cornett, M. M., & Tehranian, H. (1992). Changes in corporate performance associated with bank acquisitions. *Journal of Financial Economics, 31*(2), 211–234.

Corrado, C. J. (1989). A nonparametric test for abnormal security-price performance in event studies. *Journal of Financial Economics, 23*(2), 385–395.

Corrado, C. J., & Truong, C. (2008). Conducting event studies with Asia-Pacific security market data. *Pacific-Basin Finance Journal, 16*(5), 493–521.

Corrado, C. J., & Zivney, T. L. (1992). The specification and power of the sign test in event study hypothesis tests using daily stock returns. *Journal of Financial and Quantitative Analysis, 27*(3), 465–478.

Correa, R. (2009). Cross-border bank acquisitions: is there a performance effect? *Journal of Financial Services Research, 36*(2–3), 169–197.

Cowan, A. R. (1992). Nonparametric event study tests. *Review of Quantitative Finance and Accounting, 2*(4), 343–358.

Cowan, A. R. (1993). Tests for cumulative abnormal returns over long periods: simulation evidence. *International Review of Financial Analysis, 2*(1), 51–68.

Crouzille, C., Lepetit, L., & Bautista, C. (2008). How did the Asian stock markets react to bank mergers after the 1997 Financial Crisis? *Pacific Economic Review, 13*(2), 171–182.

Cybo-Ottone, A., & Murgia, M. (2000). Mergers and shareholder wealth in European banking. *Journal of Banking & Finance, 24*(6), 831–859.

Cyree, K. B., & DeGennaro, R. P. (2002). A generalized method for detecting abnormal returns and changes in systematic risk. *Review of Quantitative Finance and Accounting, 19*(4), 399–416.

Daniel, K., Titman, S., & Wei, K. C. J. (2001). Explaining the cross-section of stock returns in Japan: factors or characteristics? *The Journal of Finance, 56*(2), 743–766.

Daniels, K. N., & Shin Jensen, M. (2005). The effect of credit ratings on credit defaults swap spreads and credit spreads. *The Journal of Fixed Income, 15*(4), 16–33.

DeLong, G. L. (2001). Stockholder gains from focusing versus diversifying bank mergers. *Journal of Financial Economics, 59*(2), 221–252.

DeLong, G. L. (2003). The announcement effects of U.S. versus non-U.S. bank mergers: do they differ? *Journal of Financial Research, 26*(4), 487–500.

DeLong, G. L., & DeYoung, R. (2007). Learning by observing: information spillovers in the execution and valuation of commercial bank M&As. *The Journal of Finance, 62*(1), 181–216.

Desai, A. S., & Stover, R. D. (1985). Bank holding company acquisitions, stockholder returns, and regulatory uncertainty. *Journal of Financial Research, 8*(2), 145–156.

DeYoung, R. (1997). Bank mergers, x-efficiency, and the market for corporate control. *Managerial Finance, 23*(1), 32–47.

DeYoung, R., Evanoff, D. D., & Molyneux, P. (2009). Mergers and acquisitions of financial institutions: a review of the post-2000 literature. *Journal of Financial Services Research, 36*(2–3), 87–110.

Dodd, P., & Warner, J. B. (1983). On corporate governance: A study of proxy contests. *Journal of Financial Economics, 11*(1–4), 401–438.

Dong, H., Song, F. M., & Tao, L. (2011). *Regulatory arbitrage: evidence from bank cross-border M&As.* SSRN Working Paper Series.

Dontis-Charitos, P., Molyneux, P., & Staikouras, S. K. (2011). Does the stock market compensate banks for diversifying into the insurance business?. *Financial Markets, Institutions & Instruments, 20*(1), 1–28.

Drees, F., Keisers, M., & Schiereck, D. (2006). Zum Erfolg von Sparkassenfusionen: Aktuelle kasuistische Evidenz. *Zeitschrift für öffentliche und gemeinwirtschaftliche Unternehmen, 29*(1), 24–49.

Dubofsky, D. A., & Fraser, D. R. (1989). Regulatory Change and the Market for Bank Control. In B. E. Gup (Ed.), *Bank Mergers: Current Issues and Perspectives* (pp. 121–139). Norwell: Kluwer.

Eckbo, B. E. (1983). Horizontal mergers, collusion, and stockholder wealth. *Journal of Financial Economics, 11*(1–4), 241–273.

Eckbo, B. E. (1985). Mergers and the market concentration doctrine: evidence from the capital market. *The Journal of Business, 58*(3), 325–349.

Eckbo, B. E. (1992). Mergers and the value of antitrust deterrence. *The Journal of Finance, 47*(3), 1005–1029.

Egger, P., & Hahn, F. R. (2010). Endogenous bank mergers and their impact on banking performance: some evidence from Austria. *International Journal of Industrial Organization, 28*(2), 155–166.

Ekkayokkaya, M., Holmes, P., & Paudyal, K. (2009). The Euro and the changing face of European banking: evidence from mergers and acquisitions. *European Financial Management, 15*(2), 451–476.

Elsas, R. (2007). *Preemptive distress resolution through bank mergers.* SSRN Working Paper Series.

Elsas, R., Hackethal, A., & Holzhäuser, M. (2010). The anatomy of bank diversification. *Journal of Banking & Finance, 34*(6), 1274–1287.

Elyasiani, E., & Mansur, I. (1998). Sensitivity of the bank stock returns distribution to changes in the level and volatility of interest rate: A GARCH-M model. *Journal of Banking & Finance, 22*(5), 535–563.

Engle, R. F., & Ng, V. K. (1993). Measuring and testing the impact of news on volatility. *The Journal of Finance, 48*(5), 1749–1778.

Fama, E. F., Fisher, L., Jensen, M. C., & Roll, R. (1969). The adjustment of stock prices to new information. *International Economic Review, 10*(1), 1–21.

Fama, E. F., & French, K. R. (1992). The cross-section of expected stock returns. *The Journal of Finance, 47*(2), 427–465.

Fama, E. F., & French, K. R. (1993). Common risk factors in the returns on stocks and bonds. *Journal of Financial Economics, 33*(1), 3–56.

Fama, E. F., & French, K. R. (1996). Multifactor explanations of asset pricing anomalies. *The Journal of Finance, 51*(1), 55–84.

Figueira, C., & Nellis, J. (2009). Bank merger and acquisitions activity in the EU: much ado about nothing? *The Service Industries Journal, 29*(7), 875–886.

Finnerty, J. D., Miller, C. D., & Chen, R.-R. (2013). The impact of credit rating announcements on credit default swap spreads. *Journal of Banking & Finance, 37*(6), 2011–2030.

Fixler, D. J., & Zieschang, K. D. (1993). An index number approach to measuring bank efficiency: an application to mergers. *Journal of Banking & Finance, 17*(2–3), 437–450.

Focarelli, D., Panetta, F., & Salleo, C. (2002). Why do banks merge? *Journal of Money, Credit and Banking, 34*(4), 1047–1066.

Frame, W. S., & Lastrapes, W. D. (1998). Abnormal returns in the acquisition market: the case of bank holding companies, 1990–1993. *Journal of Financial Services Research, 14*(2), 145–163.

Fried, H. O., Lovell, C. A. K., & Yaisawarng, S. (1999). The impact of mergers on credit union service provision. *Journal of Banking & Finance, 23*(2–4), 367–386.

Fuller, K., Netter, J., & Stegemoller, M. (2002). What do returns to acquiring firms tell us? Evidence from firms that make many acquisitions. *The Journal of Finance, 57*(4), 1763–1793.

Galil, K., & Soffer, G. (2011). Good news, bad news and rating announcements: an empirical investigation. *Journal of Banking & Finance, 35*(11), 3101–3119.

Gleason, K. C., & Mathur, I. (1998). Wealth effects of international acquisitions by US banks. *Financial Markets, Institutions & Instruments, 7*(5), 54–69.

Goddard, J., Molyneux, P., & Zhou, T. (2012). Bank mergers and acquisitions in emerging markets: evidence from Asia and Latin America. *The European Journal of Finance, 18*(5), 419–438.

Gold, C. (1997). *Gebietsreformbeeinflußte Fusionen bayerischer Sparkassen: empirische Analyse betriebswirtschaftlicher Effekte.* Dissertation, University of Göttingen.

Greatrex, C. A. (2008). *The credit default swap market's reaction to earnings announcements*. Fordham University Department of Economics Discussion Paper Series, (2008–06).

Gropp, R., Gruendl, C., & Guettler, A. (2014). The impact of public guarantees on bank risk-taking: evidence from a natural experiment. *Review of Finance, 18*(2), 457–488.

Gupta, A., & Misra, L. (2007). Deal size, bid premium, and gains in bank mergers: the impact of managerial motivations. *Financial Review, 42*(3), 373–400.

Hadlock, C., Houston, J. F., & Ryngaert, M. D. (1999). The role of managerial incentives in bank acquisitions. *Journal of Banking & Finance, 23*(2–4), 221–249.

Hagendorff, J., Collins, M., & Keasey, K. (2007). Bank governance and acquisition performance. *Corporate Governance: An International Review, 15*(5), 957–968.

Hagendorff, J., Collins, M., & Keasey, K. (2008). Investor protection and the value effects of bank merger announcements in Europe and the US. *Journal of Banking & Finance, 32*(7), 1333–1348.

Hagendorff, J., Hernando, I., Nieto, M. J., & Wall, L. D. (2012). What do premiums paid for bank M&As reflect? The case of the European Union. *Journal of Banking & Finance, 36*(3), 749–759.

Hagendorff, J., & Keasey, K. (2009). Post-merger strategy and performance: evidence from the US and European banking industries. *Accounting & Finance, 49*(4), 725–751.

Hagendorff, J., & Keasey, K. (2012). The value of board diversity in banking: evidence from the market for corporate control. *The European Journal of Finance, 18*(1), 41–58.

Haleblian, J., Kim, J.-y., & Rajagopalan, N. (2006). The influence of acquisition experience and performance on acquisition behavior: evidence from the U.S. commercial banking industry. *Academy of Management Journal, 49*(2), 357–370.

Hankir, Y., Rauch, C., & Umber, M. P. (2011). Bank M&A: A market power story? *Journal of Banking & Finance, 35*(9), 2341–2354.

Hannan, T. H., & Wolken, J. D. (1989). Returns to bidders and targets in the acquisition process: evidence from the banking industry. *Journal of Financial Services Research, 3*(1), 5–16.

Hart, J. R., & Apilado, V. P. (2002). Inexperienced banks and interstate mergers. *Journal of Economics and Business, 54*(3), 313–330.

Haun, B. (1996). *Fusionseffekte bei Sparkassen: Empirische Analyse der Zielerreichung*. Wiesbaden: Deutscher Universitätsverlag.

Haynes, M., & Thompson, S. (1999). The productivity effects of bank mergers: evidence from the UK building societies. *Journal of Banking & Finance, 23*(5), 825–846.

Hernando, I., Nieto, M. J., & Wall, L. D. (2009). Determinants of domestic and cross-border bank acquisitions in the European Union. *Journal of Banking & Finance, 33*(6), 1022–1032.

Hoshino, Y., & Turnbull, S. J. (2002). Further study on the performance of mergers among credit associations in Japan. *Review of Pacific Basin Financial Markets and Policies, 5*(3), 395–416.

Hosono, K., Sakai, K., & Tsuru, K. (2006). *Consolidation of cooperative banks (Shinkin) in Japan: motives and consequences*. RIETI Discussion Series 06-E-034.

Houston, J. F., James, C. M., & Ryngaert, M. D. (2001). Where do merger gains come from? Bank mergers from the perspective of insiders and outsiders. *Journal of Financial Economics, 60*(2–3), 285–311.

Houston, J. F., Lin, C., & Ma, Y. (2012). Regulatory arbitrage and international bank flows. *The Journal of Finance, 67*(5), 1845–1895.

Houston, J. F., & Ryngaert, M. D. (1994). The overall gains from large bank mergers. *Journal of Banking & Finance, 18*(6), 1155–1176.

Houston, J. F., & Ryngaert, M. D. (1997). Equity issuance and adverse selection: a direct test using conditional stock offers. *The Journal of Finance, 52*(1), 197–219.

Hudgins, S. C., & Seifert, B. (1996). Stockholder returns and international acquisitions of financial firms: an emphasis on banking. *Journal of Financial Services Research, 10*(2), 163–180.

Hughes, J. P., Lang, W. W., Mester, L. J., Moon, C.-G., & Pagano, M. S. (2003). Do bankers sacrifice value to build empires? Managerial incentives, industry consolidation, and financial performance. *Journal of Banking & Finance, 27*(3), 417–447.

Hughes, J. P., Lang, W. W., Mester, L. J., & Moone, C.-G. (1999). The dollars and sense of bank consolidation. *Journal of Banking & Finance, 23*(2–4), 291–324.

Huizinga, H. P., Nelissen, J. H. M., & Vander Vennet, R. (2001). *Efficiency effects of bank mergers and acquisitions in Europe*. Tinbergen Institute Discussion Paper 01–088/3.

Hull, J., Predescu, M., & White, A. (2004). The relationship between credit default swap spreads, bond yields, and credit rating announcements. *Journal of Banking & Finance, 28*(11), 2789–2811.

Imbierowicz, B., & Wahrenburg, M. (2013). Wealth transfer effects between stockholders and bondholders. *The Quarterly Review of Economics and Finance, 53*(1), 23–43.

Ismail, A., & Davidson, I. (2005). Further analysis of mergers and shareholder wealth effects in European banking. *Applied Financial Economics, 15*(1), 13–30.

Ismail, A., & Davidson, I. (2007). The determinants of target returns in European bank mergers. *The Service Industries Journal, 27*(5), 617–634.

Ismailescu, I., & Kazemi, H. (2010). The reaction of emerging market credit default swap spreads to sovereign credit rating changes. *Journal of Banking & Finance, 34*(12), 2861–2873.

James, C. M., & Wier, P. (1987a). An analysis of FDIC failed bank auctions. *Journal of Monetary Economics, 20*(1), 141–153.

James, C. M., & Wier, P. (1987b). Returns to acquirers and competition in the acquisition market: the case of banking. *Journal of Political Economy, 95*(2), 355–370.

Jeon, Y., & Miller, S. M. (2007). Births, deaths, and marriages in the U.S. commercial banking industry. *Economic Inquiry, 45*(2), 325–341.

Jorion, P., & Zhang, G. (2007). Good and bad credit contagion: evidence from credit default swaps. *Journal of Financial Economics, 84*(3), 860–883.

Kaen, F. R., & Tehranian, H. (1989). New Hampshire bank mergers: the returns to acquiring bank shareholders. In B. E. Gup (Ed.), *Bank Mergers: Current Issues and Perspectives* (pp. 141–155). Norwell: Kluwer.

Kane, E. J. (2000). Incentives for banking megamergers: what motives might regulators infer from event-study evidence? *Journal of Money, Credit and Banking, 32*(3), 671–701.

Keisers, M. (2009). *Selected essays on the success of mergers and acquisitions.* Frankfurt am Main: Peter Lang.

Kim, J.-Y., & Finkelstein, S. (2009). The effects of strategic and market complementarity on acquisition performance: evidence from the U.S. commercial banking industry, 1989–2001. *Strategic Management Journal, 30*(6), 617–646.

King, M. R. (2009). *Time to buy or just buying time? The market reaction to bank rescue packages.* BIS Working Papers, (No. 288).

Kiymaz, H. (2004). Cross-border acquisitions of US financial institutions: Impact of macroeconomic factors. *Journal of Banking & Finance, 28*(6), 1413–1439.

Kiymaz, H. (2013). Cross-border mergers and acquisition and country risk ratings: evidence from U.S. financials. *The International Journal of Business and Finance Research, 7*(1), 17–29.

Klomp, J., & de Haan, J. (2012). Banking risk and regulation: does one size fit all? *Journal of Banking & Finance, 36*(12), 3197–3212.

Knapp, M., Gart, A., & Becher, D. A. (2005). Post-merger performance of bank holding companies, 1987–1998. *Financial Review, 40*(4), 549–574.

Koetter, M. (2008). An assessment of bank merger success in Germany. *German Economic Review, 9*(2), 232–264.

Kolaric, S., & Schiereck, D. (2013). Shareholder wealth effects of bank mergers and acquisitions in Latin America. *Management Research: The Journal of the Iberoamerican Academy of Management, 11*(2), 157–177.

Kolaric, S., & Schiereck, D. (2014). Performance of bank mergers and acquisitions: a review of the recent empirical evidence. *Management Review Quarterly, 64*(1), 39–71.

Kondova Georgiev, G., & Burghof, H.-P. (2007). *The impact of bank mergers on efficiency: Empirical evidence from the German banking industry.* Paper presented at the 2007 EFMA Annual Meeting, Vienna.

Kwan, S. H., & Eisenbeis, R. A. (1999). Mergers of publicly traded banking organizations revisited. *Economic Review, 84*(4), 26–37.

Kwan, S. H., & Wilcox, J. A. (1999). Hidden cost reductions in bank mergers: Accounting for more productive banks. *Working Papers in Applied Economic Theory, Federal Reserve Bank of San Francisco.*

Lang, G., & Welzel, P. (1996). Efficiency and technical progress in banking Empirical results for a panel of German cooperative banks. *Journal of Banking & Finance, 20*(6), 1003–1023.

Lang, G., & Welzel, P. (1998). Technology and cost efficiency in universal banking: a "Thick Frontier"-Analysis of the German banking industry. *Journal of Productivity Analysis, 10*(1), 63–84.

Lang, G., & Welzel, P. (1999). Mergers among German cooperative banks: a panel-based stochastic frontier analysis. *Small Business Economics, 13*(4), 273–286.

Laudi, P. (2003). *Fusionen von Genossenschaftsbanken: Zielerreichung von Unternehmensverschmelzungen und deren Alternativen*. Bremen: Wolfdruck Verlag.

Lehnert, T., & Neske, F. (2006). On the relationship between credit rating announcements and credit default swap spreads for European reference entities. *Journal of Credit Risk, 2*(2), 83–90.

Lensink, R., & Maslennikova, I. (2008). Value performance of European bank acquisitions. *Applied Financial Economics, 18*(3), 185–198.

Lepetit, L., Patry, S., & Rous, P. (2004). Diversification versus specialization: an event study of M&As in the European banking industry. *Applied Financial Economics, 14*(9), 663–669.

Lin, L., & Huang, C.-Y. (2009). Optimal size of the financial services industry in Taiwan: a new DEA-option-based merger simulation approach. *The Service Industries Journal, 29*(4), 523–537.

Lin, P.-w. (2005). An empirical analysis of bank mergers and cost efficiency in Taiwan. *Small Business Economics, 25*(2), 197–206.

Linder, J. C., & Crane, D. B. (1993). Bank mergers: integration and profitability. *Journal of Financial Services Research, 7*(1), 35–55.

Lorenz, J.-T. (2006). *European Banking M&A: Die Kapitalmarktperspektive.* Wiesbaden: Deutscher Universitätsverlag.

Lorenz, J.-T., Beitel, P., & Schiereck, D. (2006). Erfolgsdeterminanten aus Sicht der Käuferbanken bei großen europäischen Bankzusammenschlüssen. *Finanzbetrieb, 8*(11), 695–707.

Ma, J., Pagan, J. A., & Chu, Y. (2012). Wealth effects of bank mergers and acquisitions in Asian emerging markets. *Journal of Applied Business Research, 28*(1), 47–58.

Madura, J., & Wiant, K. J. (1994). Long-term valuation effects of bank acquisitions. *Journal of Banking & Finance, 18*(6), 1135–1154.

Mayordomo, S., Peña, J. I., & Schwartz, E. S. (2014). Are all credit default swap databases equal? *European Financial Management, 20*(4), 677–713.

McIntosh, J. (2002). A welfare analysis of Canadian chartered bank mergers. *Canadian Journal of Economics, 35*(3), 457–475.

Micu, M., Remolona, E. M., & Wooldridge, P. D. (2004). The price impact of rating announcements: evidence from the credit default swap market. *BIS Quarterly Review* (June 2004), 55–65.

Mikkelson, W. H., & Partch, M. M. (1988). Withdrawn security offerings. *The Journal of Financial and Quantitative Analysis, 23*(2), 119–133.

Milbourn, T. T., Boot, A. W. A., & Thakor, A. V. (1999). Megamergers and expanded scope: theories of bank size and activity diversity. *Journal of Banking & Finance, 23*(2–4), 195–214.

Mititelu, E. A., & Hunger, A. (2009). *Der Erfolg von M&A-Transaktionen im europäischen Bankensektor.* Berlin: Duncker & Humblot.

Morgan, D. P., & Stiroh, K. J. (2005). *Too big to fail after all these years.* Federal Reserve Bank of Bank of New York Staff Report No. 220.

Mußhoff, J. (2007). *Erfolgreiche M&A-Transaktionen in der europäischen Bankenindustrie.* Wiesbaden: Deutscher Universitätsverlag.

Mußhoff, J., Jahns, C., & Schiereck, D. (2007a). Wertschaffung durch feindliche M&A-Transaktionen in der europäischen Bankenindustrie? Das Beispiel BNP und Paribas (Teil I). *Kredit und Kapital, 40*(3), 407–450.

Mußhoff, J., Jahns, C., & Schiereck, D. (2007b). Wertschaffung durch feindliche M&A-Transaktionen in der europäischen Bankenindustrie? Das Beispiel BNP und Paribas (Teil II). *Kredit und Kapital, 40*(4), 553–582.

Neely, W. P. (1987). Banking acquisitions: Acquirer and target shareholder returns. *Financial Management, 16*(4), 66–74.

Nelson, D. B. (1991). Conditional heteroskedasticity in asset returns: A new approach. *Econometrica, 59*(2), 347–370.

Norden, L., & Weber, M. (2004). Informational efficiency of credit default swap and stock markets: the impact of credit rating announcements. *Journal of Banking & Finance, 28*(11), 2813–2843.

Novy-Marx, R. (2013). The other side of value: the gross profitability premium. *Journal of Financial Economics, 108*(1), 1–28.

O'Hara, M., & Shaw, W. (1990). Deposit insurance and wealth effects: The value of being "Too Big to Fail". *The Journal of Finance, 45*(5), 1587–1600.

Ongena, S., & Penas, M. a. F. (2009). Bondholders' wealth effects in domestic and cross-border bank mergers. *Journal of Financial Stability, 5*(3), 256–271.

Otchere, I., & Ip, E. (2006). Intra-industry effects of completed and cancelled cross border acquisitions in Australia: a test of the acquisition probability hypothesis. *Pacific-Basin Finance Journal, 14*(2), 209–230.

Packer, F., & Suthiphongchai, C. (2003). Sovereign credit default swaps. *BIS Quarterly Review*(December 2003), 79–88.

Palia, D. (1993). The managerial, regulatory, and financial determinants of bank merger premiums. *The Journal of Industrial Economics, 41*(1), 91–102.

Penas, M. a. F., & Unal, H. (2004). Gains in bank mergers: evidence from the bond markets. *Journal of Financial Economics, 74*(1), 149–179.

Peng, Y.-H., & Wang, K. (2004). Cost efficiency and the effect of mergers on the Taiwanese banking industry. *The Service Industries Journal, 24*(4), 21–39.

Peristiani, S. (1997). Do mergers improve the x-efficiency and scale efficiency of U.S. banks? Evidence from the 1980s. *Journal of Money, Credit and Banking, 29*(3), 326–337.

Pettway, R. H., & Trifts, J. W. (1985). Do banks overbid when acquiring failed banks? *Financial Management, 14*(2), 5–15.

Pilloff, S. J. (1996). Performance changes and shareholder wealth creation associated with mergers of publicly traded banking institutions. *Journal of Money, Credit and Banking, 28*(3), 294–310.

Pilloff, S. J., & Santomero, A. M. (1998). The value effects of bank mergers and acquisitions. In Y. Amihud & G. Miller (Eds.), *Bank Mergers & Acquisitions* (pp. 59–78). Boston: Kluwer.

Prager, R. A., & Hannan, T. H. (1998). Do substantial horizontal mergers generate significant price effects? Evidence from the banking Industry. *The Journal of Industrial Economics, 46*(4), 433–452.

Radomski, B. (2008). *Fusionen deutscher Sparkassen: Eine Anwendung der Data Envelopment Analysis (DEA).* Hamburg: Verlag Dr. Kovač.

Rezitis, A. N. (2008). Efficiency and productivity effects of bank mergers: evidence from the Greek banking industry. *Economic Modelling, 25*(2), 236–254.

Rhoades, S. A. (1993). Efficiency effects of horizontal (in-market) bank mergers. *Journal of Banking & Finance, 17*(2–3), 411–422.

Rhoades, S. A. (1994). *A summary of merger performance studies in banking, 1980–93, and an assessment of the "Operating Performance" and "Event Study" methodologies.* Staff economic studies 167, Board of Governors of the Federal Reserve System, Washington, D.C.

Rhoades, S. A. (1998). The efficiency effects of bank mergers: an overview of case studies of nine mergers. *Journal of Banking & Finance, 22*(3), 273–291.

Rose, P. S. (1987). The impact of mergers in banking: Evidence from a nationwide sample of federally chartered banks. *Journal of Economics and Business, 39*(4), 289–312.

Schaeck, K., Zhou, T., & Molyneux, P. (2010). *'Too-Big-to-Fail' and its impact on safety net subsidies and systemic risk.* CAREFIN Research Paper No. 09/2010.

Schiereck, D., & Strauss, M. (2000). Zum Ankündigungseffekt großer Bankfusionen. *Mergers and Acquisitions Review, 11*, 421–425.

Scholtens, B., & de Wit, R. (2004). Announcement effects of bank mergers in Europe and the US. *Research in International Business and Finance, 18*(2), 217–228.

Schwert, G. W., & Seguin, P. J. (1990). Heteroskedasticity in stock returns. *The Journal of Finance, 45*(4), 1129–1155.

Seidel, G. R. (1995). *Kritische Erfolgsfaktoren bei Unternehmensübernahmen: Eine Analyse der US-Bankenbranche.* Wiesbaden: Gabler.

Shaffer, S. (1993). Can megamergers improve bank efficiency?. *Journal of Banking & Finance, 17*(2–3), 423–436.

Shivakumar, L., Urcan, O., Vasvari, F. P., & Zhang, L. (2011). The debt market relevance of management earnings forecasts: evidence from before and during the credit crisis. *Review of Accounting Studies, 16*(3), 464–486.

Singal, V. (1996). Airline mergers and competition: an integration of stock and product price effects. *The Journal of Business, 69*(2), 233–268.

Singh Mann, B., & Kohli, R. (2008). An empirical analysis of bank mergers in India: a study of market driven versus non-market driven mergers. *Decision, 35*(1), 47–73.

Song, M. H., & Walkling, R. A. (2000). Abnormal returns to rivals of acquisition targets: a test of the 'acquisition probability hypothesis'. *Journal of Financial Economics, 55*(2), 143–171.

Soussa, F., & Wheeler, T. (2006). *Do announcements of bank acquisitions in emerging markets create value?* Bank of England Working Paper No. 315.

Stillman, R. (1983). Examining antitrust policy towards horizontal mergers. *Journal of Financial Economics, 11*(1–4), 225–240.

Subrahmanyam, V., Rangan, N., & Rosenstein, S. (1997). The role of outside directors in bank acquisitions. *Financial Management, 26*(3), 23–36.

Sufian, F., & Majid, M.-Z. A. (2007). Bank mergers performance and the determinants of Singaporean banks' efficiency. *Gadjah Mada International Journal of Business, 9*(1), 19–39.

Sushka, M. E., & Bendeck, Y. (1988). Bank acquisition and stockholders' wealth. *Journal of Banking & Finance, 12*(4), 551–562.

Tebroke, H.-J. (1993). *Größe und Fusionserfolg von Genossenschaftsbanken. Eine theoretische und empirische Analyse der Auswirkungen von Betriebsgröße und fusionsbedingter Betriebsgrößenerweiterung auf die Ergebnisstruktur von Kreditgenossenschaften*. Köln: Müller Botermann.

Tourani Rad, A., & Van Beek, L. (1999). Market valuation of European bank mergers. *European Management Journal, 17*(5), 532–540.

Toyne, M. F., & Tripp, J. D. (1998). Interstate bank mergers and their impact on shareholder returns: evidence from the 1990s. *Quarterly Journal of Business and Economics, 37*(4), 48–58.

Trifts, J. W., & Scanlon, K. P. (1987). Interstate bank mergers: The early evidence. *Journal of Financial Research, 10*(4), 305–313.

Uhlenbruck, K., & De Castro, J. O. (2000). Foreign acquisitions in Central and Eastern Europe: outcomes of privatization in transitional economies. *Academy of Management Journal, 43*(3), 381–402.

Vander Vennet, R. (1996). The effect of mergers and acquisitions on the efficiency and profitability of EC credit institutions. *Journal of Banking & Finance, 20*(9), 1531–1558.

Waheed, A., & Mathur, I. (1995). Wealth effects of foreign expansion by U.S. banks. *Journal of Banking & Finance, 19*(5), 823–842.

Wall, L. D., & Gup, B. E. (1989). Market valuation effects of bank acquisitions. In B. E. Gup (Ed.), *Bank Mergers: Current Issues and Perspectives* (pp. 107–120). Norwell: Kluwer.

Weese, A. (2007). *Bankenzusammenschlüsse in Europa. Die Relevanz der Wahl der Akquisitionswährung als Erfolgsfaktor*. Wiesbaden: Deutscher Universitätsverlag.

Werden, G. J. (2008). Unilateral Competitive Effects of Horizontal Mergers I: Basic Concepts and Models. *Issues in Competition Law and Policy*.

Wheelock, D. C., & Wilson, P. W. (2004). Consolidation in US banking: Which banks engage in mergers? *Review of Financial Economics, 13*(1–2), 7–39.

Wutz, A. (2002). *Effizienz des Bankensektors: Eine empirische Analyse am Beispiel der bayerischen Genossenschaftsbanken.* München: Bayerischer Raiffeisen- und Volksbanken Verlag.

Yu, I.-W., Fung, K.-P., & Tam, C.-S. (2010). Assessing financial market integration in Asia – Equity markets. *Journal of Banking & Finance, 34*(12), 2874–2885.

Zhang, H. (1995). Wealth effects of US bank takeovers. *Applied Financial Economics, 5*(5), 329–336.

Zollo, M., & Leshchinkskii, D. (2000). *Can firms learn to acquire? Do markets notice?* The Wharton Financial Institution Center, Philadelphia.

Zollo, M., & Singh, H. (2004). Deliberate learning in corporate acquisitions: post-acquisition strategies and integration capability in U.S. bank mergers. *Strategic Management Journal, 25*(13), 1233–1256.

Appendix

Table A-1: List of all M&A events

Announcement date	Acquirer name	Acquirer nation	Target name	Target nation	Deal value (mio. US$)	ES[a]	RES[b]	CDS[c]
3/27/1995	Mitsubishi Bank	Japan	Bank of Tokyo	Japan	33,787.73	Yes	Yes	No
6/2/1995	Advance Bank Australia	Australia	State Bank of South Australia	Australia	522.17	Yes	Yes	No
7/31/1995	Westpac Banking	Australia	Challenge Bank	Australia	503.23	Yes	Yes	No
9/20/1995	Bank of Scotland	United Kingdom	Bank of Western Australia	Australia	680.40	Yes	Yes	No
4/19/1996	Westpac Banking	Australia	Trust Bank New Zealand	New Zealand	874.77	Yes	Yes	No
4/23/1996	Schweizerischer Bankverein	Switzerland	Standard Chartered-Asian Private Asset Management	Hong Kong	226.92	Yes	Yes	No
10/14/1996	St George Bank	Australia	Advance Bank Australia	Australia	2,223.90	Yes	Yes	No
4/2/1997	Westpac Banking	Australia	Bank of Melbourne	Australia	1,129.54	Yes	Yes	No
3/18/1998	ABN-AMRO	Netherlands	Bank of Asia	Thailand	181.50	Yes	Yes	No
7/28/1998	National Bank of New Zealand	New Zealand	Countrywide Banking	New Zealand	498.82	Yes	No	No
8/21/1998	ANZ Banking Group	Australia	Primary Industry Bank Australia	Australia	173.85	Yes	Yes	No
12/16/1998	DBS Bank	Singapore	Kwong On Bank	Hong Kong	459.92	Yes	Yes	No
2/2/1999	Colonial	Australia	National Bank of Fiji	Fiji	4.85	Yes	Yes	No
4/19/1999	ABN-AMRO	Netherlands	Bank America-Asian Retail	Taiwan	200.00	Yes	Yes	No
4/28/1999	Standard Chartered	United Kingdom	Nakornthon Bank	Thailand	319.33	Yes	Yes	No
6/22/1999	Toyo Trust & Banking Company	Japan	Sanwa Trust & Banking Company	Japan	163.60	Yes	Yes	No
7/29/1999	UOB	Singapore	Westmont Bank	Philippines	78.45	Yes	Yes	No
8/6/1999	MayBank	Malaysia	Pacific Bank	Malaysia	329.00	Yes	Yes	No
10/6/1999	UOB	Singapore	Radanasin Bank	Thailand	382.51	Yes	Yes	No
10/11/1999	Southern Bank	Malaysia	Ban Hin Lee Bank	Malaysia	284.20	Yes	Yes	No
10/14/1999	Sumitomo Bank	Japan	Sakura Bank	Japan	45,494.36	Yes	Yes	No
10/21/1999	MLC (Lend Lease)	Australia	Canadian Eastern	Hong Kong	160.88	Yes	Yes	No
11/16/1999	Colonial	Australia	Trust Bank of Tasmania	Australia	96.24	Yes	Yes	No

Table A-1 (continued)

Announcement date	Acquirer name	Acquirer nation	Target name	Target nation	Deal value (mio. US$)	ES[a]	RES[b]	CDS[c]
11/26/1999	HDFC Bank	India	Times Bank(Bennett Coleman Co)	India	50.50	Yes	Yes	No
1/6/2000	Southern Bank	Malaysia	United Merchant Finance	Malaysia	110.54	Yes	Yes	No
3/10/2000	Commonwealth Bank of Australia	Australia	Colonial	Australia	5,906.21	Yes	Yes	No
3/13/2000	Sanwa Bank	Japan	Tokai Bank	Japan	14,983.74	Yes	Yes	No
4/27/2000	Standard Chartered	United Kingdom	ANZ Grindlays Bank	Australia	1,339.86	Yes	Yes	No
5/10/2000	HKCB Holdings	Hong Kong	Hong Kong Buidlining-Residential	Hong Kong	108.07	Yes	Yes	No
7/5/2000	Sanwa Bank	Japan	Toyo Trust & Banking	Japan	4,372.39	Yes	Yes	No
7/10/2000	Commonwealth Bank of Australia	Australia	Bank BII Commonwealth	Indonesia	7.75	Yes	Yes	No
8/2/2000	HSBC	United Kingdom	PCI Savings Bank	Philippines	22.11	Yes	Yes	No
9/1/2000	Standard Chartered	United Kingdom	Chase Manhattan-HK Banking	Hong Kong	1,319.95	Yes	Yes	No
9/28/2000	Sanwa Bank	Japan	Senshu Bank	Japan	575.46	Yes	Yes	No
11/21/2000	Bank of East Asia	Hong Kong	FPB Bank Holding	Hong Kong	559.98	Yes	Yes	No
12/22/2000	Kookmin Bank	South Korea	H&CB	South Korea	3,402.02	Yes	Yes	No
3/16/2001	Fukuoka City Bank	Japan	Bank of Nagasaki	Japan	17.08	Yes	Yes	No
3/23/2001	RHB Bank	Malaysia	Bank Utama (Malaysia)	Malaysia	474.52	Yes	Yes	No
4/11/2001	DBS Group Holdings	Singapore	Dao Heng Bank Group(Guoco)	Hong Kong	5,679.70	Yes	Yes	No
5/3/2001	Standard Bank	South Africa	Jardine Fleming Bank, Hong Kong	Hong Kong	120.00	Yes	Yes	No
6/12/2001	Oversea-Chinese Banking Corporation	Singapore	Keppel Capital Holdings	Singapore	3,753.91	Yes	Yes	No
7/13/2001	Commerzbank	Germany	Bank Finconesia	Indonesia	5.00	Yes	Yes	No
9/24/2001	St George Bank	Australia	Deutsche Bank-Margin Lending	Australia	179.03	Yes	Yes	No
10/5/2001	ANZ Banking Group	Australia	Bank of Hawaii-PNG, Vanuatu	Fiji	49.73	Yes	Yes	No

Table A-1 (continued)

Announcement date	Acquirer name	Acquirer nation	Target name	Target nation	Deal value (mio. US$)	ES[a]	RES[b]	CDS[c]
10/25/2001	Taishin International Bank	Taiwan	Dah An Commercial Bank	Taiwan	267.73	Yes	Yes	No
3/12/2002	Kanto Bank	Japan	Tsukuba Bank	Japan	61.99	Yes	Yes	No
4/23/2002	Westpac Banking	Australia	Rothschild AU Asset Management	Australia	173.84	Yes	Yes	No
8/8/2002	Fubon Financial Holding	Taiwan	Taipei Bank	Taiwan	2,346.52	Yes	No	No
8/19/2002	Hana Bank	South Korea	Seoul Bank,	South Korea	952.85	Yes	Yes	No
9/30/2002	Nishi-Nippon Bank	Japan	Fukuoka City Bank	Japan	1,279.99	Yes	Yes	No
11/15/2002	Hokuriku Bank	Japan	Ishikawa Bank	Japan	429.83	Yes	Yes	No
4/7/2003	Wing Hang Bank	Hong Kong	Chekiang First Bank	Hong Kong	615.61	Yes	Yes	No
4/14/2003	HSBC	United Kingdom	AMP-Residential Mortgage	New Zealand	112.00	Yes	Yes	No
5/26/2003	Hokugin Financial Group	Japan	Hokkaido Bank Ltd	Japan	1,799.65	Yes	Yes	No
6/19/2003	Shinhan Financial Group	South Korea	Chohung Bank	South Korea	2,824.12	Yes	Yes	No
7/2/2003	Chinatrust Financial Holding	Taiwan	Grand Commercial Bank	Taiwan	1,729.16	Yes	Yes	No
9/8/2003	Fubon Financial Holding	Taiwan	International Bank of Asia	Hong Kong	415.36	Yes	No	No
10/31/2003	Hana Bank	South Korea	Qingdao International Bank	China	16.00	Yes	Yes	No
11/10/2003	Citigroup	United States	Bank of China-NPL	China	600.00	Yes	Yes	No
11/26/2003	BNP Paribas	France	Intl BK of Paris & Shanghai	China	23.00	Yes	Yes	No
1/28/2004	Thai Military Bank	Thailand	DBS Thai Danu Bank	Thailand	512.80	Yes	Yes	No
2/23/2004	Citigroup	United States	Koram Bank	South Korea	2,621.22	Yes	Yes	Yes
4/30/2004	Shin Kong Financial Holding	Taiwan	United Credit Commercial Bank	Taiwan	159.70	Yes	No	No
7/26/2004	Taishin International Bank	Taiwan	Tenth Credit Coop Association	Taiwan	42.56	Yes	Yes	No
9/27/2004	Standard Chartered	United Kingdom	Sumitomo Mitsui Banking-Indian Operations	India	17.00	Yes	Yes	No

Table A-1 (continued)

Announcement date	Acquirer name	Acquirer nation	Target name	Target nation	Deal value (mio. US$)	ES[a]	RES[b]	CDS[c]
10/29/2004	Dongwon Financial Holdings	South Korea	Korea Investment & Securites Company	South Korea	493.77	Yes	Yes	No
11/19/2004	Kiyo Bank	Japan	Wakayama Bank	Japan	42.25	Yes	No	No
12/9/2004	Union Bank of Taiwan	Taiwan	Chung Shing Commercial Bank	Taiwan	221.57	Yes	Yes	No
1/10/2005	Standard Chartered	United Kingdom	Korea First Bank	South Korea	3,277.60	Yes	Yes	No
2/18/2005	Mitsubishi Tokyo Financial Group	Japan	UFJ Holdings	Japan	41,431.03	Yes	Yes	No
4/19/2005	Shin Kong Financial Holding	Taiwan	Macoto Bank	Taiwan	569.25	Yes	No	No
6/15/2005	Standard Chartered	United Kingdom	American Express-Commercial Banking	Bangladesh	24.50	Yes	Yes	No
6/17/2005	Solomon Mutual Savings Bank	South Korea	Hanmaum Savings & Finance	South Korea	54.29	Yes	Yes	No
6/20/2005	Centurion Bank	India	Bank of Punjab	India	80.51	Yes	Yes	No
11/7/2005	State Bank of India	India	Bank IndoMonex	Indonesia	5.00	Yes	Yes	Yes
12/6/2005	Sberbank Rossii	Russian Fed	Texakabank	Kazakhstan	100.00	Yes	No	Yes
12/8/2005	Yamaguchi Bank	Japan	Momiji Holdings	Japan	635.07	Yes	Yes	No
12/22/2005	Standard Chartered	United Kingdom	ICICI Bank NPL	India	20.17	Yes	Yes	Yes
5/12/2006	Bank of Fukuoka	Japan	Kumamoto Family Bank	Japan	521.26	Yes	Yes	No
8/9/2006	Standard Chartered	United Kingdom	Union Bank	Pakistan	413.00	Yes	Yes	Yes
8/15/2006	Bank of Queensland	Australia	Pioneer Permanent Building Society	Australia	37.93	Yes	Yes	No
8/21/2006	Centurion Bank of Punjab	India	Lord Krishna Bank	India	64.5	Yes	Yes	No
9/6/2006	IDBI	India	United Western Bank	India	18.31	Yes	Yes	Yes
9/29/2006	Standard Chartered	United Kingdom	Hsinchu International Bank	Taiwan	1,150.88	Yes	Yes	Yes
11/13/2006	Jinheung Mutual Savings Bank	South Korea	Kyunggi Mutual Savings Bank	South Korea	10.77	Yes	Yes	No

Table A-1 (continued)

Announcement date	Acquirer name	Acquirer nation	Target name	Target nation	Deal value (mio. US$)	ES[a]	RES[b]	CDS[c]
12/8/2006	Bank of India	India	Bank Swadesi Tbk	Indonesia	25.00	Yes	Yes	Yes
12/11/2006	ICICI Bank	India	Sangli Bank	India	67.94	Yes	Yes	No
12/21/2006	Wing Hang Bank	Hong Kong	Inchroy Credit Corp	Hong Kong	180.07	Yes	Yes	No
3/5/2007	ABN-AMRO	Netherlands	Prime Commercial Bank	Pakistan	234.21	Yes	Yes	Yes
5/2/2007	Fukuoka Financial Group	Japan	Shinwa Bank	Japan	625.46	Yes	Yes	No
6/15/2007	Solomon Mutual Savings Bank	South Korea	Hanjin Mutual Savings Bank	South Korea	28.73	Yes	Yes	No
6/20/2007	Bank of America	United States	BPI-NPL	Philippines	5.50	Yes	Yes	Yes
6/21/2007	Bank Austria Creditanstalt	Austria	ATF Bank JSC	Kazakhstan	1,661.00	Yes	Yes	No
7/12/2007	Korea Mutual Savings Bank	South Korea	Bumin Mutual Savings Bank	South Korea	34.94	Yes	Yes	No
8/9/2007	Bendigo Bank	Australia	Adelaide Bank	Australia	1,649.29	Yes	Yes	No
8/9/2007	Fukuoka Financial Group	Japan	Shinwa Bank	Japan	835.80	Yes	Yes	No
8/31/2007	Bank of Queensland	Australia	Home Building Society	Australia	484.57	Yes	Yes	No
11/14/2007	Kookmin Bank	South Korea	Hannuri Investment & Securities	South Korea	292.00	Yes	Yes	No
12/6/2007	Shinsei Bank	Japan	Shinki Co	Japan	69.03	Yes	Yes	Yes
1/11/2008	Standard Chartered	United Kingdom	Yeahreum Mutual Savings Bank	South Korea	160.3	Yes	Yes	Yes
1/16/2008	ORIX Corp	Japan	Metrobank	Philippines	114.10	Yes	Yes	Yes
2/11/2008	Citibank	United States	Suncorp-Metway Credit Card Business	Australia	14.41	Yes	Yes	Yes
2/22/2008	HDFC Bank	India	Centurion Bank of Punjab	India	2,386.62	Yes	Yes	No
2/22/2008	Bank of Ikeda	Japan	Senshu Bank	Japan	1,074.48	Yes	Yes	No
3/31/2008	HK Mutual Savings Bank	South Korea	Dongkwang Savings Bank	South Korea	33.25	Yes	Yes	No
5/13/2008	Shonai Bank	Japan	Hokuto Bank	Japan	40.30	Yes	Yes	No
5/13/2008	Westpac Banking	Australia	St George Bank	Australia	17,932.98	Yes	Yes	Yes
5/26/2008	China Merchants Bank	China	Wing Lung Bank	Hong Kong	4,555.25	Yes	Yes	No
10/7/2008	Standard Chartered	United Kingdom	Asia Trust & Invest-Certain	Taiwan	103.49	Yes	Yes	Yes

Table A-1 (continued)

Announcement date	Acquirer name	Acquirer nation	Target name	Target nation	Deal value (mio. US$)	ES[a]	RES[b]	CDS[c]
10/8/2008	Commonwealth Bank of Australia	Australia	Bank of Western Australia	Australia	1,405.32	Yes	Yes	Yes
10/28/2008	BCA	Indonesia	Bank UIB	Indonesia	24.58	Yes	Yes	No
1/26/2009	Tokusima Bank	Japan	Kagawa Bank	Japan	370.70	Yes	Yes	No
4/6/2009	Bank of East Asia	Hong Kong	ICEA Finance Holdings	Hong Kong	48.01	Yes	Yes	No
4/28/2009	Kanto Tsukuba Bank	Japan	Ibaraki Bank	Japan	77.99	Yes	Yes	No
4/30/2009	Ta Chong Bank	Taiwan	Second Credit Cooperative of Kaohsiung	Taiwan	14.58	Yes	Yes	No
5/4/2009	Kookmin Bank	South Korea	Khmer Union Bank	Cambodia	7.92	Yes	Yes	Yes
6/19/2009	State Bank of India	India	State Bank of Indore	India	5.32	Yes	Yes	Yes
7/1/2009	Nomura Trust & Banking	Japan	NikkoCiti Trust and Banking	Japan	196.67	Yes	Yes	No
7/13/2009	Bendigo & Adelaide Bank	Australia	Tasmanian Banking Services	Australia	3.89	Yes	Yes	No
7/29/2009	National Australia Bank	Australia	Goldman Sachs-Australian Business	Australia	80.85	Yes	Yes	Yes
8/4/2009	ANZ Banking Group	Australia	RBS-Asian Retail Banking	Taiwan	550.00	Yes	Yes	Yes
9/29/2009	ICBC	China	ACL Bank	Thailand	539.12	Yes	Yes	Yes
10/15/2009	Oversea-Chinese Banking Corporation	Singapore	ING Asia Private Bank	Singapore	1,462.79	Yes	No	No
10/29/2009	Punjab National Bank	India	Danabank	Kazakhstan	23.77	Yes	Yes	No
11/6/2009	Chuo Mitsui Trust Holdings	Japan	Sumitomo Trust & Banking	Japan	9,148.93	Yes	Yes	No
2/19/2010	BRI	Indonesia	BANK AGRO	Indonesia	36.99	Yes	Yes	No
5/18/2010	ICICI Bank	India	Bank of Rajasthan	India	608.47	Yes	Yes	Yes
6/16/2010	Faysal Bank	Pakistan	RBS Pakistan	Pakistan	50.46	Yes	Yes	No
7/30/2010	Juroku Bank	Japan	Gifu Bank	Japan	50.23	Yes	Yes	No
9/20/2010	UOB	Singapore	HSBC Holdings-banknotes Business	Hong Kong	15.00	Yes	No	No
10/26/2010	Bendigo & Adelaide Bank	Australia	Rural Bank	Australia	162.81	Yes	Yes	No
11/16/2010	Hana Financial Group	South Korea	Korea Exchange Bank	South Korea	3,477.06	Yes	Yes	Yes

Table A-1 (continued)

Announcement date	Acquirer name	Acquirer nation	Target name	Target nation	Deal value (mio. US$)	ES[a]	RES[b]	CDS[c]
2/18/2011	Woori Financial Holdings	South Korea	Samhwa Mutual	South Korea	548.34	Yes	No	Yes
5/16/2011	Jeonbuk Bank	South Korea	Woori Capital	South Korea	101.22	Yes	Yes	No
10/27/2011	Hyundai Securities	South Korea	Daeyeong Mutual Savings Bank	South Korea	86.79	Yes	Yes	No
12/16/2011	Bendigo & Adelaide Bank	Australia	Bank of Cyprus Australia	Australia	129.58	Yes	Yes	No
1/17/2012	State Bank of India	India	Chinatrust Commercial Bank Assets	Taiwan	14.87	Yes	Yes	Yes
2/1/2012	Kotak Mahindra Bank	India	Barclays-India Credit Card Business	India	61.07	Yes	Yes	No
3/28/2012	Kiwoom Securities	South Korea	Sam Shin Mutual Saving & Financial	South Korea	31.108	Yes	Yes	No
6/14/2012	Hana Financial Group	South Korea	Korea Savings Bank	South Korea	347.97	Yes	Yes	Yes
6/22/2012	SinoPac Financial Holdings	Taiwan	Pacific Securities	Taiwan	123.18	Yes	Yes	No
10/22/2012	L&T Finance Holdings Ltd	India	FamilyCredit	India	22.41	Yes	Yes	No
12/31/2012	Chinatrust Commercial Banking	Taiwan	Tokyo Star Bank	Japan	528.74	Yes	Yes	Yes
5/7/2013	KB Financial Group	South Korea	Yehansoul Mutual Savings Bank	South Korea	34.40	Yes	Yes	Yes
5/21/2013	CITIC Securities	China	China Asset Management	China	260.79	Yes	Yes	Yes
6/13/2013	Goldman Sachs Group	United States	Suncorp Group	Australia	108.15	Yes	Yes	Yes
7/2/2013	Bank of Tokyo-Mitsubishi UFJ	Japan	Bank of Ayudhya	Thailand	5,315.45	Yes	Yes	Yes
7/24/2013	Sumitomo Mitsui Banking	Japan	Societe Generale Private Bank	Japan	199.54	Yes	Yes	No
9/18/2013	China Banking	Philippines	Plantersbank	Philippines	34.99	Yes	Yes	No
10/10/2013	Westpac Banking	Australia	Capital Finance Australia	Australia	1,466.77	Yes	Yes	Yes

[a] ES = Acquirer used in event study in chapter 3. [b] RES = Competitor of acquirer used in rival study. [c] CDS = Acquirer used in CDS event study in chapter 4.

Corporate Finance and Governance

Herausgegeben von Dirk Schiereck

Band 1 Sebastian Michael Gläsner: Return Patterns of German Open-End Real Estate Funds. An Empirical Explanation of Smooth Fund Returns. 2010.

Band 2 Patrick Ams: Directors' Dealings and Insider Trading in Germany. An Empirical Analysis. 2010.

Band 3 Joachim Vogt: Value Creation within the Construction Industry. A Study of Strategic Takeovers. 2011.

Band 4 Fabian Braemisch: Underpricing, Long-Run Performance, and Valuation of Initial Public Offerings. 2011.

Band 5 Matthäus Markus Sielecki: Creating and Governing an Integrated Market for Retail Banking Services in Europe. A Conceptual-Empirical Study of the Role of Regulation in Promoting a Single Euro Payments Area. 2011.

Band 6 Arne Wilkes: Determinants of Credit Spreads. An Empirical Analysis for the European Corporate Bond Market. 2011.

Band 7 Dirk Schiereck / Martin Setzer (Hrsg.): Bankerfolg und Akquisitionen. Aktuelle Erkenntnisse zur Konsolidierung und Restrukturierung der Finanzindustrie. 2011.

Band 8 Steffen Meinshausen: M&A Activity, Divestitures and Initial Public Offerings in the Fashion Industry. 2012.

Band 9 Malte Helmut Raudszus: Financial Return Risk and the Effect on Shareholder Wealth. 2012.

Band 10 Ramit Mehta: Mergers and Acquisitions in the Global Brewing Industry. A Capital Market Perspective. 2012.

Band 11 Marcel Normann: The Influence of German Top Executives on Corporate Policy and Firm Performance. 2012.

Band 12 Christoph Böhm: Risk-Adjusted Performance and Bank Governance Structures. 2013.

Band 13 Christian Thamm: Minority Shareholder Monitoring and German Corporate Governance. Empirical Evidence and Value Effects. 2013.

Band 14 Robert M. Fraunhoffer: Mergers and Acquisitions in the Energy Sector. The Impact of Synergy Disclosures on Shareholder Wealth and Operating Performance. 2013.

Band 15 Heiko Schön: Pharma M&A versus alliances and its underlying value drivers. Are M&A or alliances the right therapy for an ailing pharmaceutical industry? A capital market perspective. 2015.

Band 16 Sascha Kolaric: Bank mergers and acquisitions in the Asia-Pacific region. An investigation of the shareholder wealth effects of the financial sector consolidation and its impact on the acquirer's cost of debt. 2015.

Band 17 Ulrich Erxleben: Value Creation of Corporate Restructuring. A Market Cycle and Industry View. 2015.

www.peterlang.de

www.ingramcontent.com/pod-product-compliance
Ingram Content Group UK Ltd.
Pitfield, Milton Keynes, MK11 3LW, UK
UKHW020152290926
15471UKWH00005B/833

9 783631 670545